95264

W9-ALX-756

JUSTICE
VS.
LAW

COURTS AND POLITICS IN AMERICAN SOCIETY

Eugene W. Hickok

Gary L. McDowell

THE FREE PRESS
A Division of Macmillan, Inc.
NEW YORK

Maxwell Macmillan Canada
TORONTO

Maxwell Macmillan International
NEW YORK   OXFORD   SINGAPORE   SYDNEY

The Free Press
A Division of Macmillan, Inc.
866 Third Avenue, New York, NY 10022

Maxwell Macmillan Canada, Inc.
1200 Eglinton Avenue East
Suite 200
Don Mills, Ontario M3C 3N1

Macmillan, Inc. is part of the Maxwell Communication Group of Companies.

Printed in the United States of America

printing number
1 2 3 4 5 6 7 8 9 10

Library of Congress Cataloging-in-Publication Data

Hickok, Eugene W.
    Justice vs. law : courts and politics in American society/Eugene
W. Hickok, Gary L. McDowell.
        p.   cm.
    Includes bibliographical references and index.
    ISBN 0-02-920529-8
    1. United States. Supreme Court. 2. Political questions and
judicial power—United States. 3. Law and politics. I. McDowell,
Gary L.   II. Title.   III. Title: Justice versus law.
KF8748.H53 1993
340'. 115—dc20   93–21691
                                                      CIP

To
Kathy
and
Brenda

I am always suspicious of an advocate who comes before the Supreme Court saying this is a court of justice; it is a court of law.

—Attributed to Justice Oliver Wendell Holmes

The suggestion that the function of the judge is to deliver justice, in the sense of meting out what he personally conceives to be justice, quite apart from the Constitutution or law, I would have to reject.

—Justice William H. Rehnquist

CONTENTS

PREFACE

The courts of America are an institution of paradox. On the one hand, they are intimately involved in the daily affairs of the people, yet on the other, they carry out their duties largely behind a veil of public ignorance. Few outside the legal profession even pretend to understand the intricacies of the judicial process; jurisprudence is as mystical a subject as the general public can imagine. "Thus it happens," as Henry Home wrote in the eighteenth century, "that the knowledge of the law, like the mysteries of some Pagan Deity, is confined to its votaries; as if others were in duty bound to blind and implicit submission."

The purpose of this book is to pull back that veil and to reveal the mysteries for what they are: ordinary institutional contrivances designed to shape and direct the politics of the nation. As a result, the judicial process is inevitably a forum wherein differing visions of the just society come into conflict. While the cases and controversies that come before the courts are contests between two reasonably well defined adverse litigants, each with a personal stake in the resolution of the dispute, the judgments handed down often go far beyond those litigants and affect American society and politics in the broadest sense.

When Jane Roe sued to have the right to abort an unwanted fetus it was a very personal matter; the result, however, was very public. American politics and law have been consumed with *Roe* v. *Wade* ever since.

When the motion picture industry endeavored to protect copyrights against easy duplication by video cassette recorders, the reason was narrow in the sense of protecting the rights of individuals. The result, however, had an impact in nearly every living room in America.

When the California Coastal Commission sought to protect public access to beaches by easements against property owners, it

was trying to serve the public interest, not harm individual homeowners. Yet those homeowners saw it differently: they sued that
such a public policy unconstitutionally deprived them of their
property without just compensation as required by the
Constitution. They won, thereby transforming public policy by asserting their rights in court.

Similarly, when a little girl named Linda Brown sued the school
board of Topeka, Kansas, four decades ago so that she could at-
tend the public school of her choice regardless of her race, the resolution of *Brown* v. *Board of Education* changed the face of
American society.

The examples can be multiplied without end—from the death
penalty, to rights of parental visitation, to police procedure, to
school assignments. The fact is, judicial decisions shape public policy. But they do more: They also define public understanding not
only as to the nature and extent of judicial power, but concerning
the substantive issues of law and public policy as well.

Since the beginning of the American republic, the courts have
been the scene where the great public tugs-of-war have taken
place. The question of whether Congress had the power to establish a national bank that so divided the Federalists and the
Jeffersonians; the question of slavery that nearly shattered the
union; the advent of economic liberalism and the progressive efforts to tame the social aftereffects of the industrial revolution; the
Great Depression and FDR's New Deal; and, of course, the civil
rights movement of the 1960s all had their days in court.

To suggest that courts are political bodies is not to disparage
them; they are political bodies in the highest sense of the word.
They are institutions designed to maintain the rule of law; without
them, as Alexander Hamilton once put it, "the laws are a dead letter." Thus what courts do—and how they do it—is of primary importance to the political health of the nation.

The great French commentator on America, Alexis de
Tocqueville, once noted that in a very important sense, the courts
are essential to the maintenance of the idea that law transcends the
passions and the politics of the moment; the courts in America,
Tocqueville sagely observed, wield enormous power, but it is a
power derived only from their "moral force." As Hamilton said in

The Federalist, the judges neither brandish the sword nor control the purse strings of the nation; their power is the power of disinterested judgment. For the courts to work as planned, they must have the political respect of the people; without it, their power will vanish.

In recent years, the courts have tottered ever nearer the abyss of public disrespect. The courts have become not merely arenas where concrete cases and controversies (albeit with social implications) are decided but places where abstract legal theories are pushed by this side and that. Through the judicial process has come, as Judge Robert Bork so tellingly described it, a battle for the legal culture of America.

Through the cases brought, the briefs filed, and the arguments made, ideological plaintiffs have endeavored to supplant the status quo with new visions of the just society. While the individual adverse litigant is still necessary as a threshold matter to get into court, once there individual considerations all too often fade into insignificance. The cause becomes more important than the case. The goal is to replace a concern for concrete constitutional rights with a concern for judicially decreed constitutional values. As one lawyer has observed, this new emphasis on "public law litigation" is intended to reflect "doubt as to whether the status quo is in fact just." The object is simple: "The goal of this new mode of litigation is the creation of a *new* status quo."

The average person may well wonder why the courts and not the legislatures for so tough a task. The answer is that to the advocates of this new regime the people cannot be trusted; popular government is to be supplanted by judicial decree as shaped and directed by scholarly legal theories. In this view, the role of the courts has to be more than merely resolving disputes; the proper role is one that will give vent to what one writer has called the ethos of the polity. Old fashioned sorts might think this "ethos" would have some connection with popular judgments of right and wrong, justice and injustice. Not so: "the expressive function of the Court . . . must sometimes be in advance of and even in contrast to, the largely inchoate notions of the people generally." As the current dean of Stanford Law School once put it, the contemporary theories of law pouring from the law schools are in truth "advocacy scholarship—amicus briefs designed to persuade the court to adopt our various notions of the public good."

What informs this new constitutional moralism is an intended blurring of the question of legality and the question of justice. The litigation strategies employed are all designed to show that, in the words of one famous Federal judge, there need be "no theoretical gulf between law and morality." By infusing law with moral theory, the average judge can be expected to practice what the legal theorists preach. Politically, however, the price is high. With judges unable to give an account of their decisions except to say that they are based on what the judge thinks just, without any clear textual warrant for such a view, it has become increasingly clear that the courts have begun to behave as political institutions not in the highest but in the lowest sense of the word.

While the legal moralists have gained control of much of the law over the past thirty years or so, they carried out their program largely shielded from public view by what Henry Home called "a cloud of obscure words, and terms of art, a language perfectly unknown, except to those of the profession." Shielded, that is, until Ronald Reagan undertook to change things during his two terms in the White House. Weary of judicial activism, Reagan promised the people to appoint judges "who would act like judges, and not like a bunch of sociology majors." The result was a political battle of the first order, reaching its bloodiest skirmish in the nomination of Robert H. Bork to the Supreme Court in 1987. The Bork nomination changed, probably forever, the way the American people view the nature and extent of judicial power in American politics.

Yet still the public understanding of the courts and their role under the Constitution remains more confused than clear. The goal of this book is to correct that situation.

This book is designed to examine the nature and extent of judicial power in the United States. It is meant to introduce the nontechnical reader to the intricacies of the judicial process: the structure and organization of the courts; the important implications—and politics—of judicial selection; the impact the procedures of the courts have on the substantive outcomes of litigation; and especially the intimate relationship between the rule of men and the rule of law. Taken together, these various areas reveal a marked movement in our courts away from what one might call principled judicial decision making toward a more pragmatic approach. Rather than deciding cases on the basis of concrete principles understood as neutrally transcending the case at hand, the contemporary judge all too frequently opts for attempting to individualize justice for the case before him. Moral subjectivity all too often nudges legal objectivity out of the way.

In order to achieve its goal of exposing and explaining the current state of judicial power, the book begins with an analysis of a case called *DeShanney* v. *Winnebago County.* In this case, stemming from the awful crime of child abuse, one can see in microcosm all of the important aspects of judicial power—the effect of personnel on the direction of the law; the demands placed on judges by a written Constitution; the relationship between procedure and substance the distinction between the private law of tort at the state level and the public law of the Constitution at the national level; certain aspects of American civil procedure and the legal profession; and ultimately the limits of the demands of justice under the rule of law.

CHAPTER ONE

AN "UNDENIABLY TRAGIC" CASE

The Supreme Court Building sits atop Capitol Hill, tucked behind the Capitol on First Street, Northeast, next to the Library of Congress. In a sense, the Court's geographic place in official Washington is a metaphor for its institutional role. Beyond the Court there are no more official buildings, no more bureaucracy. To the east, Capitol Hill quietly and suddenly fades away into a depressed and dangerous area of town, more grime than glitz. Sitting as it does on the edge of power, the Court enjoys a certain freedom from the limelight. Unlike the President or Senators or even Representatives, the Justices of the Supreme Court are relatively free from public attention. They wander about the streets unbothered and largely unnoticed; they often dine just down the street at the Monocle restaurant with nary a bodyguard in sight. Yet perhaps more than any other institution in Washington, the Court often touches people's daily lives in a far more intimate way than the more public branches of the government colossus.

By mid-morning on what was a bright but chilly November day, Attorney Don Sullivan had already arrived at the Supreme Court building, enjoyed a short tour by one of the Court officers, and was gathering his thoughts. Mr. Sullivan had forsaken the big Eastern cities, like Washington, years earlier. After graduating in 1970 from Syracuse Law School, he had established practice in Onondaga County, New York. For a short time he dabbled in local politics. In 1979 he moved to Wyoming because of his love for the Rocky Mountains and the West. By the early eighties, he had a thriving practice in Cheyenne and a reputation as a talented

1

litigator. Indeed, in 1983 he was president of the Wyoming Trial Lawyers Association. Today, however, he would face any lawyer's ultimate test—presenting an oral argument before the Supreme Court of the United States. It was his first.

The legal team that had been assembled to oppose the arguments Sullivan would present to the justices was also at the Court. Mark Mingo had arrived in Washington from Milwaukee a few days before so that he could rehearse his presentation and huddle with Department of Justice attorneys, who were both sympathetic to his position and familiar with Supreme Court practice. The product of Marquette University Law School, Mingo was a partner in the law film of Simarski & Stack in Milwaukee, a firm with a solid reputation that emphasizes insurance defense litigation, product liability, civil rights, and employment law. His list of clients was impressive: Ohio Casualty Insurance Group, Employers of Wausau Group, American Family Mutual Insurance. Mingo was familiar with the strategy so often employed by attorneys representing clients who were seeking to play upon jurors' sympathies in order to win huge sums of money. He had developed his own strategies for undermining the arguments about pain and suffering. But he always had his doubts going into trial; no good lawyer wouldn't.

Mingo harbored few doubts, however, about the soundness of his legal argument in the case at hand. He was convinced his position was correct. More important, he had been able to convince two lower federal courts as well. Still, the Supreme Court had agreed to hear the case, which surprised Mingo. It meant at least four Justices were willing to hear the arguments and were, to some unfathomable degree, undecided. Justices aren't like jurors. Often, in a courtroom, a good attorney can have the jury eating out of his hand. Good attorneys control the chemistry of a trial. But this was different. This was more like law school. The Justices controlled the chemistry. During an oral argument before the Supreme Court the Justices might interrupt at any time and were known for peppering attorneys with questions, sometimes hassling them, lecturing them. The histrionics that sometimes go on at a jury trial would be put aside. At the high court, a lawyer's case rests on the strength of his argument and the willingness of the

Justices to buy it. It is the ultimate challenge of good lawyering. While passion and sentiment no doubt play a role, to win in the Supreme Court one has to bend the logic of the law to fit the facts of the day.

Whatever anxiety Mingo felt about the task ahead was somewhat assuaged by the confidence displayed by the Justice Department attorney who was to present the government's argument in support of the Milwaukee counselor's position. Donald Ayer, at the age of thirty-nine, was a veteran of Supreme Court practice and was quickly becoming a major player in Washington. A graduate of Stanford University and Harvard Law School, since 1986 Ayer had served as principal deputy to the Solicitor General of the United States, the nation's trial attorney and the individual responsible for presenting the federal government's position before the federal courts. Prior to coming to Washington he had been a United States Attorney in California. Ayer's knowledge of the Court was based on more than his experience as an attorney. In 1976 he had clerked for then Associate Justice William Rehnquist. He knew how the Court functioned, how Justices molded their arguments, their sympathies, and their biases.

By half past noon on November 2, 1988, the attorneys who would present their oral arguments in the case of *DeShaney, a minor, by his guardian ad litem, et al.* v. *Winnebago County Department of Social Services, et al.*, had arrived at the Courtroom. The lawyers were familiar with one another, they knew each other's arguments, had read and reread each other's briefs. There was little that Sullivan could say this day that might surprise Mingo, little that Mingo might offer during his presentation that might catch Sullivan off guard. Donald Ayer had digested everything that had been written by both attorneys and the judges who had heard the case in the lower courts. His job today was to offer the government's position regarding the case, to emphasize the constitutional stakes involved in resolving this particular controversy. He would be brief—he had been given only a few minutes by the Court—and probably would not be questioned by the Justices. Unlike Sullivan and Mingo, he was relaxed.

The courtroom in the Supreme Court Building is imposing. The long, half-hexagonal bench where the nine justices sit catches the attention immediately. The nine justices sit in high-back leather chairs, each custom-made according to the individual justice's wishes. A small brass plate on the back of each chair identifies whose seat it is. They sit according to seniority on the Court, with the Chief Justice in the center chair. Attorneys facing the bench confront the most senior Justice just to their left of the Chief Justice and the most junior to the far right.

The room is heavy with the air of history and tradition. It is a dignified, a most solemn place. A velvet curtain hangs behind that Justices' chairs. When the clerk calls the Court to order, the nine Justices suddenly emerge, like black-robed apparitions, from behind that curtain and take their seats. Next to each chair on the bench sits a brass spittoon, an ornament from a long-forgotten era in which oral arguments before the nation's highest court might go on for days. Attorneys who will present their arguments to the Court sit at long tables directly in front of and below the Justices' bench. Goose-quill pens and pewter inkwells grace the tables. When presenting their arguments, attorneys stand at a lectern. They do not pace. They direct their argument to the Justices. Each attorney is allowed a set period of time to present his case, usually a half-hour. At the lectern, two lights—one white and one red—warn counsel of the constraints of time. When the white light comes on, the attorney knows there are five minutes left in his allotted time. When the red light flashes, counsel must stop immediately.

Off to the left of the attorneys' table is a small area set aside for attorneys who are members of the bar of the District of Columbia and who wish to watch oral argument. Behind the attorneys' table is a larger area set aside for visitors to the Court. Here is where the hordes of tourists sit, as well as interested citizens.

Every case that comes before the Supreme Court is a story of real people engaged in real conflict; each has something to win, something to lose, by being there. The Court does not deal in hypotheticals or academic debate; it long ago refused to offer merely "advisory opinions." According to the Constitution, the Court sits to resolve only actual cases and controversies. To reach this Court of last resort the issues that have been debated in lower courts must contain unresolved questions that bear upon national policy, questions that pose, in the language of the law, a federal question.

At half-past noon on this November day in 1988, oral arguments concerning the permissibility of random, warrantless drug tests for railroad employees were concluding. Moments later the advocates in the *DeShaney* case approached the bench. At 12:54 P.M. the clerk calls the Court to order. The Chief Justice, William Rehnquist, speaks:

"We'll hear argument now in No. 87-154, *Joshua DeShaney* v. *Winnebago County Department of Social Services.*"

At the invitation of the Chief Justice, Don Sullivan rises to address the Court. After speaking the words every attorney addressing the Supreme Court has uttered when commencing oral argument—"Mr. Chief Justice, and may it please the Court"—Sullivan begins:

> We are here contending today not for a broad constitutional mandate to the states to do all good things to all people, nor do we contend for a broad constitutional duty to prevent harm or all sadness, nor do we contend for a broad constitutional duty to protect all children in all cases.

Justice Byron White mumbles something, which Sullivan has a difficult time deciphering. Ruffled a bit, he returns to his well-prepared argument:

> We do suggest that there is one and only one exquisitely narrow circumstance where there is an affirmative duty . . .

Sullivan's goal is to lay out the argument that the Constitution's Due Process Clause, contained in the Fourteenth Amendment, should have protected Joshua DeShaney from his father. Before he can begin to mount the argument, the Chief Justice interrupts him and asks sarcastically: "You derive all of this from the language of the Due Process Clause?" The debate begins.

Far away, in Wisconsin, nine-year-old Joshua DeShaney sits, severely retarded, close to brain dead, the victim of his father's vicious beatings. At the age of four, young Joshua had had an IQ of

114. Institutionalized because of the severity of his condition, he now has the mental capacity of less than a twelve-month-old child. Today the Supreme Court is hearing the tragic story of poor Joshua.

Joshua DeShaney was born to Melody and Randy DeShaney in Cheyenne, Wyoming, in 1979. Randy DeShaney was a troubled man. Having completed his enlisted service in the Air Force with an honorable discharge, he had difficulty holding down a job. Both he and Melody were unhappy in their marriage. They agreed they had married too young. Perhaps that was why the couple were drifting apart. Gradually it became apparent to both that a divorce was inevitable. Randy began to seek comfort in alcohol. He and Melody were divorced in 1980 when Joshua was less than a year old.

Melody and Joshua traveled to Phoenix where she found employment. Randy moved to Wisconsin to be close to his family. The pressure of managing two jobs and taking care of Joshua became overwhelming for Melody. She and Randy agreed that Randy should have custody of the child. And so Randy took Joshua and settled in the town of Neenah located in Winnebago County, not far from Oshkosh.

Almost immediately, Randy met and married a woman, Chris. The marriage soured, and the couple quickly divorced. Randy became associated with rumors of excessive drinking and the use of street drugs. And so by the age of twenty-seven DeShaney could look back on a history of alcohol abuse, disorganized family life, sporadic employment, meager finances and two failed marriages plus a growing record of run-ins with the police. There was something else going on that almost nobody knew anything about. Almost as soon as Randy DeShaney had arrived in Neenah, he had begun abusing his little son Joshua. It was his way of dealing with the frustrations of life and the agitation created by a child.

The rumors of abuse first surfaced in 1982. During the divorce proceedings that ended the second marriage, DeShaney's second wife mentioned to her attorney and to police that her husband had abused Joshua. According to the second Mrs. DeShaney, Randy had "hit the boy causing marks and [was] a prime case for child abuse." The police then notified the Winnebago County Department of Social Services. Wisconsin law outlines specific policies to be followed in cases where children are believed to be endangered. A child protection unit was charged with following up on the former Mrs. DeShaney's allegations. The child protection unit, a special division of the Department of Social Services, is charged with identifying and protecting endangered children. In this case, it proceeded to contact Randy DeShaney and to interview him about the allegations. DeShaney denied the assertions. Although procedures call for the child protection team to see the child when abuse is suspected, on this occasion it did not see Joshua. Apparently convinced that Mr. DeShaney was telling the truth, or at least lacking any compelling evidence to the contrary, the unit left the DeShaney residence. The investigation ended with the interview, and the case file was closed.

Approximately one year later, in January 1983, Joshua was brought to the Theda Clark Medical Center in Winnebago County by his father's live-in girlfriend, Maria DeShaney, the ex-wife of Randy's brother. Suffering from a number of bruises and abrasions, the child was admitted to the hospital. The doctor who examined Joshua, Dr. Robert Gehringer, immediately suspected child abuse and contacted the Department of Social Services. Officials at the DSS then sought and obtained an order from Wisconsin juvenile court placing Joshua in the temporary custody of the hospital.

For three days a child protection team worked together to determine the extent of Joshua's injuries and what had caused them. Dr. Gehringer was joined by a clinical psychologist, Dr. Donald Derozier, and two employees of the Department of Social Services, Ann Kemmeter, a social services caseworker, and her supervisor, Cheryl Stelse. Tom Hoare, a social worker employed by the Theda Clark Medical Center, assisted the team. Keith Nelson, a detective with the Neenah police department, worked with John Bodnar, assistant counsel for Winnebago County, to determine whether or not evidence existed to pursue a claim of child abuse.

After three days of investigation and analysis, the team assembled to decide whether or not to pursue the case. Dr. Gehringer felt strongly that Joshua had indeed been beaten by someone—

either his father or his father's girlfriend. But the attorney for
Winnebago County seemed unsure of the findings of the doctors
and the social workers. According to Mr. Bodnar, the evidence
was insufficient to warrant pursuing a child protection action at
that time. Joshua would have to be returned to the custody of his
father. Ann Kemmeter agreed with counsel's decision and
recorded her thoughts in her case file:

> I therefore recommend that the temporary physical custody order
> and any further allegations against this family be dismissed at this
> time, but will refer it back into Court should there be any further
> injuries to this child of an unexplained origin.

Bodnar was uncomfortable with the decision to return the child
but felt compelled to abide by Wisconsin law. Worried that Joshua
might be subjected to mistreatment, Bodnar drafted an agreement
to present to Randy DeShaney in an attempt to protect the child
against further injury. The terms of the agreement called for
Randy DeShaney to seek counseling, for Joshua to be enrolled in
the Head Start Program so that the Department of Social Services
could monitor his condition, and for Maria, the live-in girlfriend,
to be removed from the DeShaney residence. The child protection
team presented Randy with the agreement, and he said he would
work with the team to ensure that the conditions of the agreement were met. Young Joshua was returned to his father. Within
three weeks, the county court had closed the case.

One month later Ann Kemmeter, the Department of Social
Services caseworker was notified that Joshua had been admitted to
the hospital again and that child abuse was again suspected as the
cause of minor injuries. An informal investigation conducted while
Joshua was at the hospital had failed to uncover conclusive evidence that child abuse had taken place, however, so no formal action was taken by Kemmeter or her department.

For the next several months Ann Kemmeter visited the
DeShaney home regularly in an attempt to determine the degree
to which the terms of the agreement were being met and to check
on the condition of little Joshua. In May 1983, during one of her
visits, she noticed a bump on Joshua's head. When asked about it,

Randy DeShaney said the child had fallen in the bathroom and hit his head. The bump was not severe, but it did cause Kemmeter to continue to be suspicious. Joshua at this time had not been enrolled in Head Start, and Kemmeter noted that in her report as well. In addition, Maria, the live-in girlfriend, continued to reside at the DeShaney home, in violation of the agreement.

In July 1983 Kemmeter visited the DeShaney home again. Marie was still residing there, Joshua was still not enrolled in Head Start. A few days later a Head Start worker who had been sent by Kemmeter visited the DeShaney home and found four-year-old Joshua alone in the house. Mrs. Kemmeter was notified immediately, but no action was taken by the Department of Social Services.

In September of that year, Kemmeter visited the DeShaney home but found it empty. A neighbor informed her that the family had left for the hospital because Joshua was having a problem with his eyes. Later she learned that Joshua had been treated at Theda Clark Medical Center for a scratched cornea and released.

Visiting the DeShaney's home in early November 1983, Kemmeter noticed a scrape on Joshua's chin. She thought it looked a bit peculiar and wrote in her files that she felt it might have been a cigarette burn but that she could not be sure. Later that month Joshua was again admitted to the hospital and treated for a number of minor injuries, including a cut on his forehead, a bloody nose, a swollen ear, and bruises on the backs of both of his shoulders. Randy and Maria told the doctors and nurses attending to Joshua that he had fallen down the stairs. Ann Kemmeter was notified by the hospital but no action was taken by the Department of Social Services. On her next several visits to the DeShaney home she was told that young Joshua was ill and could not see her. She protested but took no action.

On March 7, 1984, Ann Kemmeter visited the DeShaneys but was told that Joshua was again ill and she could not see him. According to Mr. DeShaney, Joshua had fainted in the bathroom and was resting. He gave no reason for his son's fainting, and Kemmeter did not force the issue. The next day Joshua DeShaney was brought to the emergency room at Mercy Medical Center. He was in a deep coma, with extensive old and new bruises over most of his body. Dr. B. F. Kayali and Dr. Marc Letellier rushed him into surgery in an attempt to save his life.

The surgeons found evidence of earlier severe head injuries. Massive pools of yellow liquid, the byproduct of older intercranial hemorrhages, convinced the doctors that Joshua had sustained several serious head injuries over a period of time. The yellow liquid suggested to them that old blood clots had been in place long enough for the red blood cells to have chemically decomposed, and only the yellow bilirubin element remained. The membrane covering the brain was stained blue as a result of the standing and pooling of blood in the brain and skull. The doctors were convinced that Joshua had suffered serious and permanent brain damage caused by physical trauma to the head over an extended period. He had suffered what Dr. Kayali described as "an acute, extensive subdural hematoma."

In addition to the injuries to Joshua's head, the child had severe bruising over 50 to 75 percent of his thighs and buttocks. Although Joshua had suffered no broken bones, his body was badly beaten and his brain had been severely damaged. Both Kayali and Letellier doubted he would recover.

According to Joshua's father, the child had fallen down the stairs when he was sent down to the basement "to get a hammer for me to pound a nail." After he fell he was screaming and seemed out of control, so DeShaney had picked Joshua up and shook him and slapped his face in order to "bring him around." DeShaney admitted to police at the time that he may have "shaken Joshua too hard, causing his injuries" but he did not admit to abuse. When asked about the bruises on Joshua's thighs and buttocks, DeShaney responded that "Joshua usually needed spanking" and that "Joshua is a child that usually needed discipline."

Both Kayali and Letellier felt Joshua's injuries were inconsistent with a fall and that the child's overall physical condition suggested to them that he had been the victim of ongoing abuse for some time.

At a preliminary hearing before Judge William Carver, held in early June, Randy DeShaney was charged with injury by conduct regardless of life and two counts of child abuse. His defense attorney, Thomas Fink, immediately moved to dismiss the charges, claiming Joshua had lost consciousness while falling down the stairs because of injuries sustained hours earlier. Fink argued that there was no evidence that DeShaney had inflicted harm on the boy. "We have an injury so we need a scapegoat," Fink told the press. Judge Carver denied the motion. Randy DeShaney was arraigned a week later.

For months DeShaney and his attorney worked to defeat the charges. Fink entered into plea bargaining with the prosecution. During those negotiations, Fink became convinced that prosecutors believed they could persuade a jury to convict DeShaney. Knowing this, he advised his client to plead no contest.

In early February 1985 Randy DeShaney appeared before Judge Robert Hawley to receive sentencing. Tom Fink had asked Judge Hawley for probation for his client, or at least to allow the penalties for the crimes to run concurrently. Assistant District Attorney Eugene Bartman sought the maximum sentence.

Citing the "reprehensible" conduct of DeShaney and a report that concluded that DeShaney demonstrated "anger and hostility in close personal relationships"; a lengthy list of disturbance calls about DeShaney; and allegations that he had beaten not only his son but his girlfriend (albeit she had refused to press charges), and referring time and again to the tragic condition of little Joshua, Judge Hawley sentenced Randy DeShaney to the maximum of two back-to-back two-year prison terms for child abuse and reckless behavior. "The court feels this offense is extremely aggravated and that the public has to be protected."

Little Joshua had been brought to the emergency room on March 8, 1984. Almost one year later, on March 4, 1985, Melody DeShaney, Joshua's natural mother, filed a complaint in the U.S. District Court for the Eastern District of Wisconsin. Melody DeShaney, who had not been informed of her son's condition until the day he was brought, so severely injured, to the emergency room, was seeking compensatory and punitive damages under the Due Process and Equal Protection Clauses of the Fourteenth Amendment of the Constitution, as authorized under Title 42 of the United States Code, sections 1983, 1985, 1988. Her lawyers argued that the facts surrounding the tragedy were such that federal and constitutional law was violated, as well as Wisconsin law. They asserted that individuals acting "under color of state statute" had caused a deprivation of Joshua's "rights, privileges, and immunities" as a citizen. On June 20, 1986, that court issued a summary judgment holding that the relationship between the state and Joshua did not give rise to a constitutionally protected right of protection. The court determined that the state, or more precisely officials of the state, had not caused the harm to Joshua—his father had—and that no violation of federal law had taken place. According to the court, while individuals acting on behalf of the state had indeed entered into something of a relationship with Joshua, this did not imply that what happened to the child was the state's fault.

Within a month the case was appealed to the Seventh Circuit Court of Appeals. That court heard the case in January 1987. In February it issued its opinion, upholding the lower court and arguing that "while the authorities inexplicably failed to act on mounting, and eventually overwhelming, evidence that Joshua was in great danger from his father, the child had no constitutionally protected right which was violated thereby." That Joshua had been the victim of child abuse was never questioned. But according to the court, state officials had not caused the abuse, hence the state could not be held liable for it. Moreover, while the state had indeed attempted to protect Joshua's welfare, the nature of the relationship between the state and Joshua did not mean that the child had a right to expect protection from his father—a right that the state had failed to protect.

The Supreme Court granted certiorari, exercising its discretion to hear the case on appeal, that summer. It scheduled oral arguments for early in the autumn term. The legal road from Wisconsin to Washington had been long and rough.

CHAPTER TWO

JOSHUA'S QUEST FOR JUSTICE AND THE LOGIC OF THE LAW

On March 4, 1985, Curry First of Milwaukee, Joshua DeShaney's court-appointed guardian, and Don Sullivan, who had been retained by Melody DeShaney, filed suit in the United States District Court for the Eastern District of Wisconsin; the complaint ran to sixty-three counts and cited five causes of action which the plaintiffs alleged gave them the right to sue in federal court. Beneath the plethora of charges the point of the complaint was unambiguous: money.

Melody DeShaney was seeking a total of $100,000,000 in damages for herself and for her son—$50,000,000 in compensatory damages and another $50,000,000 in punitive damages for the misconduct of the county social workers involved in Joshua's case, whose behavior was called "extreme, bizarre, unjustifiable, unwarranted and utterly unacceptable in a civilized society." The defendants had to be held up as a grim example so that other public officials similarly situated would take notice. It was suggested that $50,000,000 would make the point rather emphatically. Justice demanded nothing less, the plaintiffs claimed.

In the view of the plaintiffs, the State of Wisconsin would not allow justice to be done—at least not to the tune of $100,000,000. While the state provided a mechanism for the redress of such wrongs as those alleged in the complaint, it set the limit on damages available at a mere $50,000. The only way around this obstacle was to make a federal case out of it; under certain federal laws there would be no cap on the amount of damages a plaintiff might recover from a benevolent jury and a deep-pocketed state.

The first threshold the DeShaneys had to clear was to argue that they had a legitimate federal cause of action that could be properly heard and decided in a federal court. In other words, they needed *standing* to sue. The claim made by the DeShaneys was that the behavior of the Winnebago County Department of Social Services, the State of Wisconsin, and those state and county employees who had had a role in the decisions affecting Joshua had violated his civil rights and had denied him the protections afforded by the Due Process and Equal Protection Clauses of the Fourteenth Amendment to the U.S. Constitution. As a result, the DeShaneys argued, they were entitled to relief under section 1983 of Title 42 of the United States Code.

Section 1983 had been enacted in 1871 as part of the Ku Klux Klan Act as a way of providing damages to those whose civil rights were violated by violent resistance to the outcome of the Civil War. Indeed, Section 1983 was a prime example of why the Fourteenth Amendment had been adopted in the first place. In the wake of the War Between the States, Congress had undertaken to reconstruct the Union and to pass legislation that would protect the former slaves within the states where they resided. It was widely believed that the Supreme Court of the United States was likely to strike down such legislation; such federal intrusions into the domestic affairs of the states violated traditional notions of federalism and state sovereignty. In order to allow such legislation, the Constitution was amended in 1868 and the traditional understanding of the federal balance of the Constitution was altered. Two sections of the Fourteenth Amendment in particular had that effect, the first and the fifth:

> *Section 1* All persons born or naturalized in the United States, and subject to the jurisdiction thereof, are citizens of the United States and of the State wherein they reside. No State shall make or enforce any law which shall abridge the privileges or immunities of the citizens of the United States; nor shall any State deprive any person of life, liberty, or property, without due process of law; nor deny to any person within its jurisdiction the equal protection of the laws. . . .
>
> *Section 5* The Congress shall have power to enforce, by appropriate legislation, the provisions of this article.[1]

With the new legislative power granted in this fifth section, Congress saw fit to pass the legislation that would become, when codified, Section 1983:

> Every person who, under color of any statute, ordinance, regulation, custom, or usage of any State or Territory, subjects, or causes to be subjected, any citizen of the United States or other person within the jurisdiction thereof to the deprivation of any rights, privileges, or immunities secured by the Constitution and laws, shall be liable to the party injured in an action at law, suit in equity, or other proper proceeding for redress.

Related to this provision, and necessary for it to have effect, is Section 1343 of Title 28 of the United States Code. Because federal courts are courts of limited jurisdiction, they depend upon Congress to confer whatever jurisdiction they have by legislation. The pertinent parts of Section 1343 provide:

> The district courts shall have original jurisdiction of any civil action authorized by law to be commenced by any person: . . . (3) To redress the deprivation under color of any State law, statute, ordinance, regulation, custom, or usage, of any right, privilege or immunity secured by the Constitution of the United States or by any Act of Congress providing for equal rights of citizens or of all persons within the jurisdiction of the United States.

In plain English, Section 1983 created a means by which individuals could sue when state officials, in the conduct of official business, violated their rights, and they could collect damages. Section 1343 gave original jurisdiction to federal courts to hear and decide those suits.

It was under those provisions that the lawyers for Melody and Joshua DeShaney sought to convince the Federal District Court that their clients were deserving of the remedies afforded by the laws and Constitution of the United States and should not be restricted to the more niggardly provisions of the State of Wisconsin. The essence of their argument was simple and direct. The defendants had been involved with Joshua to such a degree that they "knew or by the existence of even slight care reasonably should have known . . . of the strong likelihood and great danger of child abuse being committed upon Joshua DeShaney." Their failure to act to protect Joshua constituted a deprivation of his liberty without due process of law in clear disregard of the Due Process Clause of the Fourteenth Amendment.[2] Their negligence was so great as to be a constitutional violation, hence they were not protected by any doctrine of immunity that might otherwise shield public officials from suits for damages when they are in fact carrying out their duties in good faith. The defendants, by their inaction, were directly responsible for Joshua's fate and should be made to pay.

On March 26, 1985, the defendants responded to the complaint point by point, denying every allegation made by the plaintiffs. Beyond the particulars of the plaintiffs' complaint the defendants posited their "Affirmative Defenses," arguing, first, that the plaintiffs had failed to state a cause of action upon which relief could be granted (in effect, that neither the Fourteenth Amendment nor Section 1983 provided the grounds for their suit) and, second, that "the actions taken by the defendants Ann Kemmeter and Cheryl Stelse were within the good faith exercise of governmental authority and that the defense of qualified individual immunity is applicable to said defendants." In other words, they may have erred, but they did so in the course of duty, not through negligence. The defendants asked for a judgment dismissing the plaintiffs' complaint on its merits. On June 20, 1986, Judge Reynolds dismissed the complaint and filed a summary judgment denying that the claims raised constituted a legitimate cause of action under Section 1983.

The essence of Judge Reynolds's decision to dismiss derived from his reading of prior cases, wherein a Section 1983 claim depended upon there having been a "special relationship" between the claimant and the governmental entity from which damages were sought. Judge Reynolds said:

> This case is not sufficiently similar to such cases to support a finding that a special relationship existed between Joshua DeShaney and the public defendants. Neither Joshua nor his father were in

state custody either at the time of or immediately prior to the beating. None of the public defendants were present when the beating took place. Nor can the Court say, even after drawing all the inferences to which plaintiffs are entitled, that the public defendants deliberately exposed Joshua to known danger.

Further, he argued:

The fact that the Theda Clark Regional Medical Center held Joshua under a protective custody order for three days some thirteen months prior to the March 1984 beating indicates no more than that efforts were made at the time to protect a child in the legal custody of one of his natural parents from possible child abuse. Such temporary custody more than one year prior to the incident complained of did not give rise to a relationship with the public defendants sufficiently similar to the relationship between the state and a prisoner incarcerated in one of its penal institutions so as to hold such defendants liable under Section 1983.

As a district judge, Judge Reynolds was bound not only by the relevant holdings of the Supreme Court but also by those of the Seventh Circuit Court of Appeals, his home circuit. The law of the Seventh Circuit was clear: Section 1983 did not provide a remedy for violations of a duty to care arising out of tort law; such injuries were remediable only under state tort law in the state courts.

THE APPEAL

The DeShaneys appealed to the Seventh Circuit Court of Appeals. The case was argued on January 13, 1987, before Circuit Judges Richard A. Posner and John L. Coffey and Senior District Judge Robert A. Grant.

The crux of the DeShaney appeal was that the Department of Social Services, by its earlier actions pertaining to Joshua, had entered into a "special relationship" with him analogous to the sort of relationship that exists between an incarcerated prisoner and the state or a confined mental patient and the state; in brief, the claim would be that the Department of Social Services had assumed responsibility for Joshua's well-being and were thus duty-bound by the Due Process Clause to make certain no harm came to him.

The claim was not far-fetched. Indeed, in two very significant cases the United States Supreme Court had inclined in precisely that direction. In *Estelle* v. *Gamble* (1976), the Court, in an opinion by Justice Thurgood Marshall that was joined by Chief Justice Warren Burger and Associate Justices William Brennan, Potter Stewart, Byron White, Lewis Powell, and William Rehnquist (Justice Harry Blackmun concurred in the judgment and Justice John Paul Stevens dissented), held that "deliberate indifference to a prisoner's serious illness or injury states a cause of action under Section 1983."[3]

Similarly, in 1982 a unanimous Court held in *Youngberg* v. *Romeo* that Section 1983 extended to involuntarily committed mental patients. "Persons who have been involuntarily committed are entitled to more considerate treatment and conditions of confinement than criminals whose conditions of confinement are designed to punish."[4] The Constitution, the Court held, demanded "minimally adequate training" to enable the profoundly retarded defendant, Nicholas Romeo, to function without "undue restraint" within the institution to which he had been confined.[5] The Court said, in an opinion by Justice Powell, that "the minimally adequate training required by the Constitution is such training as may be reasonable in light of respondent's liberty interests in safety and freedom from unreasonable restraints."[6]

Given that Section 1983 was in many ways "a statute that has burst its historical bounds," as Justice Powell would say in another case, the DeShaneys hoped that the Court of Appeals would find that increasingly versatile statute capacious enough to embrace their cause. After all, the sympathy that seemed to inform the reasoning of the Supreme Court in *Youngberg* certainly should extend to facts as shocking to the conscience as child abuse.

But there was another peg upon which the DeShaneys' lawyers hung their hopes. In 1985 a panel of the Third Circuit Court of Appeals had held in *Estate of Bailey by Oare* v. *County of York*[7] that "once the State is aware that a particular child may be abused, a special relationship arises between it and the child and places on the State a constitutional duty to protect the child from the abuse."[8] Yet the three judges sitting in *Estate of Bailey* had divided over this basic question. It was at least possible that Judges Posner, Coffey, and Grant could be persuaded to follow the lead of the majority of the Third Circuit panel and stretch the meaning of Section 1983 to cover Joshua DeShaney, thus altering the standing law of the Seventh Circuit. But such was not to be. On February 12, 1987, the court, in a unanimous decision and with an opinion written by Judge Posner, dashed the DeShaneys' hopes for an easy time of it.

In the view of the Court, there were "two possible theories on which the defendants . . . might be thought to have violated Joshua DeShaney's Fourteenth Amendment rights." The first, Judge Posner said, was that Joshua had a right to be protected by the Department of Social Services; the second was that the defendants were themselves somehow "complicit" in the beatings that had been inflicted upon Joshua by his father. "The first theory," Posner quickly concluded, "is foreclosed by the rule, well established in this circuit, that the state's failure to protect people from private violence, or other mishaps not attributable to the conduct of its employees, is not a deprivation of constitutionally protected property or liberty."[9] The reason, according to Judge Posner, is that "the Constitution is a charter of negative rather than positive liberties." In other words, the Constitution does not obligate government to do things as much as it restrains government from doing things.

> The state does not have a duty enforceable by the federal courts to maintain a police force or a fire department, or to protect children from their parents. The men who framed the original Constitution and the Fourteenth Amendment were worried about government's oppressing the citizenry rather than about its failing to provide adequate social services. For such failures, political remedies (along with such legal remedies as states might see fit to provide in their own courts) were assumed to be adequate.[10]

The second theory was a trickier matter. Conceding that the injuries inflicted upon Joshua had indeed "deprived him of his liberty within the meaning that the courts have given this word in the due process clauses," the fundamental question was "whether the state shares responsibility for this deprivation, in a federal constitutional sense, with Joshua's father."[11] There was no denying that Ann Kemmeter had "inexplicably failed to act on mounting, and eventually overwhelming, evidence that Joshua was in great peril from his father." Yet a simple question remained: Did the Constitution require her to act, and by her failure did she thus deprive Joshua of his constitutional right? To that question the court found an equally simple answer: no. "It is unlikely that Ann Kemmeter's well intentioned but ineffectual intervention did Joshua any good at all, but it is most unlikely that it did him any harm. She merely failed to protect him from his bestial father." Posner's logic was as clear as it was chilling: "That the state's inaction may have brought about a trivial increase in the probability that Joshua would be severely injured by his father does not enable a conclusion that the state deprived Joshua of his right to bodily integrity." More to the point, the judge concluded, "if the defendants, though blameworthy, did not cause Joshua's injuries, they cannot be said to have deprived him of his liberty; deprivation implies causation."[12]

Unlike the prisoner in *Estelle* or the mental patient in *Youngberg*, the state in *DeShaney* had not placed Joshua in a situation of its making where he would be at risk, as it would have, for example, had it placed him in a state-supervised foster home. The facts could not be made to reach so far:

> The Department of Social Services did not place Joshua in his father's custody; a Wyoming juvenile court did that. It is true that three days after temporarily placing Joshua in the custody of the hospital to which he was brought in January 1983, the Department returned him to his father. . . . But there is no evidence that the Department was reckless in returning Joshua to the custody of his father back in January 1983. If at that time the Wisconsin authorities had tried to terminate Randy's parental rights, he might well have sued them under 42 U.S.C.1983, charging an unconstitutional deprivation of his rights as a father, as in *Lossman* v. *Pekarske* . . . where another Wisconsin father suspected of child abuse brought just such a suit; or under state law, relying on such

[Wisconsin state court] cases as *LaChapell* v. *Mawhinney* . . . which held that as a general rule a child's best interests are served by living in a parent's home, rather than in the home of a more distant relative or in a foster home.[13]

Posner concluded:

To place every state welfare department on the razor's edge, where if it terminates parental rights it is exposed to a section 1983 suit (as well as a state-law suit) by the parent and if it fails to terminate those rights it is exposed to a section 1983 suit by the child, is unlikely to improve the welfare of American families, and is not grounded in constitutional text of principle.[14]

In its opinion the Seventh Circuit Court rejected out of hand the interpretation of the Third Circuit Court in *Estate of Bailey*. The notion posited there of a "special relationship" existing between the state welfare authorities and a child deemed likely to be abused was too extreme; it was supported neither by the language of the Due Process Clause nor by more general principles of constitutional law. The Third Circuit had simply created the doctrine out of whole cloth, going far beyond what any other circuit had decided and surely beyond what the Supreme Court had ever held.[15] Moreover, the doctrine, if embraced, would serve only to "inject the federal courts into an area in which they have little knowledge or experience: that of child welfare."[16] The federal design of the Constitution alone argued against so expansive a reading.

On February 25, 1987, the plaintiffs filed a petition for a rehearing *en banc*—meaning that it would be heard by the entire Seventh Circuit Court of Appeals. On April 21 that petition was denied, the Court order noting simply: "All of the judges on the original panel have voted to deny the petition, and none of the active members of the court has requested a vote on the suggestion for rehearing en banc." There was only one step left to the DeShaneys, and on July 17, 1987, they filed a petition for a writ of certiorari before the Supreme Court of the United States. Certiorari was granted on March 21, 1988.

SECTION 1983

Since 1895 the Supreme Court has had the use of the writ of certiorari. It is a writ that lies solely in the discretion of the Court; it is granted only if at least four justices agree that the case at issue raises questions important enough to merit a review by the highest Court. When a writ of certiorari is granted (and roughly 90 percent of all such petitions are denied each term), the Supreme Court orders the lower court to send the record of the case up to the Court for its review. However, the granting of the writ in no way assures that oral arguments will actually be scheduled or that the Court will reach the merits of the prior decision. Nor does the denial of certiorari reflect the considered judgment of the Supreme Court that the lower courts got it right; the Court simply cannot review every case for which appeal is made from the courts below.[17] Yet there is no denying that the internal politics of the Court has a bearing on what kinds of cases succeed in the application process.

Between March 1985, when the DeShaneys first filed their complaint, and March 1988, when the Supreme Court granted their petition for a writ of certiorari, the Court had undergone a transformation. Chief Justice Warren Burger had stepped down in June 1986. President Ronald Reagan had nominated the most conservative member of the Court, Associate Justice William H. Rehnquist, to replace him; the President in turn had nominated Judge Antonin Scalia of the United States Court of Appeals for the District of Columbia Circuit to fill Rehnquist's old seat. After a bruising confirmation battle, both Rehnquist and Scalia were confirmed, giving the Court a decidedly more conservative cast.

Reagan, after all, had pledged to stem the tide of what he derided as judicial activism by nominating jurists who would be unwilling to follow the policy-making paths that had been cleared for the Court by Chief Justice Earl Warren. His first appointment to the Court, Justice Sandra Day O'Connor in 1981, was less a fulfillment of Reagan's ideological promise than it had been the result of electoral reality as he planned for a second term. She was conservative, but hardly a dyed-in-the-wool restrainer. But after his reelection in 1984, Reagan had power to spare when it came to judicial appointments. By 1986, with the Department of Justice under his longtime ally Attorney General Edwin Meese III picking judicial nominees, Reagan was determined to keep his promise. As he summed it up that year, he was going to appoint to judgeships only those who would act like judges "and not like a bunch of sociology majors."

In June 1987 Reagan had yet another vacancy to fill on the high court. Justice Lewis Powell, widely regarded as the moderate fulcrum of an already ideologically teetering Court, announced his retirement. By then the state of affairs was not politically the same as it had been during the hard-fought confirmation of Rehnquist; it was worse. In November 1986 the Republicans had relinquished control of the Senate to the Democrats. The Senate Judiciary Committee under Joseph Biden of Delaware was far different from what it had been under Strom Thurmond of South Carolina. Further, the campaign for the 1988 presidential race had already begun, and two Democratic members of the committee, Biden and Senator Paul Simon of Illinois, were announced candidates for their party's nomination. But with only a moment's hesitation President Reagan turned to the man who had come to symbolize the sort of jurisprudence Reagan admired: Judge Robert H. Bork, also of the United States Court of Appeals for the District of Columbia Circuit.

By the end of September, Judge Bork's nomination had been crushed under the ideological onslaught of Reagan's liberal opponents, both within Congress and without. After the controversy surrounding his second choice, Judge Douglas Ginsburg, who withdrew after admitting past marijuana use, Reagan settled on Judge Anthony Kennedy of the Ninth Circuit Court of Appeals. Widely regarded as a "safe" conservative nomination within the Administration, Kennedy was confirmed overwhelmingly in December by a Senate still politically exhausted from the battle over Bork. Thus by March 1988, when the Court granted the DeShaneys' petition, the Supreme Court was an institution inclined much more toward a posture of judicial restraint than toward activism.

Most significant for the DeShaneys' case was the fact that the center chair of Chief Justice was now filled by William Rehnquist.

Not only was he one of the two most judicially conservative members of the newly reconstituted Court (Justice Scalia being the other), but he had been waging a long fight to restrict precisely the sort of creative interpretations of Section 1983 that the DeShaneys were about to urge on the Justices. In many ways, the case of *DeShaney* v. *Winnebago County Department of Social Services* would provide the perfect occasion for Rehnquist to curb what he viewed as the excesses that had come to define too many of the Court's judgments concerning both Section 1983 and the Due Process Clause of the Fourteenth Amendment. His abiding respect for federalism and state sovereignty demanded nothing less.

The judicial controversies over Section 1983 had begun in earnest in 1961 in the case of *Monroe* v. *Pape*.[18] In *Monroe* the Court considered the reach of Section 1983 regarding the actions of public officials "under the color" of state law. The facts were troubling, to say the least. Police officers for the city of Chicago, without any warrant for search or arrest, broke into the Monroe home in the wee hours of the morning, roused the family from their beds, and made them stand naked in the living room while the officers ransacked the entire house. The father was allegedly struck several times with a flashlight by Detective Pape, called "nigger" and "black boy," and then finally hauled into the police station where he was held on "open charges" for ten hours while the police interrogated him about a murder that had occurred two days earlier. The Monroes had filed suit under what was then called Section 1979 of the Revised Statutes, later Section 1983.

The question before the Court was twofold. First, did the Congress that enacted Section 1983 intend "to give a remedy to parties deprived of constitutional rights, privileges and immunities by an official's abuse of his position"; second, did the statute render a municipality liable for damages? To the first query the Court concluded that such was indeed the intention of the Congress that passed the law. To the second question, as to municipal liability, Justice William O. Douglas wrote for the Court that Congress did not intend "to bring municipal corporations within the ambit" of the law.[19]

The only dissent in the case came from Justice Felix Frankfurter; it was a blistering denunciation of the Court's judgment holding that Section 1983 extended liability to public officials who abuse their power. The crux of Frankfurter's complaint was not that the alleged actions could not raise constitutional questions. The problem in *Monroe* was that the statute under which the suit was brought was too specific to include the instant complaint. Reviewing the legislative history of the statute, Frankfurter was convinced that there was never an intention to include "acts in defiance of state law and which no settled state practice, no systematic pattern of official action or inaction, no 'custom or usage, of any State,' insulates from effective and adequate reparation by the State's authorities."[20]

[R]espect for principles which this Court has long regarded as critical to the most effective functioning of our federalism should avoid extension of a statute beyond its manifest area of operation into applications which invite conflict with the administration of local policies. Such an extension makes the extreme limits of federal constitutional power a law to regulate the quotidian business of every traffic policeman, every registrar of elections, every city inspector or investigator, every clerk in every municipal licensing bureau in this country. The text of the statute, reinforced by its history, precludes such a reading.[21]

The Court, Frankfurter argued, had abstracted the 1871 statute from its proper historical context in order "to attribute twentieth century conceptions of the federal judicial system to the Reconstruction Congress."[22] And therein lay the danger:

We cannot expect to create an effective means of protection for human liberties by torturing an 1871 statute to meet the problems of 1960. . . . It is not a work for courts to melt and recast this statute. "Under color" of law meant by authority of law in the nineteenth century. No judicial sympathy, however strong, for the needs now felt can give the phrase—a phrase which occurs in a statute, not in a constitution—any different meaning in the twentieth.[23]

The decision in *Monroe* v. *Pape* excluding municipalities from the reach of Section 1983 would stand as good law for seventeen years. But in June 1978, in an opinion by Justice William Brennan, the Court overruled that portion of *Monroe*. In *Monell* v. *New York City Department of Social Services* (a class action suit brought by a group of women against the official policy of the Department of Social Services that demanded that pregnant employees must take unpaid leaves of absence before any medical reason for so doing) the Court wrought a revolution in federalism:

> Our analysis of the legislative history of the Civil Rights Act of 1871 compels the conclusion that Congress *did* intend municipalities and other local government units to be included among those persons to whom Section 1983 applies. Local governing bodies, therefore, can be sued directly under Section 1983 for monetary, declaratory, or injunctive relief where . . . the action that is alleged to be unconstitutional implements or executes a policy statement, ordinance, regulation, or decision officially adopted and promulgated by that body's officers.[24]

There was, however, a minimal threshold, although it was not as clear or as high as the Court first implied:

> [A] local government may not be sued under Section 1983 for an injury inflicted solely by its employees or agents. Instead, it is when the execution of a government's policy or custom, whether made by its lawmakers or by those whose edicts or acts may fairly be said to represent official policy, inflicts the injury that the government as an entity is responsible under Section 1983.[25]

To Justice Rehnquist, then six years on the Court, the logic of Brennan's opinion could not go unchallenged. Rehnquist's dissent, joined by Chief Justice Burger, would foreshadow, in some ways, the clash between Brennan and Rehnquist a decade later in *DeShaney*. That debate would center on what Brennan would see as a properly evolving conception of decency and what Rehnquist would hold to be a perversion of the written Constitution in order to make it conform to the ideological predilections of the Court. The future Chief Justice said:

The decision in *Monroe* v. *Pape* was the fountainhead of the torrent of civil rights litigation of the last 17 years. Using Section 1983 as a vehicle, the courts have articulated new and previously unforesee-able interpretations of the Fourteenth Amendment. At the same time, the doctrine of municipal immunity enunciated in *Monroe* has protected municipalities and their limited treasuries from the conse-quences of their officials' failure to predict the course of this Court's constitutional jurisprudence. None of the members of this Court can foresee the practical consequences of today's removal of that protection. Only the Congress, which has the benefit of the advice of every segment of this diverse Nation, is equipped to con-sider the results of such a drastic change in the law. It seems all but inevitable that it will find it necessary to do so after today's deci-sion.[26]

But it would not be enough to leave this area of the law to con-gressional action; Section 1983 would continue to provide a "tor-rent of civil rights litigation" and countless demands for the Court to discover "previously unforeseeable interpretations of the Fourteenth Amendment." And within the confines of the cases and controversies that came before the Court it would be possible to shackle the Court somewhat from wandering even farther away from the historic meaning of both Section 1983 and the Fourteenth Amendment. In a series of cases that, looking back, would prove to be a preface to the Court's decision in *DeShaney,* Justice Rehnquist set out to drain much of the judicially fer-mented substance from the Due Process Clause and thereby to limit the extent of Section 1983.

From the time of the decision in *Monell* the primary question that would vex the Court would be how and when ordinary negli-gence on the part of public officials might constitute a cause of ac-tion under Section 1983 as a violation of the Due Process Clause of the Fourteenth Amendment. Just prior to the *Monell* decision the Court had brushed up against the issue; but in *Procunier* v. *Navarette* (1978)[27] it chose to sidestep it and limited the scope of its inquiry to the narrower facts of that case. The next year the Court decided to grapple with the question more forthrightly, al-though not in a comprehensive way.

In *Baker* v. *McCollan* (1979) the Court was confronted by a claim that a false imprisonment constituted a deprivation of liberty under the Due Process Clause and thus constituted a cognizable claim for damages under Section 1983.[28] The false imprisonment had resulted from Leonard McCollan's having altered the driver's license of his brother, Linnie Carl McCollan. Leonard had attached his photograph to Linnie's license. When Linnie was stopped for a traffic violation he was arrested on an outstanding warrant, which in fact had been issued against Leonard but in Linnie's name on the basis of the false driver's license. Despite Linnie's protests that he was innocent, he was held in jail for four days. When Sheriff Baker realized he had the wrong man, Linnie was immediately set free. Linnie brought suit against Sheriff Baker, claiming that through the negligence of the sheriff's department Linnie McCollan had been unconstitutionally deprived of his liberty.

At first it seemed the Court could not avoid addressing the question of negligence directly; surely being incarcerated wrongly for four days constituted a deprivation of Linnie McCollan's rights. But again the Court hedged. Writing for the majority, Justice Rehnquist acknowledged that "the question whether an allegation of simple negligence is sufficient to state a cause of action under Section 1983 is more elusive than it appears at first blush. It may well not be susceptible of a uniform answer across the entire spectrum of conceivable constitutional violations which might be the subject of a Section 1983 action."[29] But before grappling with that question, Justice Rehnquist argued, there was a threshold requirement of whether the plaintiff had indeed been deprived of a right secured by the Constitution and laws of the United States. In the view of the Court, Linnie McCollan had not been able to clear that hurdle.

The Court argued that there had been no deprivation of McCollan's rights carried out "under the color" of state law. Indeed, the arrest warrant under which his wrongful imprisonment was carried out was "facially valid." The error was not the fault of the Sheriff in acting on the warrant once Linnie had been stopped; the warrant was based legitimately on the evidence available to the authorities at the time. While McCollan had indeed been deprived of his liberty for a four-day period, "it was pursuant to a warrant conforming, for purposes of our decision, to the requirements of the Fourth Amendment."[30] McCollan's innocence of the charge was, Rehnquist argued, "largely irrelevant to his claim of deprivation of liberty without due process of law." Put more bluntly: "The Constitution does not guarantee that only the guilty will be arrested."[31]

The essential point of the opinion of the Court in *McCollan* was that "false imprisonment does not become a violation of the Fourteenth Amendment merely because the defendant [Sheriff Baker] is a state official."[32] That was not to suggest, the Court assured McCollan, that he was without the possibility of remedy for what was clearly a "wrongful" imprisonment. It was only to point out that the relief to be sought was under state tort law in the state courts.

The question of negligence would not go away. In 1981 the Court turned once again to the task of trying to posit some guidelines for Section 1983 claims in *Parratt* v. *Taylor*.[33] The facts of *Parratt* bordered on the trivial. The respondent, Taylor, an inmate at the Nebraska Penal and Correctional Complex, had ordered hobby materials through the mail for $23.50; the materials were lost after they arrived at the prison. Taylor sued under Section 1983, claiming that his property had been negligently lost by prison officials in violation of the Fourteenth Amendment. In particular, he claimed that he had been unconstitutionally deprived of his property without due process of law. The District Court had upheld his claim; the Court of Appeals affirmed that decision. The State's appeal was supported by a horde of state attorneys general as "friends of the court" in *amici curiae* briefs.

Again writing for the Court, Justice Rehnquist attempted to sharpen the focus. Taylor had presented a claim, he conceded, that "satisfies three prerequisites of a valid due process claim: the petitioners acted under color of a state law; the hobby kit falls within the definition of property; and the alleged loss, even though negligently caused, amounted to a deprivation." However, Rehnquist went on, by themselves those three facts could not establish a violation of the Fourteenth Amendment; more was needed. In particular, the deprivation under the color of state law had to be effected without due process of law. Citing his opinion in *Baker* v.

McCollan, Rehnquist reiterated the maxim that the Fourteenth Amendment only protects against deprivations "without due process of law."[34] Taylor's loss "did not occur as the result of some established state procedure. Indeed, the deprivation occurred as a result of the unauthorized failure of the agents of the state to follow established state procedure."[35]

Before reversing the lower courts on that ground, however, Rehnquist had stumbled into a potentially dangerous thicket: What standards might there be to determine negligence within the meaning of due process of law and Section 1983? The issue was whether the state of mind or intention of the public official accused of wrongdoing was an issue in such Section 1983 litigation. A criminal statute analogous to Section 1983, for example, had specified that any deprivation of rights had to be done "willfully."[36] "Nothing in the language of Section 1983 or its legislative history limits the statute solely to intentional deprivations of constitutional rights." Nor, Rehnquist noted, had the Court ever found the statute to contain a state-of-mind requirement, as had the criminal law. The conclusion was clear: "Both *Baker* v. *McCollan* and *Monroe* v. *Pape* suggest that Section 1983 affords a 'civil remedy' for deprivations of federally protected rights caused by persons acting under color of state law without any express requirement of a particular state of mind."[37] In brief, negligence might indeed be sufficient to legitimate a Section 1983 claim provided the rights violated by the negligent actions were clearly rights protected by the Constitution or laws of the United States.

Of the other five opinions filed in the case, only that of Justice Powell would prove to be of significance. Powell could not bring himself to agree with the reasoning of Rehnquist's opinion; he concurred in the judgment but offered his own way of thinking about these issues. He was to the point: "Unlike the Court, I do not believe such negligent acts by state officials constitute a deprivation of property within the meaning of the Fourteenth Amendment, regardless of whatever subsequent procedure a State may or may not provide."[38] In a sense, Powell's opinion seemed more like what was usually expected of Rehnquist than had Rehnquist's own opinion; it was an opinion rooted in the text and intention of the Constitution:

In the due process area, the question is whether intent is required before there can be a "deprivation" of life, liberty, or property. In this case, for example, the negligence of the prison officials caused respondent to lose his property. Nevertheless, I would not hold that such a negligent act, causing unintended loss of or injury to property, works a deprivation in the *constitutional sense*. Thus no procedure for compensation is constitutionally required.

Further, Powell explained:

A "deprivation" connotes an intentional act denying something to someone, or, at the very least, a deliberate decision not to act to prevent a loss. The most reasonable interpretation of the Fourteenth Amendment would limit due process claims to such active deprivations.[39]

To adopt this standard, one already adopted by "an overwhelming number of lower courts," Powell argued, would avoid "trivializing the right of action provided in Section 1983."

That provision was enacted to deter real *abuses* by state officials in the exercise of governmental powers. It would make no sense to open the federal courts to lawsuits where there had been no affirmative abuse of power, merely a negligent deed by one who happens to be acting under color of state law.[40]

The importance of concurring and dissenting opinions is that they may, in time, come to convince a new majority of the Court as to the rightness of their reasoning. Such was to be the fate of Justice Powell's concurrence in *Parratt* v. *Taylor*. Five years later the Court returned to the question of negligence within the context of Section 1983 claims and abandoned the view it had enunciated in *Parratt* in favor of Justice Powell's notion. The injury for which Section 1983 damages were sought in *Daniels* v. *Williams* had resulted when the claimant, an inmate in a Richmond, Virginia jail, tripped over a pillow allegedly left on a stairwell by jail personnel.

In assessing the petitioner's claim, Justice Rehnquist went immediately to the point, overruling at least a sliver of the logic in *Parratt*: "We conclude that the Due Process Clause is simply not implicated by a *negligent* act of an official causing unintended loss of or injury to life, liberty, or property."[41] The question boiled down to the original meaning and purpose of the Due Process Clause:

> Historically, this guarantee of due process has been applied to *deliberate* decisions of government officials to deprive a person of life, liberty, or property. . . . No decision of this Court before *Parratt* supported the view that negligent conduct by a state official, even though causing injury, constitutes a deprivation under the Due Process Clause. This history reflects the traditional and common-sense notion that the Due Process Clause, like its forbear in the Magna Carta . . . was "intended to secure the individual from the arbitrary exercise of the powers of government."

Turning to the case at hand, Rehnquist concluded:

> Far from an abuse of power, lack of due care suggests no more than a failure to measure up to the conduct of a reasonable person. To hold that injury caused by such conduct is a deprivation within the meaning of the Fourteenth Amendment would trivialize the centuries-old principle of due process of law. . . . Our Constitution deals with the large concerns of the governors and the governed, but it does not purport to supplant traditional tort law in laying down rules of conduct to regulate liability for injuries that attend living together in society. . . . The only tie between the facts of this case and anything governmental in nature is the fact that respondent was a sheriff's deputy at the Richmond city jail and petitioner was an inmate confined in that jail. . . . [W]hile the Due Process Clause of the Fourteenth Amendment obviously speaks to some facets of this relationship . . . we do not believe its protections are triggered by lack of due care by prison officials . . . .Where a government official's act causing injury to life, liberty, or property is merely negligent, "no procedure for compensation is *constitutionally* required."[42]

Justice Rehnquist had been able to hold the Court together in *Daniels* v. *Williams;* no one dissented. Yet there were fissures of dissatisfaction in the cases that had come before it. In *Baker* v. *McCollan,* Marshall, Stevens, and Brennan had dissented; in *Parratt,* Marshall had dissented, but only in part; and in *Daniels* both Stevens and Blackmun had concurred only in the judgment. But the fissures broadened to cracks in a case that came just after *Daniels, Davidson* v. *Cannon*.[43] In *Davidson* the lines were drawn that would later divide the Court in *DeShaney* v. *Winnebago County;* Rehnquist had passed the boundary beyond which the most liberal members of the Court—Blackmun, Marshall, and Brennan—were not willing to go.

The difference for the liberal dissenters in *Davidson* between that case and *Daniels* was that while the claim presented in *Daniels* had been trivial, that in *Davidson* was not. Davidson was an inmate in the New Jersey State Prison; he had been first threatened and then attacked by a fellow inmate, one McMillian. Upon being threatened, Davidson had sent a note on December 19, 1980, to a civilian hearing officer in the prison who passed it along to the defendant Cannon, the Assistant Superintendent of the prison. Cannon, in turn, had passed the note on to his fellow defendant in the Section 1983 suit, James, a Corrections Sergeant. As reported by the Court in its opinion, Davidson's note was not ambiguous. Davidson wrote:

> When I went back to the unit after seeing you McMillian was on the steps outside the unit. When I was going past him he told me "I'll fuck you up you old mother-fucking fag. Go up to your cell, I be right there." I ignored this and went to another person's cell and thought about it. Then I figured I should tell you so "if " anything develops you would be aware.
>
> I'm quite content to let this matter drop but evidently McMillian isn't.
>
> > Thank you,
> > R. Davidson[44]

Cannon testified that he did not think the situation urgent insofar as Davidson had not come directly to him, as he had in the past. James, when receiving the note from Cannon, put it aside unread and later left for the day, not having returned to it; neither Cannon nor James worked on December 20 or 21. On December 21 McMillian attacked Davidson with a fork, as the Court reported, "breaking his nose and inflicting other wounds to his face, neck, head, and body." Davidson sued under Section

1983, claiming that the prison officers' behavior had violated his rights under the Eighth and Fourteenth Amendments. The District Court, after a bench trial, held that although the petitioner had not made his case for an Eighth Amendment violation, he did succeed under the Fourteenth Amendment's Due Process Clause. The Court awarded Davidson $2,000 in compensatory damages under its reading of *Parratt* v. *Taylor.* The Third Circuit Court of Appeals reversed, holding that *Parratt* did not extend Section 1983 remedies "for the type of negligence found in this case."[45]

For Rehnquist and the majority for which he wrote (Burger, White, Powell and O'Connor) the issue was simple:

> In *Daniels,* we held that the Due Process Clause of the Fourteenth Amendment is not implicated by the lack of due care of an official causing unintended injury to life, liberty, or property. In other words, where a government official is merely negligent in causing the injury, no procedure for compensation is constitutionally required.

As went Daniels's claim, so must go Davidson's:

> Respondents' lack of due care in this case led to serious injury, but that lack of care simply does not approach the sort of abusive government conduct that the Due Process Clause was designed to prevent. . . . Far from abusing governmental power, or employing it as an instrument of oppression, respondent Cannon mistakenly believed that the situation was not particularly serious, and respondent James simply forgot about the note. The guarantee of due process had never been understood to mean that the State must guarantee due care on the part of its officials. . . . As we held in *Daniels,* the protections of the Due Process Clause, whether procedural or substantive, are just not triggered by lack of due care by prison officials.[46]

The main dissent was written by Justice Blackmun. It was, in a sense, a boiling over of sentiment that had been simmering all along. Although he had concurred in both *McCollan* and *Parratt,* Blackmun had been careful to carve out a position that differed from the opinions of Rehnquist in those cases. In *McCollan,* for example, Blackmun sought to make clear that the opinion he was joining would not foreclose future Due Process Clause claims under the "shocks the conscience" test of *Rochin* v. *California.* There was more to the meaning of the Due Process Clause, Blackmun argued, than merely the particular provisions of the Bill of Rights. He was inclined to agree with Justice John Marshall Harlan when, in *Poe* v. *Ullman,* he argued that the meaning of "liberty" in that clause "is a rational continuum which, broadly speaking, includes a freedom from all substantial arbitrary impositions and purposeless restraints."[47]

Blackmun had concurred in both the judgment and the opinion of *Parratt* but felt obligated, he said, "to write separately to emphasize my understanding of its narrow reach."[48] The fundamental issue in *Parratt,* he insisted was "the deprivation only of property." The rule laid down by the Court concerning negligence, Blackmun insisted, would not, in his view, be "applicable to a case concerning deprivation of life or of liberty." For Blackmun there is a hierarchy of rights under the Fourteenth Amendment; property comes in last place.[49] The problem with *Davidson,* for Blackmun, was that it sought to elevate the "sensible rule of thumb" that mere negligence would not meet the demands of Section 1983 into an "inflexible constitutional dogma." Blackmun saw no justification for such a "rigid view" of the standard of liability.[50]

The great difference between *Daniels* and *Davidson,* Blackmun argued, derived from the sort of injury Davidson had suffered and how it could have been avoided. A pillow inadvertently left on a stairwell was merely negligent; not following up on a prisoner's fearful report of a threat made against him went beyond simple negligence. There was evidence to suggest, Blackmun insisted, that the behavior of Cannon and James was "sufficiently irresponsible to constitute reckless disregard of Davidson's safety." Even though negligence had been held "insufficient to cause a deprivation under the Fourteenth Amendment, recklessness must be sufficient."[51] The fact that both Cannon and James had been forewarned about "a real and known possibility of violence" was what changed the "constitutional complexion" of the case.[52]

But there was more than simply the forewarning of violence against Davidson. Perhaps even more troubling to Blackmun was the fact that Davidson had first been deprived of any means of self-protection, and the prison had not fulfilled its obligation to protect him.

> When the State of New Jersey put Robert Davidson in its prison, it stripped him of all means of self-protection. It forbade his access to a weapon . . . It forbade his fighting back. . . . It blocked all avenues of escape. The State forced Davidson to rely solely on its own agents for protection. When threatened with violence by a fellow inmate, Davidson turned to the prison officials for protection, but they ignored his plea for help. As a result, Davidson was assaulted by another inmate.[53]

It was this obligation to protect that most clearly distinguished *Daniels* from *Davidson:*

> When the State incarcerated Daniels, it left intact his own faculties for avoiding a slip and fall. But the State prevented Davidson from defending himself, and therefore assumed responsibility to protect him from the dangers to which he was exposed.[54]

And this was the core of Blackmun's dissent in *Davidson:*

> [W]here the State renders a person vulnerable and strips him of his ability to defend himself, an injury that results from a state official's negligence in performing his duty is peculiarly related to the governmental function.[55]

There was yet another concern for Blackmun, and that was the danger of eroding the purposes for which Section 1983 was originally enacted. Fearing that the State would not provide an adequate avenue for redress of violations of rights by the state, Congress sought to pave a federal remedial road. Blackmun pointed out: "The very purpose of Section 1983 was to interpose the federal courts between the States and the people, as guardians of the people's federal rights."[56] This was precisely the problem in

Davidson. By statute the State of New Jersey had explicitly provided for the immunity of officials like Cannon and James in cases like Davidson's: "Neither a public entity nor a public employee is liable for . . . any injury caused by . . . a prisoner to any other prisoner."[57] Such immunity closed off to Davidson an avenue for redress in the state courts after the alleged deprivation of his liberty took place, as had been possible in *McCollan, Parratt,* and *Daniels.* "Lacking a meaningful post-deprivation remedy in state court," Blackmun concluded, "Davidson was deprived of his liberty without due process of law."[58]

Given the doctrinal movement of the Court from *McCollan* to *Parratt* to *Daniels* to *Davidson,* especially in light of the changes among the Justices themselves, there should have been little doubt what the next jurisprudential step was likely to be when the Court granted certiorari in *DeShaney* v. *Winnebago County Department of Social Services.* Yet the liberal bloc of the Court remained intact. If Justice Brennan could be persuaded of the worthiness of Joshua's claim (he had dissented, after all, in both *McCollan* and *Davidson,* even though he had joined Rehnquist in *Parratt* and *Daniels*), it might be enough to carry the day. There remained, as well, the emotional advantage the plaintiffs enjoyed: An innocent four-year-old boy beaten by his father was a far more sympathetic petitioner than the usual convicts with which the Court had to deal. Thus there was at least hope that the Court could be swayed by Brennan and his constant reliance on "evolving conceptions of decency" as the proper standard for constitutional interpretation. Perhaps even Rehnquist would find these facts too grim to ignore.

THE BRIEFS

By the time the Court set aside time for oral argument in *DeShaney* v. *Winnebago County* on November 2, 1988, both sides had marshaled their forces. The plaintiffs, the DeShaneys, were supported in their quest by an *amicus curiae* brief filed by the American Civil Liberties Union on behalf of the ACLU's Children's Rights Project and several other organizations.[59] Each had an ongoing interest in the rights of children, particularly those who found themselves in Joshua DeShaney's sad circumstance. Each believed the Seventh Circuit Court of Appeals had erred in its denial of liability under Section 1983.

Winnebago County had an even more impressive army of supporters. *Amicus curiae* briefs had been filed by the National School Boards Association; the States of New York, Connecticut, Maryland, Oregon, Pennsylvania, and Wisconsin; the National Association of Counties; the Council of State Governments; the United States Conference of Mayors; the National Conference of State Legislatures; the National League of Cities; the International City Management Association; and, finally, the United States Department of Justice. A formidable assemblage stood in support of the defendants. Needless to say, not all of the interest in behalf of Winnebago County was a matter of the highest principle; if the DeShaneys prevailed, the costs to state and local governments would be potentially astronomical and certainly crippling. The stakes were very high indeed.

Having had their plea twice rebuffed, the DeShaneys had honed their argument considerably. Rather than claim a general liability under Section 1983 for a violation of the Fourteenth Amendment broadly construed, they now insisted that they were concerned only with an "exquisitely narrow issue," the question of a constitutional deprivation of due process only as implicated in the protection of children from violence. That issue alone, they told the Court, was the claim presented, nothing more.

They rested their appeal to the Supreme Court on another collection of cases that had been emerging in the lower courts. As stated in their brief: "Every circuit which has considered this issue, with the sole exception of this present case, has in a variety of child concern contexts affirmed the need and the right of the child to special consideration from the state." In *Doe* v. *New York City Department of Social Services*, for example, the Second Circuit had held that the Fourteenth Amendment guarantees a child a certain affirmative duty of protection when the child has been placed in a foster home. "When individuals are placed in custody or under the care of the government," the court said, "their governmental custodians are sometimes charged with affirmative duties, the nonfeasance of which may violate the Constitution."[60]

Similarly, the Fourth Circuit Court of Appeals in *Jensen* v. *Conrad* had held that "a right to affirmative protection need not be limited by a determination that there was a 'custodial relationship.' " [61] The reason they could so hold, the court said, arose from an earlier decision they had handed down, *Fox* v. *Custis.*

In *Fox,* a case that dealt with actions by parolees under the supervision of the Virginia Department of Corrections, the court had said an affirmative right of protection could arise out of "special custodial or other relationships created or assumed by the state in respect of particular persons." In both *Fox* and *Jensen,* the Fourth Circuit left the door ajar. "Were the issue properly before this court on different facts," the panel ruled, "there would be nothing to preclude further definition of the meaning of that term followed by a ruling that the facts of that case fell within the meaning of 'special relationship.' " [62]

The DeShaneys seized upon *Jensen* insofar as that opinion had undercut to a degree yet another earlier case, that of *Bowers* v. *DeVito,* a Seventh Circuit opinion written by the same Judge Posner who had denied their claim on appeal.[63] In *Bowers* Posner had foreshadowed his opinion in *DeShaney* by arguing that "there is no constitutional right to be protected by the state against being murdered by criminals or madmen. It is monstrous if the state fails to protect its residents against such predators but it does not violate the due process clause of the Fourteenth Amendment or, we suppose, any other provision of the Constitution." The reason, said the judge, is simple: "The Constitution is a charter of negative liberties; it tells the state to let people alone; it does not require the federal government or the state to provide services, even so elementary a service as maintaining law and order."[64]

But Judge Posner seemed to have left a slight gap, one which the Fourth Circuit's opinions in *Fox* and *Jensen* had exploited to their advantage, the DeShaneys now argued. "We do not want to pretend," Posner had written, "that the line between action and inaction, between inflicting and failing to prevent the infliction of harm, is clearer than it is. If the state puts a man in a position of danger from private persons and then fails to protect him, it will not be heard to say that its role was merely passive; it is as much an active tortfeasor as if it had thrown him into a snake pit."[65]

That, of course, was precisely what the DeShaneys were arguing:
that by sending Joshua back to his "bestial father" the state had in
effect "thrown him into a snake pit."

As they had in the court below, the DeShaneys once again relied on the Third Circuit ruling in *Estate of Bailey by Oare* v.
County of York, which had rested, in part, upon the *dictum* of the
court in *Jensen*. Aleta Bailey, like Joshua DeShaney, had been subjected to the violence of child abuse; the DeShaneys sought to
pound home the striking similarities in their brief as well as to
point out how much more obvious Joshua's situation had been:

> There, as here, a small child lived with a natural parent and the par-
> ent's paramour. There, as here, there was an accusation of the para-
> mour's having struck the child, and an initial hospitalization and
> examination. There, as here, the examining medical staff felt they
> were dealing with an abuse situation and so advised the child pro-
> tection agency. There, as here, the recommendation was made that
> the paramour be kept away from the child. There, as here, the wel-
> fare agency initially arranged for placement away from the home,
> and then returned the child to the home. There, the agency did not
> investigate or know where the paramour was or what the home
> conditions were, whereas here that information was at hand and
> was adverse to the child's interests and to the agency's own recom-
> mendations. There the child died within a month, whereas here the
> child continued to be abused systematically while the DSS contin-
> ued to annotate the observed signs of abuse and neglect for almost
> a year and a half.

Bailey afforded them an opportunity to distinguish cases like
that of Aleta Bailey and Joshua DeShaney from that which had
given rise to another controlling Supreme Court decision,
Martinez v. *California.*[66] In *Martinez* a fifteen-year-old girl was
murdered by a parolee five months after he was released from
prison. The family of the decedent sued under Section 1983,
claiming that the state knew or should have known that the
parolee was likely to present a clear and present danger to the
community, given his history as a sex offender. Further, the family claimed it had a legitimate federal case because the state of
California had provided immunity to such state law claims.[67] In a

unanimous opinion by Justice Stevens, the Court rejected that claim:

> [W]e cannot accept the contention that this statute deprived Thomas's victim of her life without due process of law because it condoned a parole decision that led directly to her death.

But, as is often the case, the Court could not resist injecting a bit of ambiguity into its holding. And it was this ambiguity upon which subsequent cases, such as *Bailey*, would try to rest. Justice Stevens wrote:

> We need not and do not decide that a parole officer could never be deemed to "deprive" someone of life by action taken in connection with the release of a prisoner on parole.[68]

When the Third Circuit Court of Appeals turned to the claim raised by the estate of Aleta Bailey, a majority held that the circumstances leading to Bailey's death fell "on the other side of the line suggested in *Martinez*."[69] More to the point: "The significant difference between this case and *Martinez* is the fact that the victim in *Martinez* was a member of the public at large while here the agency was aware of a 'special danger' to Aleta."[70] This, the DeShaneys argued, was precisely the situation of Joshua's misfortune.

By the time their case found its way into the Supreme Court, the DeShaneys had yet another lower court opinion they believed was apposite to their claim. Shortly after the Seventh Circuit had denied their appeal in 1987, the Eleventh Circuit considered the same issues as those in *Bailey* and, like the court in *Bailey*, found that there were certain children's rights that could be violated by the gross neglect or deliberate indifference of a child protection agency. *Taylor* v. *Ledbetter* offered the DeShaneys yet another hook on which to hang their argument: A state's statutory scheme that created a right to protection could not be violated without a clear violation of due process of law.[71] The court in *Taylor* argued that the there were clear "liberty interests" such as being free from the infliction and unnecessary pain and a fundamental right to physical safety that were protected by the due process clauses of the Fifth and Fourteenth Amendments. When a state agency assumes "the responsibility of finding and keeping the child in a safe environment," it assumes an obligation "to insure the continuing safety of that environment."[72]

To the *Taylor* court, it was not a formal legal relationship—such as that in *Estelle* or *Youngberg*—that gave rise to the state's obligation to provide a safe environment. In light of the decisions in such cases as *Bowers* and *Fox,* it was clear that such a right to protection could arise "out of special custodial or other relationships created or assumed by the state in respect of particular persons."[73]

The DeShaneys, then, had several things in their favor. The federal courts were ambivalent with regard to the two important factors that weighed heavily in their argument: the degree to which the intentions of the state officials matter in determining 1983 liability, and the characteristics of the relationship that has to exist between the state and an individual that will create an entitlement protected by the Fourteenth Amendment. In addition, of course, was the special significance attached to the fact that this was a case of the welfare of a child, not an adult. This, coupled with the tragic facts surrounding the case, led the attorneys for the DeShaneys to be hopeful as they prepared for their hearing before the Supreme Court.

In their brief, they therefore argued:

> [T]he statute specifically mandates that social workers and others with reasonable cause to suspect child abuse *shall* report such, Sec. 48.981(2); persons required to report, such as social workers, *shall* immediately contact designated officials, Sec.48.981(3); county DSS upon receiving a report *shall* commence an appropriate and thorough investigation within twenty-four hours, Sec.48.981(3)(c); and a DSS investigator having grounds *shall* place the child in protective custody, Sec.48.981(3)(c)(5).

The crux of the matter, the DeShaneys went on, is that such rules and regulations are not discretionary, and it was at this level that Winnebago County failed to meet its statutory duty to Joshua:

These acts are not elective but mandatory; the mandate goes not to how "perfectly" they are carried out, but to the stark obligation to perform them. In this case, factually, these unequivocal mandates were ignored, and ignored repeatedly. It is not simply that they were done poorly; rather, they were not done at all, and were omitted without excuse or sense.[74]

The real burden of the DeShaneys' claim was to prove that the officials of the Department of Social Services were guilty not merely of neglect but of something worse. Granting that it was inconceivable that Ann Kemmeter and Cheryl Stelse in any way wished Joshua any harm, especially the gruesome harm that eventually befell him, granting, that is, that they never within the meaning of the law "intended" to cause Joshua any injury, still, their behavior went beyond the ordinary and legal understanding of negligence. Conveniently, the Supreme Court had left open the possibility that it would view such transgressions differently. In *Daniels* v. *Williams,* Justice Rehnquist had signaled that such a question remained theoretically open: "Despite his claim about what he might have pleaded, petitioner [Daniels] concedes that the respondent [Williams] was at most negligent. Accordingly, this case affords us no occasion to consider whether something less than intentional conduct, such as recklessness or "gross negligence," is enough to trigger the protections of the Due Process Clause."[75] As the DeShaneys argued in their petition for certiorari, they saw their case as providing precisely the factual situation to allow the Court to resolve that still-nagging question of negligence.

The DeShaneys repeatedly emphasized the inherent narrowness of their claim, that it was simply the next logical jurisprudential step in a line of cases that stretched back nearly thirty years to *Monroe* v. *Pape.* But beneath the arguments pressing the unexceptional character of their suit lay the heart of what they were trying to accomplish, and it was truly radical. Their quest was nothing less than to turn the Constitution from, as Judge Posner had termed it, a charter of negative liberties into an expansive charter of positive liberties. Put more precisely, the core of the DeShaneys' argument was that the Due Process Clause of the Fourteenth Amendment was not merely a restriction on the exercise of state power but an obligation for certain state services, that there was "a constitutionally protected right under the Fourteenth Amendment to at least minimum standards of protection from physical abuse and neglect."

Making such an argument persuasive depended upon a successful blurring of the line—at once legal and commonsensical—between state action and inaction. Whereas the Due Process Clause historically had been understood to extend only to official actions of state governments and their officials, the DeShaneys now argued that due process of law also prohibited certain kinds of state *inaction*. Put slightly differently, the Due Process Clause, by prohibiting certain sorts of state inaction, would now be read as in fact mandating state action in those areas. If this argument could persuade the Court, the Fourteenth Amendment would be transformed into a mighty engine for judicially engineered social reform. Beyond the instant claim of Joshua DeShaney, the constitutional stakes were extremely high; what hung in the balance was nothing less than a radical reformation of the Constitution's most fundamental principles: federalism and separated powers. There were others in the legal community who recognized how high the stakes were and quickly moved to aid the DeShaneys' quest.

The *amicus curiae* brief filed by the American Civil Liberties Union had a specific purpose: to urge the Court to enhance the "substantive" component of the Due Process Clause to expand the "right" to personal security they argued the Court had fashioned in *Youngberg* v. *Romeo* to include children like Joshua DeShaney, children with whom child welfare and protection agencies have entered into a "special relationship" by having once taken notice of them.

For nearly half a century the Court had spent much of its time weaving new protections under the guise of the guarantee of due process of law provided in the Fifth and Fourteenth amendments. What was once understood to be a guarantee to individuals of certain governmental processes due to them had been transformed by the Court into having a "substantive" component. The meaning of "substantive due process" was nothing more than an enhancement of the power of judicial review to disallow state legislation or actions when there was no particular provision in the

Constitution's text that clearly prohibited such actions or legislation. What that means in plain language is that the Court will determine whether actions by the states were "reasonable" or not. Thus had the Court contrived certain "tests" of constitutionality such as Justice Frankfurter's "shocks the conscience test" in *Rochin* v. *California.*

This world of "substantive due process" was the world in which Joshua DeShaney's case had made its way. In *Daniels,* Justice Stevens had seen fit to sketch the outlines of what was meant by "Due Process." The Due Process Clause of the Fourteenth Amendment, Stevens noted, "is the source of three different kinds of constitutional protection":

> First, it incorporates specific protections defined in the Bill of Rights. Thus, the State, as well as the Federal Government, must comply with the commands in the First, and Eighth Amendments; so too, must the State respect the guarantees in the Fourth, Fifth and Sixth Amendments. Second, it contains a substantive component, sometimes referred to as "substantive due process" which bars certain arbitrary government actions "regardless of the fairness of the procedures used to implement them." Third, it is a guarantee of fair procedure, sometimes referred to as "procedural due process": the State may not execute, imprison, or fine a defendant without giving him a fair trial, nor may it take property without providing appropriate procedural safeguards.[76]

It was the second sort of protection that the DeShaneys sought and whose reach the American Civil Liberties Union was endeavoring to broaden. In particular, the ACLU hoped to obliterate altogether the distinction between action and inaction as a standard of what constituted due process of law. The impact of such a move, if the Court could be persuaded to make it, would go far beyond little Joshua DeShaney.

In no small part, the confusion over the distinction between action and inaction, between omission and commission, in cases such as Joshua's had been exacerbated by Judge Posner, who, it will be recalled, had observed in *Bowers* v. *DeVito* that it should not be pretended that "the line between action and inaction, between inflicting and failing to prevent the infliction of harm is clearer than it is."[77] This was a thought the ACLU was determined to take to the very limits of its logic. The "distinction between action and inaction," it argued, "is ultimately illusory . . . In many constitutional contexts, the line between omission and commission simply makes no sense."[78]

With this distinction between action and inaction denied, it was much easier to make their central claim that "the existence of a right to personal security in a particular case does not turn on the formal legalisms of custody or confinement, but rather on the degree to which the state has assumed responsibility for the protection of a specific individual when that individual—here a small child—is unable to protect himself and the state's assumption of responsibility effectively precludes others from protecting him."[79] Put most bluntly: "The right to personal security . . . is, by definition, a right to be protected from the state's failure to act."[80] The ACLU's conclusion was thus simple to reach:

> The illusory attempt to distinguish omission from commission is a diversion from the real issues in this case. If Joshua DeShaney had a right to personal security and the state's failure to protect him was grossly negligent, then liability should be available.[81]

The arguments put forth by the DeShaneys and their supporters confirmed one of the most abiding maxims in American law: When the law is against you, argue the facts. Perhaps even more strikingly, the defendants drew their bearings from the other half of that maxim: When the facts are against you, argue the law. To rebut the emotional appeal of Joshua's case—an "undeniably tragic" case, as Chief Justice Rehnquist would later describe it—Winnebago County and its friends in court sought to make clear the lines and limits of the law. Those lines and limits, they would argue, however compelling the facts of the DeShaneys' case, simply excluded their claim before the federal courts.

The defense offered by the defendants consisted of four parts. First, the defendants never "deprived" Joshua of his liberty in any constitutional sense of the word; second, the defendants never had the intention to inflict harm that is necessary to trigger a

Fourteenth Amendment violation; third, the injuries were not caused by anyone acting under the color of state law; and fourth, the individual defendants were entitled to qualified immunity insofar as they were carrying out their duties in good faith.

The core of the argument was that the standards for what constitutes a constitutional deprivation under the Due Process Clause of the Fourteenth Amendment had been much too finely drawn by the Court to stretch to fit Joshua's claim. The fundamental issue was simple and powerful: "The harm to Joshua DeShaney was inflicted by his father, whose actions were not merely independent of any governmental entity or person, but in flat derogation of government policy." To state a valid claim under the Fourteenth Amendment and Section 1983 a petitioner is obligated to demonstrate that his injuries were inflicted by the state or agents of the state; the Due Process Clause does not protect citizens at large from harm inflicted by their fellow private citizens.

The DeShaneys, the defendants argued, "cannot avoid the constitutional requirement of state, rather than private, action merely by rephrasing [the] complaint to attack official failures to prevent private deprivations." The inability of the government to achieve perfection in the administration of its services "simply cannot be equated with the kind of 'affirmative abuse of power' needed to establish a due process violation." Not only was the distinction between action and inaction not illusory, as the ACLU had argued, but it was the very essence of the Constitution's design. The effort by the DeShaneys "to transform a privately inflicted harm into a governmental deprivation stretches the Due Process Clause well beyond its breaking point." What's more, the defense argued, such a transformation would "drastically alter the role of the Constitution in ordering governmental action." The Supreme Court itself, the defendants were quick to point out, had said as much as recently as 1982 in the case of *Lugar* v. *Edmondson Oil Co.*:

> Careful adherence to the "state action" requirement preserves an area of individual freedom by limiting the reach of Federal law and Federal judicial power. *It also avoids imposing on the State, its agen-*

cies or officials, responsibility for conduct for which they cannot fairly be blamed. A major consequence is to require the courts to respect the limits of their own power as directed against state governments and private interests. Whether this is good or bad policy, it is a fundamental fact of our political order.[82]

With any luck, the Supreme Court would still cling to this understanding of state action, an understanding that should clearly push Joshua's case outside the litigational boundaries of the Constitution.

The DeShaney case differed dramatically from *Estelle* and *Youngberg,* the defendants insisted, in that Joshua was not in the custody of the state or its agents when the harm was inflicted. Only in instances when the state has deprived an individual of his liberty does it have an affirmative obligation to provide care. The idea that Joshua satisfied this requirement because he had been briefly placed in custody when abuse was first suspected was at best far-fetched. The defendants said: "The criterion of *prior* custody is clearly too broad to reflect active State infliction of harm. Obviously the State does not become a lifetime guarantor of an individual's safety by having once taken him into custody." Tough as the facts of any case may appear, not every private wrong has a constitutional remedy; reason, not emotion, must guide constitutional adjudication.

The second main issue, but one the Court would not need to reach if the DeShaneys could not clear the state action threshold, was the question of negligence. The DeShaneys' claim that there were stages beyond simple negligence which fell short of clear intent but were still sufficient to satisfy the Section 1983 requirement of causation ignored the law. The Court in *Daniels* had made clear that the Due Process Clause historically had been applied only to "*deliberate* decisions of government officials to deprive a person of life, liberty, or property."[83] The Court should not waver now, the defendants urged:

Negligence in whatever form, whether slight, gross, or denominated as "recklessness," does not amount to conduct that is "deliberate." Nor does it rise to conduct "used for the purpose of

oppression." The government simply cannot attempt to suppress
without an intent to do so—especially in a "failure to protect" situation, where it is necessary to distinguish between a decision not to
devote limited resources to a particular task, on the one hand, and
a decision to oppress particular individuals on the other.

The best test remained that of "deliberate indifference," which
had been first enunciated in *Estelle*. It was a workable measure:

> To trigger the protections of the Fourteenth Amendment, any
> failure to act must be based on a state of mind such that the actor
> can fairly be said to have deliberately and purposefully disregarded
> the constitutionally protected right of another. Only that kind of
> conscious indifference to the rights of another can be fairly said to
> equate itself with conduct that is employed "as an instrument of
> oppression" or that amounts to "abusive governmental conduct."

The integrity of the Constitution and the judicial process demanded, the defendants concluded, adherence to such a reasonable test:

> To predicate due process protections on a distinction as artificial as
> that between negligence and "gross" negligence (or "reckless-
> ness")—as Petitioners would do—would be to overrule *Daniels*
> and *Davidson sub silentio* ["under silence"—without notice taken].
> The line between these varying standards is simply too imprecise to
> provide any meaningful constitutional guidance, especially in a case
> predicated on governmental inaction.[84]

When mistakes do occur in the administration of governmental services, which hindsight now suggested occurred in Joshua's case,
those mistakes are to be dealt with in state tort law, not federal constitutional law. No one denied that mistakes could be addressed in
court; the only question was which court, and under which law.

Beyond the hurdles posed by state action and state of mind,
there was yet another question: Did Joshua's injuries result from
the "policy or custom" of the governmental entity involved? If so,
the state and county would be liable for damages as well as the

two social workers, Ann Kemmeter and Cheryl Stelse. To this the defendants' answer was quick and clear: no. Indeed, every aspect of the official policies and laws implicated by the DeShaneys' claims were unambiguously aimed at preventing such abuse as that suffered by little Joshua. Further, even after *Monell* there remained a realm of protection for municipalities under Section 1983 suits. The "central proposition" of *Monell* remained good law, the defendants said: "Because Section 1983 liability must be predicated on active infliction, a municipality cannot be held liable for the constitutional torts of employees over whom it has [quoting *Monell*] 'the mere right to control without any control or direction having been exercised.'" Even if it could be proved that Kemmeter and Stelse had violated Joshua's rights, the state and county were not liable for their wrongs.

There was another stone to be fitted into place, one that would shield Stelse and Kemmeter as well. However unpleasant the outcome, they had, in fact, exercised their professional judgment in good faith. After all, they had to balance two conflicting concerns: Joshua's right to be protected on the one hand, and his father's rights under court-awarded custody on the other. Their balancing of such conflicting interests did not play out well, but in no sense could either Stelse or Kemmeter be rightly accused of not acting in good faith; their constant monitoring of the situation, despite what Judge Posner had called their "inexplicable" decision not to do more, argued that they were not remiss in the discharge of their duties. This "good faith" immunity was a matter of Wisconsin law.[85]

There was one final matter the defendants had to address in responding to the claims the DeShaneys put before the Court. That was the new claim, rooted in their reading of *Taylor* v. *Ledbetter*, that the failure to enforce state law was a violation of the Due Process Clause of the Fourteenth Amendment. Whatever the merits of such a claim—and the defendants denied the claim on the merits—the petitioners had not raised the claim before either in the District Court or before the Seventh Circuit Court of Appeals. Nor had it been presented in the DeShaneys' petition for certiorari before the Supreme Court. It was simply too late, on procedural grounds, to raise it now.

For those reasons, the defendants asked that the judgment of the Court of Appeals be affirmed. They were not alone. The various groups that joined them as *amici curiae* shared their concerns as to where a decision to overrule the Court of Appeals in *DeShaney* v. *Winnebago County* would lead. The bottom line, as a matter of judicial policy, was simple: "[T]here is no principled basis for distinguishing child welfare services from other protective services. As a result, reversal in this case would constitutionalize analogous duties of other government employees, including parole officers, police officers, and paramedics."[86] There was no way to distinguish because all governmental actors were subject to the same weaknesses: "Each must necessarily make inherently subjective appraisals [and] is equally capable of coming to the wrong conclusion in a particular case, because of flawed information, mistake in judgment or other error."[87] Given this fact, it was imperative that the Court not remove the shield of qualified immunity which afforded such public servants as Kemmeter and Stelse protection from liability.

To allow such public officials to be sued for damages under Section 1983 would open "a broad avenue of liability" that would, in time, lead to all sorts of public service suits. The result would not be to provide generous remedies for those who would be able to prevail in court; the long-term effect would be that such services would simply cease to be provided. The instant case of child welfare services would be the primary case in point:

> Constitutional liability for allegedly incompetent social work could diminish the availability as well as the quality of state social services. Given the disturbing facts of any child abuse case, million-dollar verdicts against government agencies and officials are likely. These verdicts, as well as litigation costs incurred regardless of the verdict, would necessarily direct state expenditures away from the provision of services. . . . The financial consequences of liability could substantially impair, if not destroy, foster care services in many states.[88]

Public officers would find themselves in a damned-if-you-do, damned-if-you-don't dilemma of "being sued for either doing too much or too little."[89] Should the DeShaneys prevail, the effect would be to confuse "knowledge of potential risk with a constitutional duty to prevent the harm." There would be no limit to the new suits short of the Justices' own predilection. The Constitution could not be expected to provide any principled guidance on such a fuzzy question. Thus to overrule the lower court would be "to open a Pandora's box of liability."[90]

Beyond the immediate economic concerns facing many of those who filed as *amici curiae* there were also deeper issues, questions about the nature and extent of judicial power under the Constitution. Given the precedential nature of the common law tradition, one can never be sure how far cases may be made to extend; the history of the Supreme Court was, in many ways, a history of what James Madison once called "constructive ingenuity." The deepest concern with a case like *DeShaney* is how to cordon off the logic the Court might use and keep it tied rather closely to the basic facts; there would be no guarantee that the Court would not, in time, take the ruling far beyond the limited universe of child welfare or even state services more generally. Better to be safe than sorry.

Part of the strategy in which all the *amici* shared was to remind the Court of the proper limits of the power of the federal courts. At a minimum this meant to persuade the Justices that "sympathy should not substitute for law."[91] The essence of the constitutional system, they argued, is that "a breach of some kind of moral duty" is not the same thing as "a breach of a constitutional right."[92] Nor is constitutionality linked to the gravity of the offense: "The seriousness of the injury does not determine whether the Constitution is implicated."[93] Indeed, even something as important as child welfare and preventing child abuse does not rise above other policy concerns in the eyes of the Constitution. "[T]he importance of a service does not turn it into a fundamental right merely because the state opts to offer the service."[94] By definition, the Constitution is limited in its prescriptions and proscriptions, it "does not protect against all wrongs."[95] Perhaps sadly, the wrong suffered by Joshua DeShaney was simply one of those to which the Constitution does not reach.

Among those writing in support of the defendants against the DeShaneys' claims was the U.S. Government. The appearance of the Solicitor General in a case to which the United States is not a party is always an indication of the importance of the issues raised. That is underscored when, as in *DeShaney*, the government requests and is granted time to present its views during oral argument. Often referred to as the "Tenth Justice", the Solicitor General is the nation's chief litigator in the courts; the office is widely regarded as one of great integrity, and its views are taken very seriously by the Supreme Court. Still, the Solicitor General is a presidential appointee and an integral member of the President's political team. The notion of the Solicitor General as a tenth Justice—that, somehow, he is an independent agent of the Court—ignores the decidedly political character of his office. A case such as *DeShaney* v. *Winnebago County* was joined, at least in part, because the issues presented would allow the Reagan Administration an opportunity to nudge the Supreme Court (a Court, it must be remembered, that now boasted four Reagan appointees) away from a more expansive notion of judging toward a position of greater self-restraint. The brief the Department of Justice filed in support of Winnebago County, Ann Kemmeter, and Cheryl Stelse left no doubt where the Reagan Administration stood on such issues.

The Justice Department lawyers had narrowed the issues of the case to what they deemed most significant. The question they presented was straightforward: "Whether a county government and employees of its Department of Social Services can be held liable for violation of the Due Process Clause of the Fourteenth Amendment by failing to prevent the abuse of a child by his father." The governmental interest in the outcome derived from the fact that the Fifth Amendment—which applies only to the Federal Government as the Fourteenth applies only to the States—also has a Due Process Clause. As the Fourteenth Amendment went, so would go the Fifth, thus greatly expanding the liability of federal officers. The Federal Government had a concrete interest in the outcome of the case.

But there were also more abstract concerns at play. In particular, to hold for Joshua would mean a radical abandonment of the historic understanding of due process of law, of federalism, and of the nature and extent of judicial power under the Constitution. The government presented its arguments concisely:

Randy DeShaney, not respondents, deprived Joshua DeShaney of
his liberty. An expansive interpretation of the word "deprive",
which would cover respondents' *failure to prevent* that deprivation, is contrary to the historical purpose of the Due Process
Clause. That Clause was intended to prevent the arbitrary exercise
of the powers of government; to prevent affirmative abuses of
power; and to bar government oppression. Petitioners seek to recover not because they have suffered from any such arbitrary exercise of power, abuse of power, or oppression, but because the
power of government was *not* used to save Joshua DeShaney from
his father. Any duty to use that power, however, derives from the
common law and not the Due Process Clause. . . . [T]he fundamental purpose of the Due Process Clause [was] to prevent the
misuse of power, rather than to compel its use. . . . [I]n the sense
in which the word is ordinarily and naturally used, respondents
did not "deprive" Joshua DeShaney of personal security.[96]

To argue as the DeShaneys did, the government warned, was to
play fast and loose with the Constitution. However morally compelling the goal, the means were simply illegitimate:

Petitioners . . . seek to use the Due Process Clause to *require* certain government actions and thus to insist on a use of governmental power to relieve persons from the dangers posed by others in
society. That may be a noble goal, and a proper objective of state
tort law. But it is not the case [quoting *Daniels*] that "all common
law duties owed by government actors were somehow constitution-
alized by the Fourteenth Amendment." . . . [T]he state violates the
Due Process Clause only by acting so as to deprive a person of liberty, and not merely by passively allowing a third party to deprive
someone of liberty."[97]

As had been said many times, the states are under no obligation to
provide services to those within their borders; and therein lay the
final hitch in the DeShaneys' claim:

It is no answer to say that the Constitution, while imposing on the
States no duty to provide social welfare services, nevertheless regu-
lates the care with which such services are provided once the State

elects to provide them. The Constitutional guarantee is that the State will not—through social welfare services or any other means—"deprive any person of life, liberty, or property, without due process of law." By no feat of alchemy can that constitutional guarantee be transmuted into an assurance that the State, once it undertakes to protect against certain deprivations caused by persons other than agents of the State, will not permit any such deprivation that a competent performance of the State's undertaking would have prevented. Any such assurance is a feature of tort law that has nothing to do with the words used in or the purpose of the Due Process Clause. . . . [A] tort, in order to rise to the level of a violation of the Due Process Clause, must at a minimum involve some action of the state that creates the victim's predicament, and not just inaction in the face of a predicament that is not of the state's making.[98]

In conclusion the Solicitor General argued that the Court "should specifically reject—the notion espoused by a divided panel of the Third Circuit in *Estate of Bailey ex rel. Oare* v. *County of York* . . . that a tort suit for government inaction becomes a tenable claim under the Due Process Clause when the state undertakes to protect against, but did not create, the danger to a specific individual."[99] To allow *Bailey* to stand would only have the effect of transforming an array of state services into constitutional rights "by first affixing the label 'special relationship,' and then broadly construing that label to include as a beneficiary of constitutional protection anyone whose danger is known to a state actor whose job involves protection against that danger."[100]

The arguments for and against Joshua DeShaney's claim that he was entitled to sue under Section 1983 were spread out before the Court. The Court's own precedents and the historic understanding of both the Fourteenth Amendment and Section 1983 pulled in one direction; the horrific facts of Joshua's situation and other prior decisions, seemingly related to those circumstances, tugged in the other. It remained for the Supreme Court to sort it all out.

CHAPTER THREE

MAY IT PLEASE THE COURT

D on Sullivan returned to his argument. Chief Justice
Rehnquist had hit the point squarely. How does the
Constitution protect Joshua from his father? Had
Joshua's constitutional rights been violated? Sullivan's strategy was
relatively straightforward. First he had to convince the Court that
the relationship between the state of Wisconsin and Joshua was intimate—that the state had been actively involved in securing the
welfare of the child. Then he had to convince the Court that this
intimate relationship meant that the state had an affirmative obligation to protect the child from his father. Finally, he had to convince the Court that since the state had failed in this obligation, it
could be sued for damages. Joshua's liberty had been denied him
without due process of law. He would be forever severely retarded
because the state failed to do its job.

Sullivan understood that his argument had to be subtle. He
knew that he would be blown away by the Court if he asserted
that the state had an obligation to do good things or to intervene
in private matters. He had to emphasize the uniqueness of
Joshua's situation.

It is my view—it is our view that the protector of the child, the
raiser of the child, the person with the right and the power and authority and the duty to educate the child, teach the child, provide
medical care, all those parental things, including setting bedtime, is
the parent and not the state.

But there is another side to the coin. A child, Sullivan reasoned,
has no protection from those protectors. What happens when the
"protector becomes the predator"? The Court had long ago rec-

ognized that the Constitution governs the relationship between parent and child; that a parent can be denied, through due process of law, the liberty to raise his or her child. That being the case, Sullivan reasoned, "if the rights of the parents are recognized, why should the rights of the child be less recognized?" If parents have a constitutionally protected right to exercise their authority as parents and can be denied that right only through due process of law, then why can't it be argued that children also have some rights in the parent–child relationship, and that one of those rights is protection from parents as predators?

Growing impatient, Justice Rehnquist pushed Sullivan. "The question here is the extent to which you impose a mandatory duty on the state to act affirmatively to protect the child." The Chief Justice challenged Sullivan to find some language in the Constitution to defend his assertion that the state has an obligation to intervene in the parent–child relationship. To his way of thinking, the Fourteenth Amendment provided no such authority.

> Well, why don't we start with the language of the Fourteenth Amendment which says that a state shall not—what does it state?—deprive any person of life, liberty or property without due process of law? . . . Now, certainly we've held in many cases that the state may not deprive someone of life, but we've never held that that provision protects in the constitutional sense a private—a private attack on another person.

Sullivan agreed. The last thing he wanted to do was to come across as arguing that the Constitution was a mandate for government to ensure that individuals do good things. To argue that, he admitted, would be to argue that "the police department would have an obligation to prevent the mugging and a whole host of things that are simply unworkable and are not to be found in the Constitution." Certainly, he was not arguing for such a broad reading of the Constitution. But that is what made Joshua's case so unique. The state was intimately involved in providing for the child's well-being. Not only had Joshua's father failed him, the state had failed as well.

Associate Justice Sandra Day O'Connor saw where Sullivan was trying to take the argument.

[T]he only cases in which the Court has found an affirmative duty on the part of the state to provide basic services is in a setting like a prison or a state institution where the state has already deprived the individual of the individual's liberty and institutionalized them. . . . This is certainly a step far beyond that that you're asking us to take.

Sullivan shook his head: "The only word I would—I would differ with you is—is the word 'far.' " The state was very involved in Joshua's life. Sullivan liked the term "enmeshment" to describe the relationship of the State of Wisconsin to Joshua. The Department of Social Services, the child protection team, Ann Kemmeter—these were people who visited the DeShaney home regularly, who kept files about Joshua, who monitored his life and could chronicle his suffering. No, Joshua was not institutionalized, O'Connor was correct, but the state had become involved "in the life of this person."

O'Connor seemed genuinely stumped by Sullivan's response. She could see the argument but didn't like where it took her. To hold that the state might incur an obligation such as outlined by Sullivan would be impractical. If Sullivan's theory were upheld, it would be a deterrent to state child abuse programs. "Why would a state want to undertake a child abuse program at all if they face liability if they guess wrong?" Sullivan cited recent cases that responded to her question. The Court had determined already that negligence was not reason enough to sue for damages. But what had happened to Joshua was more than mere negligence, he maintained. Wisconsin had been a part of the problem.

Sullivan was really not making any progress in his presentation. He was responding to inquiries from Justices who were decidedly unfriendly to his argument. Rehnquist was notoriously unfriendly to arguments that sought to expand state liability, and O'Connor was perhaps the most consistent pro-state member of the Court. Sullivan had prepared for the sorts of questions the Justices were firing at him, but he had hoped that some of the members of the

Court who might be more sympathetic to his position—liberals like William Brennan, Harry Blackmun, and Thurgood Marshall—would help to move the argument along so that he was not defending himself but asserting himself. Then Justice Brennan interrupted the exchange between the attorney and O'Connor.

According to Brennan, Sullivan had to persuade the Court that Joshua had an entitlement under Wisconsin law. He looked at the attorney and asked simply, "What's your argument?" Finally Sullivan could get back to the basic points in his presentation. And Brennan helped him put that argument together:

Brennan:	Mr. Sullivan, let me put it another way. This child was severely injured.
Sullivan:	Yes, sir.
Brennan:	And the state placed him in a position of extreme danger, did it not?
Sullivan:	Eventually they did, yes, sir. And and the reason for that—
Brennan:	Well, they put him in—not eventually, but they put him in a position of extreme danger. It certainly turned out to be that way.
Sullivan:	When they—when they unilaterally returned him to the abusive father, yes, sir.
Brennan:	Now, suppose the—the state or the county, municipality knew that it was putting the child—placing the child in a situation of extreme danger. Do you have any trouble in working out liability on that situation?
Sullivan:	No, your Honor. I have no trouble. And I would further say that that's not a supposition in this case.
Brennan:	Well, I wonder why you don't argue it.

Sullivan caught Brennan's point. He needed to make the fact that the state was an accomplice in this abuse incident more explicit. Brennan wanted the attorney to turn up the heat on the state, making it more difficult for the Justices to sit there quietly and ignore the suffering that the state had helped to inflict on poor Joshua. Ann Kemmeter had known what was happening to the child. He had presented evidence in earlier trials and in his brief that demonstrated her knowledge. She had written in her files: "I always knew the phone would ring some day and Joshua would be dead." Brennan wanted that brought out in the oral argument. Sullivan quoted from Kemmeter's files. Justice Blackmun, until now silent, repeated several times for emphasis, "she knew," "or should have known."

Now Sullivan made his move. Brennan and Blackmun had paved the way for him. He wasn't arguing that Kemmeter wanted the child dead—"That would be irresponsible, and we don't make that claim." But Kemmeter had failed Joshua, certainly. The state had procedures for her to follow, "black and white absolute mandates" saying the social worker must investigate reports of child abuse when received from doctors, police, or other social workers. The facts were straightforward: The first report was investigated—for three days—and then the child was returned to his father. But Joshua was returned upon certain conditions and with the promise that the social worker, Ann Kemmeter, would initiate an investigation "should there be any further injuries to this child of an unxplained origin." Kemmeter visited the DeShaneys several times and almost every time she saw evidence that should have triggered the investigation she promised. Not only was she at fault, therefore, for failing to abide by the terms of the agreement, but the agreement was a condition leading to Joshua having been returned to his father in the first place.

> [S]he made a written promise to the child and to the family court that the very next time there was a suspicious lesion on this child, she would bring the matter back to the court for the child to be protected. She made that—that promise to the—now, the child was a toddler, so I don't mean to say that child understood that. But she made that guarantee and it was on that promise that the child I think erroneously was returned.

The very first time she visited the house, all the conditions on which the child protection team had insisted—the removal of the live-in girlfriend, the father seeking therapy, Joshua enrolled in Head Start—remained unfulfilled, nor were they ever fulfilled. That was reason enough for Kemmeter to have sought an order from family court. But then, on later visits, she saw evidence of suspicious cuts, bruises, and wounds on Joshua, and she still failed to live up to her promise. Justice Stevens summarized Sullivan's argument:

> So, your theory is not that the state placed the child in a position of extreme danger, but rather that the state failed to remove the child from a position that they should have known was extremely dangerous.

Sullivan shook his head in agreement. The state failed to act when it promised to act, and young Joshua will forever pay the costs for that. That aspect of his argument seemed to make sense, and at least some of the members of the Court seemed to be buying it. But how did that add up to a violation of the Constitution? That question came next: "Now, how do you—how do you place within the words of the Fourteenth Amendment again? How is the state depriving—depriving the child?"

> I don't understand how the state is depriving the child of anything when—when the child is already in the home and all the state has done is failed to take the child out of the home.

Sullivan responded that in this unique set of circumstances the child had no one else. "The only protector he has in the world is now the predator," and so the state must act.

"Isn't that true in every incident of child abuse?"

Yes. But in this case the evidence of abuse was overwhelming and ongoing. "I lose track of how many different doctor reports of abuse there were and how many different nurse abusive reports there were."

Justice Antonin Scalia asked if Sullivan's argument was specific regarding children. . . . What if a case worker goes in and finds an elderly person starving, would the state be liable if it did not provide food?

Sullivan tried to dismiss the Justice's inquiry by asserting, correctly, that the Constitution does not intrude into each individual life. But it does intrude with regard to the rights of parents when child abuse takes place. The parent's constitutional rights in the relationship are recognized, his substantive right to possession of the child, and his procedural rights to have witnesses and hearings, and burden of proof. "And if we have one—one equation—and the Constitution is in here for the parent and we know the Constitution recognizes the child has at least the right to be alive and more or less healthy . . ."

Chief Justice Rehnquist interrupted and returned to his earlier question.

> But that's a—that's a limitation on the state—those cases. They say the state can't do certain things. You're trying to turn that around and say that arising out of that same relationship is a duty on the state.

Sullivan, caught by the sudden turn in the discussion, and recognizing the weak spot in his argument, stammered a bit, trying to get his thoughts together. Justice Rehnquist pushed him, urging him to answer the question. Sullivan continued to mumble, Rehnquist continued to push. Finally it came out:

> Well, what I'm saying is that we recognize that the Constitution has a legitimate place in the relationship between the parent and the child. If it does, I—I suggest that it should fairly apply both ways. It doesn't make sense to me that the—the Constitution applies between the parent and the child only for the benefit of the parent. And I think that's the—that's the result.

The members of the Court seemed unmoved. "Well, Mr. Sullivan, aren't there any Wisconsin tort remedies assuming you're right?" Of course there were. Joshua could have sued under Wisconsin law for negligence and probably won $50,000, the limit set by that state. But that wasn't the point of the case. "I am not here arguing that the dollar amount makes that remedy insufficient," Sullivan responded.

> What I am saying is that under the state system, the objective, the stated objective of it, is the well-being of the child, the safety of the child, and I suggest that no after-the-fact damage action can address that question.

Justice Brennan seemed a bit befuddled by the argument. If Sullivan had tried the issue in Wisconsin, as he could have, the issue of tort liability would have been settled at the state level. His argument regarding the obligation of the state made some sense, but he still was having a difficult time tracking it to the Constitution. Why wasn't this a case of negligence by a state worker and therefore easily resolved at the state level?

Sullivan was frustrated. It wasn't merely negligence. Kemmeter knew what she was doing—she knew what the law states, what the facts were, and that she should have sought an order from family court. It was a "very conscious, a deliberative, a thought-through decision," argued Sullivan, and that is not the same thing as negligence.

The white light had been illuminated for more than three minutes. Attorney Sullivan knew he was running out of time. He wanted badly to pull his argument together, to return to the condition of poor Joshua, to reemphasize the way Wisconsin had let the child down. He also wanted to try to undermine whatever the counsel for the state might say. He asked that the remainder of his time be reserved. Chief Justice Rehnquist agreed, and Sullivan took his seat. He did not feel good about his performance.

Mark Mingo approached the lectern. He had been working on this case for as long as Sullivan. He had nursed it through the various levels of the federal branch. At each level he had prevailed. He was determined to prevail before the Supreme Court as well.

Mingo's style was different from Sullivan's. Mingo preferred to focus on the facts and the law. It was a style that seemed particularly well suited for oral argument before the Supreme Court. In a jury setting, Mingo would have to be able to counter Sullivan's extended discussion about the appalling treatment and tragic status of little Joshua. He would have had to try to move jurors to distinguish between the sympathy they felt toward the child and what the law says or doesn't say about the liability of the state. Before the federal bench, however, his argument was direct and concise. He was convinced that the petitioners had no case. He wasn't sure why the Supreme Court had agreed to hear the case— other cases from other federal districts had resolved similar disputes in a variety of ways—perhaps the justices felt the issue needed final resolution. In any event, he had listened carefully to the exchanges that had transpired during Sullivan's presentation. He counted Rehnquist, Scalia, O'Connor, and White in his corner. He had written off Brennan, Blackmun, and Marshall long since, and the way Brennan and Blackmun had tried to help Sullivan make his argument had provided evidence that he had guessed correctly. Justice Stevens gave little indication of his leanings, and his record on the Court provided little insight. Justice Anthony Kennedy, the newest member of the Court, had been virtually silent during Sullivan's oral argument. He was something of a wild card, although his work on the appeals court suggested his conservative tilt.

As Mingo began his argument, he took Sullivan straight on:

We believe this case involves an attempt by the Petitioners to transform the private wrongdoing of a natural father into state action for purposes of invoking the Fourteenth Amendment.

The issue presented to the Court was simply stated: Did the county's failure to prevent harm to the child by a third person, the child's father, constitute a violation of the Fourteenth Amendment's due process clause? The issue wasn't negligence, nor was it misfeasance or malfeasance. The issue wasn't whether Ann Kemmeter had done her job or not, or whether the child protection unit had done its job. Those were all facts beyond dispute. Virtually everyone agreed the county had not done a good job. But the issue before the Court was something else; it was now a matter of constitutional law, nothing else.

"The Fourteenth Amendment's concept of liberty does not include a right to basic protective services from the state," Mingo continued, "there is no state action in a constitutional sense which caused a deprivation in this case." Nothing Kemmeter or anyone else connected with the case did could be said to invoke the Fourteenth Amendment. Indeed, Mingo contended, nothing the county did could be suggestive of a policy or custom which led to a deprivation of the child's liberty, and besides, the employees named by the petitioners as being responsible for Joshua's condition were entitled to qualified immunity.

As Mingo saw it, Sullivan was trying to rewrite the idea behind the Fourteenth Amendment and the law that put that Amendment into action, Section 1983 of the Civil Rights Act of 1871. Section 1983 is remedial in nature. Hence, Mingo reasoned, Sullivan has to look to the Fourteenth Amendment to find what it is the Constitution is supposed to provide for Joshua that Wisconsin failed to provide and that must be remedied. The problem with Sullivan's argument, according to Mingo, was that the Fourteenth Amendment, according to the decisions of the Supreme Court, imposes no constitutional duty upon states to provide substantive services to their citizens. Moreover, should states provide services, the Amendment does not tell states how far they must go in providing those services.

Justice O'Connor wanted to know if there might be conditions under which the state could indeed be found liable under the Fourteenth Amendment. What if the child had been placed in foster care by the state and then abuse took place, would that lead to potential liability? Yes, Mingo responded. It could then be argued that the state had removed the child from his natural surroundings and placed that child in state-controlled surroundings in which the risk of harm was increased. In such an instance, it could be argued, the state had taken deliberate action that led to the deprivation of the child's liberty. The Court had said as much in earlier cases dealing with prisons and mental institutions.

Justice O'Connor started to continue her inquiry but was interrupted by Justice Stevens. After they both stepped on each other's lines, O'Connor laughed and deferred to her elder colleague. Stevens wanted to know whether or not the fact that Joshua had been in the custody of the county for three days in January of 1983—during the child's initial stay at the hospital when doctors Gehringer and Derozier had suspected abuse and obtained an order from the court giving the child protection team three days to investigate—constituted conditions similar to those outlined by O'Connor. Mingo did not hesitate a moment. The court had awarded temporary custody to the hospital, not the state, the county, or the social workers. Okay, Stevens responded, but then, when the child was returned to his father, certainly abuse was suspected, and the state returned the child anyway. Again, Mingo was adamant: "I believe from a constitutional standpoint only a county or a department of social services could return the child without facing constitutional liability." In other words, when Joshua was returned to his father, the state may have acted in a way that endangered the child and may be liable under some provisions of Wisconsin law, but Mingo did not see any federal constitutional liability. According to Mingo, the Constitution just did not speak to this issue. Stevens continued: "Even with knowledge that there's—even with knowledge of extreme danger and almost certain abuse of this kind?" Mingo would not concede that the members of the child protection unit had such knowledge. Indeed, they had suspected abuse. But, after an investigation, they felt they lacked enough evidence to keep Joshua from his father. But even assuming they had such evidence and possessed such knowledge, they would not confront constitutional liability.

By now Justice Stevens was becoming intrigued by the argument. How was this situation different from the setting of the foster home, which O'Connor had suggested? Mingo argued it was a very different setting. This was temporary custody in a hospital, primarily for observation and examination. Mingo was not sure whether the hospital was run by the state or not. But he was sure that the Department of Social Services had not had custody of Joshua. And he was eager to emphasize that all who worked on the case were convinced that evidence of abuse could not be substantiated and that the child therefore had to be returned to his father, as directed by Wisconsin law. Joshua had been returned to Randy DeShaney by order of the juvenile court.

Stevens pressed on. What if the court had issued the order in spite of the existence of evidence of serious abuse—would the state be liable then? Mingo refused to back down: "I don't believe in that instance we would have state action because we have not done anything to increase the risk of harm to that child." Justice Scalia joined the discussion, asking Mingo if the state would be liable if Joshua had been given to someone else who then abused him. Mingo replied that such a situation might indeed imply liability since Joshua was placed in a position of risk by the state. Scalia seemed to capture Mingo's argument:

So, what you're saying is what makes a difference is whether you're returning him to the status he was in before you took the temporary custody.

Mingo nodded in agreement. What mattered—the threshold question—was whether the state can be said to have increased the risk of harm to the child from what that risk was at the time the state originally took custody. Scalia led the attorney along. "Well, you were just returning it to the person who had the legal right to custody." Again, Mingo nodded his agreement. Justice Blackmun, visibly bothered by the discussion, erupted: "Which is more important than the abuse to poor Joshua?" Mingo was startled. He wasn't arguing it was more important but that parents have constitutionally protected rights which the social workers have to observe. Blackmun shook his head and shuddered: "Poor Joshua."

The courtroom fell silent for a brief moment. Mingo stood still, trying to gauge whether or not Justice Blackmun or one of his colleagues would try to continue the discussion. If the Justices chose to focus on "poor Joshua," Mingo would have a difficult time returning to the legal arguments. But Blackmun seemed honestly distressed, concerned about the small child so far away who had suffered so very much. He didn't say anything more. Mingo adjusted his thoughts and returned to his presentation, charting the Court's earlier decisions and how precedent might shed some light on the case under review.

Precedent established two instances in which state action might be found: when a state directly inflicts harm upon an individual, and when the state, acting in a custodial setting, intentionally acts to deprive a person of his liberty. Neither of those conditions pertained to this case. Justice Brennan asked sarcastically: "And under your theory, I take it if two policemen see a rape and watch it just for their own amusement, no violation of the Constitution." Mingo had to concede that such action would not violate the Constitution. Brennan wouldn't let the attorney get away so easily. "You're not—you're arguing it as well as conceding it." Briefly some of the Justices stifled a laugh.

Mingo tried to continue his argument. The attorney for the petitioners, Sullivan, had tried to argue that the special relationship

that had developed between Joshua and the state—what Sullivan
had termed "enmeshment"—constituted adequate grounds to assert state action. Sullivan had argued it was a relationship that fitted into the Court's precedents. But Mingo asserted that the
theory was flawed, since it meant that a state could be liable whenever it expresses a desire to protect an individual and has some
generalized knowledge of the victim's plight. Clearly this was well
beyond the scope of the Fourteenth Amendment and Section
1983, and earlier decisions by the Court had never gone so far.
Moreover, it would make very poor public policy:

> What their theory would do is open up local governments to mas-
> sive new areas of exposure precisely because of the fact that the
> states, if we were to accept Petitioners' theory, become liable for
> the acts of private wrongdoers.

The problem with Sullivan's enmeshment theory was that it
"fails to distinguish between privately inflicted harm and state action." Is it really correct to hold the state responsible for the actions of Randy DeShaney? Moreover, Mingo argued, Sullivan had
not argued successfully that the actions of the state supported a
Fourteenth Amendment claim. Here was a claim of inaction by
the state, not action. Sullivan's argument failed to recognize the
fact that social workers must respect the constitutional rights of
parents. Kemmeter, after all, had had to walk a fine line "to avoid
having the door slammed in her face thereby preventing any future involvement of the department." Had the social worker dis-
regarded her duty under state law? Absolutely not. The only duty
she had was to investigate when she received a report of abuse.
Abuse was reported only once. There was an immediate investigation, after which the child was returned to his father.

"But there was further information received by the social
worker?"

Kemmeter had suspected there might be abuse. She visited the
DeShaney home twelve times. But those had been informal investigations and voluntary visits. There had been only one formal investigation, which had been triggered by the initial report of
abuse.

Justice Blackmun retorted that "the social worker knew enough that under state law it was her duty to take the child out of the house or do something to remove the child from that position of danger." Mingo voiced his disagreement. Under Wisconsin law the only duty Kemmeter had was to investigate, and she had a duty to investigate only when she received a formal report of abuse. Blackmun seemed befuddled. What, after all, is the purpose behind such an investigation? Doesn't it make sense to think that if, during the course of an investigation, the state finds out certain things then it must take certain actions? Mingo pointed out that the law of Wisconsin didn't say that, although one might fairly presume that an investigator might relay information to appropriate officials.

Justice Thurgood Marshall interrupted the exchange. He had listened quietly during much of the argument. But Mingo seemed to him to be seeking refuge in the technicalities of the law. "What is the difference between formal and informal investigation?" Mingo was caught off balance. "A formal investigation is an investigation triggered by the statute." Marshall was not satisfied. "What's the difference in what the social worker does?" Mingo repeated the point he had just made. Marshall asserted that "there's no difference between a formal and an informal one." Mingo shook his head. Marshall was exasperated: "Well, what is the difference? This is my last time I'm going to ask you." Mingo squirmed and repeated the distinction he had made twice before. Marshall wouldn't have any of it. He felt Mingo was drawing paper distinctions. As he understood the attorney's argument, no matter what Kemmeter uncovered during her investigations, if no formal report was filed there could be no liability. To his way of thinking, Mingo was trying to argue that even though the social worker had not done her job, she could not be held responsible. Indeed, it was precisely because she had done such a poor job— she had failed to file a report even though, by her own admission, she felt she would one day hear Joshua was dead—that she could not be found liable.

Mingo tried to respond. Marshall cut him off. Suddenly the red light was flashing. Mingo took his seat.

Now it was time for Don Ayers, Deputy Solicitor General of the

United States, to present his argument on behalf of the federal government. He approached the lectern with the sort of ease and comfort that come from experience before the Supreme Court and the fact that he enjoyed some distance from the facts in this case. He wasn't there representing Joshua and his mother, or Wisconsin and its social workers. He was there to provide the Justices with the federal government's perspective on the questions presented by the DeShaney case. Much of his presentation would focus on the larger questions emanating from the case.

Ayer chose to focus primarily on the relationship of the federal and state governments. In his opinion, the federal constitution did not speak to the DeShaney case. Indeed, Ayer maintained, "it is reasonably clear that the area of child protection is not one that is crying out for federal constitutional oversight." Not only was there no constitutional right to protection, he asserted, but in each of the states programs have been established in response to a real concern for children and the sorts of abuse that Joshua suffered. "The state is actively intervening to do all that it can reasonably do." Moreover, there was little reason to feel federal oversight in this area would contribute very much. "There is, I think, little reason to think that federal courts have any special expertise in reviewing" the sorts of issues presented by cases like Joshua's. Indeed, it was the position of the Reagan Administration that this was an area of traditional state and local involvement and should continue as such. "It's the kind of sensitive situation that requires close, on-the-scene involvement, the exercise of discretion and the exercise of a great deal of care and concern." Asking the federal government to get involved seemed "misguided." It would add to the bureaucracy, divert financial and personnel resources, and probably discourage local agencies from doing their job.

Those were all policy arguments. They flowed almost directly from the Reagan Administration's position on federalism—the proper relationship between Washington and the states. Ayer was merely asserting the primacy of federalism as a policy principle as well as a constitutional principle. Seizing a phrase employed by the Court in an earlier case, Ayer asserted that the Due Process Clause of the Fourteenth Amendment should not be seen as a "font of tort policy." Simply put, the Due Process Clause concerns the abuse of government power. It does not oblige the government to provide a particular service, no matter how desirable such a service might be.

For the next several minutes Ayer was engaged with the members of the Court in a constitutional discussion of sorts. In an almost amiable fashion, they discussed the relationship of the states to the federal government and sought Ayer's ideas regarding how it might be possible to fashion a federal cause of action in circumstances similar to those presented in this case. It took on the air of an academic discussion. It appeared that the Justices sincerely wanted to understand the government's perspective here. Justice Brennan then attempted to focus on the particulars of the DeShaney case. Would Ayer concede that the state had knowledge enough in this instance to argue that it had a duty to protect the child from his father? Ayer didn't think so. The child was removed from his father for only a short time, and even then the father remained the legal custodian of the child. The fact that the state returned the child to his condition before the investigation—the status quo ante—is not enough to suggest that the state was the moving force behind the injury that occurred.

With that Ayer sat down.

Don Sullivan was granted one minute to address the Court. Chief Justice Rehnquist seemed irritated by now and pressed the attorney to "spell out" his due process argument. Sullivan mumbled. There was a substantive due process right "inherent in the balancing of the constitutional involvement in the child–parent relationship," he argued, by now for the fourth time. The fact that the state knew the child was in harm's way and did nothing, he said, constituted a denial of Joshua's constitutional rights. The state, "despite its power, its exclusive power, refused to help the child." That, Sullivan contended, was an abuse of the power of the state.

With that the oral argument was over. It was approaching two o'clock. Sullivan turned to shake hands with Mingo and Ayer. They had made the arguments before. Nothing new had emerged from the proceedings. The attorneys each packed up their materials and moved out of the courtroom. They had an empty feeling. Before, after earlier presentations in front of lower courts, there was always the feeling that the fight might continue. There was always the possibility of trying to prevail at the next level. Now it was over. This was the court of last resort. These arguments would not be made again. Joshua's fate was now completely out of their hands.

The Supreme Court reached its decision in *DeShaney* v. *Winnebago County* rather quickly. It handed down its opinion on February 22, 1989. Joshua lost.

The Court divided six-to-three against the claim that the Due Process Clause of the Fourteenth Amendment imposes an affirmative obligation on state and local governments to protect their citizens from harm by other citizens. The majority opinion was written by Chief Justice Rehnquist; dissenting opinions were offered by Brennan (joined by Blackmun and Marshall) and Blackmun. Rehnquist had been able to pull the ideologically ambiguous members of the Court—White, O'Connor, and Stevens—into the conservative fold, leaving only the three most liberal Justices refusing to go along. It was as clear a case of Ronald Reagan's success at transforming the Court as one could imagine.

The Court had granted certiorari, Rehnquist noted, because of confusion among the circuits, particularly the line of thinking put forth by the Third Circuit Court of Appeals in *Estate of Bailey*. Rehnquist said the Court needed to make clear what the limits to the standard of such "special relationships" between the state and its citizens were. The standard, Rehnquist pointed out, as defined by the Court earlier in *Estelle* and *Youngberg*, simply did not apply to Joshua's situation. Those cases, Rehnquist noted, "afford the petitioners no help."

> Taken together, they stand only for the proposition that when the State takes a person into its custody and holds him there against his will, the Constitution imposes upon it a corresponding duty to assume responsibility for his safety and general well-being. . . . [T]he harms Joshua suffered did not occur while he was in the State's custody, but while he was in the custody of his natural father, who was in no sense a state actor. While the State may have been aware

of the dangers that Joshua faced in the free world, it played no part in their creation, nor did it do anything to render him any more vulnerable to them.

But that was not all, in the view of the Court:

> That the State once took temporary custody of Joshua does not alter the analysis, for when it returned him to his father's custody, it placed him in no worse position than that in which he would have been had it not acted at all; the State does not become the permanent guarantor of an individual's safety by having once offered him shelter. Under these circumstances, the State had no constitutional duty to protect Joshua.

The Court went beyond the facts of the instant case in an effort to clear the constitutional waters that apparently had been muddied by its earlier opinions. What, precisely, were the lines and limits of the "special relationship" test under Section 1983? The answer was reasonably simple, Rehnquist pointed out:

> The affirmative duty to protect arises not from the State's knowledge of the individual's predicament or from its expressions of intent to help him, but from the limitation which it has imposed on his freedom to act on his own behalf. . . . [I]t is the State's affirmative act of restraining the individual's freedom to act on his own behalf—through incarceration, institutionalization, or other similar restraint of personal liberty—which is the "deprivation of liberty" triggering the protections of the Due Process Clause, not its failure to act to protect his liberty interests affirmed by other means.

The Court's decision was the inevitable outcome of the proper historical reading of the Due Process Clause. By such a reading it was impossible to conclude that a state or local government is ever "categorically obligated" to protect its citizens in most circumstances. Nothing in the language of the clause itself, Rehnquist pointed out, "requires the State to protect the life, liberty, and property of its citizens against invasion by private actors."

The Clause is phrased as a limitation on the State's power to act, not as a guarantee of certain minimal levels of safety and security. It forbids the State itself to deprive individuals of life, liberty, or property without "due process of law," but its language cannot fairly be extended to impose an affirmative obligation on the State to ensure that those interests do not come to harm through other means. Nor does history support such an expansive reading of the constitutional text. . . . Its purpose was to protect the people from the State, not to ensure that the State protected them from each other. The Framers were content to leave the extent of governmental obligation in the latter area to the democratic political processes.

The historical reading of the original intention behind the Due Process Clause demanded the outcome in Joshua's case:

If the Due Process Clause does not require the State to provide its citizens with particular protective services, it follows that the State cannot be held liable under the Clause for injuries that could have been averted had it chosen to provide them. . . . Because . . . the State had no constitutional duty to protect Joshua against his father's violence, its failure to do so—though calamitous in hindsight—simply does not constitute a violation of the Due Process Clause.

However troubling the circumstances, the fact was that the Due Process Clause "does not transform every tort committed by a state actor into a constitutional violation."

A case like Joshua's was, Rehnquist said, "undeniably tragic." And precisely because it was so tragic the Court had an obligation to resist the impulse of "natural sympathy" that might lead to reading the Constitution in such a way as "to find a way for Joshua and his mother to receive adequate compensation for the grievous harm inflicted upon them." But the fact was that the State had not inflicted the harm—Joshua's father had.

In the view of the Court, Joshua's claim was properly to be placed in the state courts or raised in state legislatures. Rehnquist pointed out that "by voluntarily undertaking to protect Joshua against a danger it concededly played no part in creating, the State acquired a duty under the state tort law to provide him with adequate protection against that danger." The federal system was such that a "State may, through its courts and legislatures, impose such affirmative duties of care and protection upon its agents as it wishes." But that is a far cry from suggesting that the Fourteenth Amendment obligated them to do so.

The first term after Rehnquist assumed the chief justiceship had found many of those who comment upon the Court and its direction seeing not a Rehnquist Court in place of the Burger Court, but a Brennan Court. Justice Brennan had for years wielded considerable clout. Since his appointment by President Eisenhower he had been an active participant in defining the liberalism that had so dominated the Court under Chief Justice Earl Warren and had continued to color many of the decisions of the Burger Court. During those years Rehnquist was often known as the "lone dissenter," the only Justice willing to buck the trend. But now all was changed. By the beginning of the October term of 1988, Brennan's influence had waned considerably. His failure at least to pull the generally liberal Justice Stevens to his side in *DeShaney* was striking, because Brennan had made a powerful, case-bound argument for allowing the DeShaneys to have their day in Federal court.

Brennan began by suggesting that the Court was peering into the case from the wrong end. By beginning with the notion that the Constitution ordains no positive rights, he argued, the Court had locked itself into the conclusion it had reached. The majority revealed a troubling "suspicion" of any claim that even seemed to depend upon such positive constitutional rights and was thus unwilling "to see that inaction can be every bit as abusive of power as action, that oppression can result when a State undertakes a vital duty and then ignores it." And that was precisely the deepest issue in Joshua's claim. What was especially puzzling to Brennan was that the Court seemed determined to decide a question no one had actually raised:

It may well be, as the Court decides . . . that the Due Process Clause as construed by our prior cases creates no general right to basic government services. That, however, is not the question presented here; indeed, that question was not raised in the complaint, urged on appeal, presented in the petition for certiorari, or addressed in the briefs on the merits. No one, in short, has asked the Court to proclaim that, as a general matter, the Constitution safeguards positive as well as negative liberties.

It would be more appropriate, Brennan argued, if the Court would simply stick to the specific facts of Joshua's case. If the majority would do that, he was convinced, they could not uphold the appeals court ruling as they did.

In particular, Brennan was appalled at the "stingy scope" the majority had given *Estelle* and *Youngberg*. As he read those cases, they were much more capacious, sufficiently so to embrace Joshua's case. "I would read *Youngberg* and *Estelle*," Brennan wrote, "to stand for the much more generous proposition that, if a State cuts off private sources of aid and then refuses aid itself, it cannot wash its hands of the harm that results from the inaction." Cases like *Estelle* and *Youngberg* could not be correctly read to draw "a neat and decisive divide between action and inaction."

> Because of the Court's initial fixation on the general principle that the Constitution does not establish positive rights, it is unable to appreciate our recognition in *Estelle* and *Youngberg* that this principle does not hold true in all circumstances.

What made Joshua's claim fit under the rubric of *Estelle* and *Youngberg*, Brennan suggested, was that Joshua had been confined by the state no less than had the prisoner in *Estelle* and the mental patient in *Youngberg*.

> Through its child welfare program . . . the State of Wisconsin has relieved ordinary citizens and governmental bodies other than the Department of any sense of obligation to do anything more than report their suspicions of child abuse to DSS. If DSS ignores or dismisses these suspicions, no one will step in to fill the gap. Wisconsin's child-protection program thus effectively confined Joshua DeShaney within the walls of Randy DeShaney's violent home until such time as DSS took action to remove him.

That was the crux of the matter for Brennan:

> Today's opinion construes the Due Process Clause to permit a State to displace private sources of protection and then, at the critical moment, to shrug its shoulders and turn away from the harm it has promised to try to prevent. Because I cannot agree that our Constitution is indifferent to such indifference, I respectfully dissent.

Not all of the dissenters were willing or able to resist that impulse of natural sympathy to do good of which Rehnquist had warned. Where Brennan sought to root his dissent in the law, Blackmun chose to reject the Court's "sterile formalism" in a blisteringly passionate dissent. He found it simply galling that "the Court purports to be the dispassionate oracle of the law, unmoved by 'natural sympathy.'" To Blackmun, the Court had a moral obligation to interpret its prior Fourteenth Amendment precedents in a way "which comports with dictates of fundamental justice and recognizes that compassion need not be exiled from the province of judging." The foundation for Blackmun's high-minded moralism was nothing more than a 1984 book entitled *Law, Psychiatry, and Morality.* He found it worth quoting:

> We will make mistakes if we go forward, but doing nothing can be the worst mistake. What is required of us is moral ambition. Until our composite sketch becomes a true portrait of humanity we must live with our uncertainty; we will grope, we will struggle, and our compassion may be our only guide and comfort.

"Poor Joshua!" Blackmun wailed. He deserved more from the Court than the mere legalisms he got from the majority. Following the suggestion by the ACLU that the distinction between action and inaction is "illusory," Blackmun sought to make the case for the obliteration of that "formalistic" distinction. The Court could not recognize the duty of the State to act because "it attempts to draw a sharp and rigid line between action and inaction." And therein lay the defect of the majority opinion:

[S]uch formalistic reasoning has no place in the interpretation of the broad and stirring Clauses of the Fourteenth Amendment. Indeed, I submit that these Clauses were designed, at least in part, to undo the formalistic legal reasoning that infected antebellum jurisprudence . . . Like the antebellum judges who denied relief to fugitive slaves . . . the Court today claims that its decision, however harsh, is compelled by existing legal doctrine.

For Blackmun, the proper role of the Court was to eschew the text and intention of the Constitution when their moral duties became clear to the Justices. Fundamental justice, not the Constitution, was to be the guide to interpretation. So extreme was Blackmun's reasoning that neither Justice Brennan nor Justice Marshall would sign on to his dissent.

JUSTICE VS. LAW

With the Court's decision, that was that. If Joshua was to find relief for the injuries inflicted upon him by his "bestial father," it would have to be in the courts of Wisconsin, somewhere under the laws of that state. Federalism had prevailed; the newly conservative Court was simply unwilling to give vent to "moral ambition" and create new rights out of whole cloth. An important precedent had been set.

But the significance of *DeShaney* v. *Winnebago County* is not limited to its facts or to the body of law to which it belongs. The case also exposes all the factors that contribute to making the judicial process simultaneously important to everyone's daily lives and utterly mystical to the average citizen. No doubt many if not most or all people who might be asked how the case should have been decided might very well have joined with Brennan and Blackmun. Fundamental notions of justice seem to cry out for such a conclusion. But in the end, the law is not simply about justice. It is about procedure, about rules and regulations and jurisdiction, about the nature of precedent. At a minimum, *DeShaney* makes clear the distinction between the just and the legal, a gulf that is often wide and unbridgeable.

To understand why the outcome in *DeShaney* is the right one requires a deeper look into the nature and extent of judicial power under a written constitution of limited powers. That look necessitates coming to grips with the inherently political nature of judicial power, the powerful role appointments to the courts play in determining how controversial cases will be decided. It also demands a reconsideration of the most fundamental of the Constitution's principles, federalism and separated powers, to understand why it is important that there not be a federal judicial remedy for every moral wrong that taints society. Finally, it requires a consideration of the increasingly influential role of "constitutional theory" in the exercise of judicial power and an attempt to answer the question posed by Judge Frank Easterbrook: Can the Constitution survive constitutional theory?

Alexis de Tocqueville once noted that in America the courts wield enormous power, but not the same power as legislatures or executives. It is, rather, power rooted more deeply, in the very "moral force" of the community. The power of the courts, from the Supreme Court down to the lowest local tribunal, derives from the belief of the people that their decisions are, in some sense, just. They are not arbitrary or capricious, but are founded upon something more than the particular judge's opinion of what is right or just. The moral force of the courts in America is drawn precisely from the fact that they are *legal* institutions guided by and beholden to a law not of their own making. If that moral force is to be sustained, it is necessary that the public understand the limits of judicial power under a Constitution that was intended, as Chief Justice John Marshall said, to be a rule for courts as well as for legislatures. Investigating what lay behind the facts and controversies of *DeShaney* can enhance that understanding, and, thereby, the moral force of the courts in American society and politics. In the chapters that follow, those fundamental issues will be examined closely.

CHAPTER FOUR

DOING JUSTICE IN THE NAME OF THE LAW

The Transformation of Due Process of Law

The split between the justices in *DeShaney* v. *Winnebago County* as to the meaning of the Due Process Clause of the Fourteenth Amendment went beyond the immediate precedents. The real division was far deeper, far more confusing. Ultimately what divided the Court was nothing less than an understanding of the nature and extent of judicial power under the written Constitution. As such, the clash of opinions in *DeShaney* was only the most recent battle in a long-running intellectual war within the Court over a basic question: Does the written Constitution impose limits upon a judge's power to effect justice?

The skirmishes over how to answer this question have been many and varied. At least since Justice James Iredell and Justice Samuel Chase did rhetorical battle in *Calder* v. *Bull* (1796), the issue has been a live one for the Court itself. In *Calder* Iredell and Chase had sketched in broad outline the two sides of the debate, an outline that has generally held its shape to this day. To Chase it seemed simply that there "are acts which the federal or state legislature cannot do without exceeding their authority. There are certain vital principles in our free republican governments, which will determine and overrule an apparent and flagrant abuse of legislative power; as to authorize manifest injustice by the positive law; or to take away that security for personal liberty or private property, for the protection whereof the government was established. An act of the legislature (for I cannot call it a law), contrary to the great first principles of the social compact, cannot be considered a rightful exercise of legislative authority."[1]

Justice Iredell could not abide Chase's unseemly confidence in judicial insight—nor his misunderstanding of judicial power under a written constitution. Iredell offered a caustic reply: "If . . . the legislature . . . shall pass a law within the general scope of their constitutional powers, the court cannot pronounce it void, merely because it is, in their judgment, contrary to the principles of natural justice." The reason, Iredell explained, was simple: "The ideas of natural justice are regulated by no fixed standard: the ablest and the purest men have differed upon the subject; and all that the court could properly say, in such an event, would be, that the legislature possessed of an equal right of opinion, had passed an act which, in the opinion of the judges, was inconsistent with the abstract principles of natural justice."[2]

It is not too much to say that the most recent representatives of the Chase and Iredell camps had come to be, by the time of *DeShaney* v. *Winnebago County,* Justices Brennan and Rehnquist, respectively. Since Rehnquist joined the Court in 1972 he had consistently staked out a position generally at odds with that of Brennan, the intellectual ballast of the liberal constitutionalism of the Warren Court. Where Brennan saw an evolving Constitution needing a constant judicial infusion of meaning, Rehnquist saw a fixed and definite body of law that demanded nothing more morally taxing for the Court than to discern the original intention of its clear provisions. The debate between Rehnquist and Brennan often spilled out of the Court itself; neither was shy about offering his views in a public forum. The larger arguments that lay just beneath the surface of the opinions in *DeShaney* had been clearly and forcefully expressed by the Justices years before Joshua's case came to their attention.

In a 1975 speech at the University of Texas Law School, then Associate Justice Rehnquist spoke to what he called the "notion" of the living Constitution. While granting both that the general language of the Constitution inevitably grants "latitude to those who would later interpret the instrument to make that language

applicable to cases that the framers might not have foreseen" and
that there "is obviously wide room for honest difference of opinion over the meaning of general phrases in the Constitution,"
Rehnquist insisted that it was left to "the popularly elected
branches of government, not the judicial branch, to keep the
country abreast of the times."[3] The Constitution created the institutional framework within which the people would be able to confront "the numerous and varied problems that the future would
bring."[4] It would be through politics that the people in their collective capacity would give vent to their moral inclinations and see
them transformed into law.

By Rehnquist's measure neither the moral judgments of the
people, either individually or collectively, nor those of any public
official had public force unless explicitly enacted into law. It is by
that action and that action alone that considerations of justice—of
right and wrong—can be transformed into legitimately binding
rules. As he put it:

> If . . . a society adopts a constitution and incorporates in that con-
> stitution safeguards for individual liberty, these safeguards indeed
> do take on a generalized rightness or goodness. They assume a
> general social acceptance neither because of any intrinsic worth nor
> because of any unique origins in someone's idea of natural justice
> but instead simply because they have been incorporated in a consti-
> tution by the people.

Moreover:

> Beyond the Constitution and the laws in our society, there simply
> is no basis other than the individual conscience of the citizen that
> may serve as a platform for the launching of moral
> judgments . . . Many of us necessarily feel strongly and deeply
> about our own moral judgments, but they remain only personal
> moral judgments until in some way given the sanction of law.[5]

This was not to argue, Rehnquist was quick to point out, that
there was no ground for moral judgments outside the law; rather,

it was only to argue that moral judgments cannot have the force of law unless *formally* enacted as law. Such a view, he concluded, does not denigrate the power of moral judgments but celebrates them by keeping them in their proper place. But there was more to it than that:

> It should not be easy for any one individual or group of individuals to impose by law their value judgments upon fellow citizens who may disagree with those judgments. Indeed, it should not be easier because the individual in question is a judge.[6]

To Justice Brennan, views like Rehnquist's ignored the true glory of the Constitution. The Constitution is not merely a document of often tedious phrases and arcane meaning; it is a moral manifesto that "embodies the aspirations to social justice, brotherhood, and human dignity that brought this nation into being."[7] In a widely noted speech at Georgetown University in 1985, Justice Brennan undertook especially to criticize those who, like Rehnquist, embraced the idea that constitutional interpretation should take its bearings from the original intentions of those who drafted and ratified the Constitution and its subsequent amendments. Such a position, Brennan argued, "feigns a self-effacing deference" to the founders, but it is in fact "little more than arrogance cloaked as humility."[8] The Justice pulled no punches: "Those who would restrict claims of right to the values of 1789 specifically articulated in the Constitution turn a blind eye to social progress and eschew adaptation of overarching principles to changes of social circumstances."[9] Such a crabbed view of constitutional interpretation was born of an equally crabbed view of the Constitution. To Brennan, the Constitution was meant to be not merely "a plan of government" but rather "an embodiment of fundamental substantive values."[10] The Constitution, he argued, is "a sublime oration on the dignity of man;" it is "a sparkling vision of the supremacy of the human dignity of every individual."[11]

The crux of Brennan's view is that the text of the Constitution was intended to have a "transformative purpose." The judges and

justices must seek "to draw meaning from the text in order to resolve public controversies" and thereby transform the status quo.
But that meaning is not the meaning that has lurked in the words
since they were first drafted and ratified; it is, rather, a meaning to
be gleaned by each age for itself. Taken on its face, the
Constitution is burdened with "majestic generalities and en-
nobling pronouncements [that] are both luminous and obscure."
In the end the nature of judicial power cannot be simply to find an
antecedent meaning in the Constitution but must be to "give
meaning to the Constitution."[12] That meaning to be judicially
given takes its substance from the rather vague standard of
"human dignity." It is the protection of this "human dignity" that
forms the essential duty of the Supreme Court, in Justice
Brennan's view.

But "human dignity" does not remain static; its very essence is
dynamic. And thus are the contours of constitutional meaning
ever changing: "The precise rules by which we have protected fundamental human dignity have been transformed over time in response to both transformations of social conditions and evolution
of our concepts of human dignity."[13] Thus the "transformative
purpose" of the Constitution, by Brennan's calculus, is to allow
judges especially to adapt fundamental principles to changed social
circumstances. The task of the judge, for Brennan, is to keep the
Constitution in tune with the times. History is the master, principle the slave.

To put it a bit more bluntly, for Justice Brennan the interpretation of the Constitution is the moral obligation of a judge not
simply to seek to discover allegedly fundamental, preexisting law,
but to articulate what each judge sees as the "vision of the individual embodied in the Constitution" according to the time and
place when the interpretation is made.[14] This comes not from the
dry and outdated historical text or intentions but from nothing
less than the judge's having "a personal confrontation with the
well-springs of our society."[15]

It is this "personal confrontation" that allows the Justices to believe that what they are upholding is not simply their own personal
moral vision, but rather "the community's interpretation."[16]
Brennan summed it up:

We current Justices read the Constitution in the only way that we can: as Twentieth Century Americans. We look to the history of the time of framing and to the intervening history of interpretation. But the ultimate question must be, what do the words of the text mean in our time? For the genius of the Constitution rests not in any static meaning it might have had in a world that is dead and gone, but in the adaptability of its great principles to cope with current problems and needs. What the constitutional fundamentals meant to the wisdom of other times cannot be the measure to the vision of our time. Similarly, what those fundamentals mean for us, our descendants will learn, cannot be their measure to the vision of their time.[17]

Since the polestar of constitutional meaning is "human dignity," and since "the demands of human dignity will never cease to evolve," the Constitution will never cease to evolve. But for Brennan such evolution is not to be sought, as it is for Rehnquist, in the collective consent of the people through the cumbersome process of amendment, but merely in the independent judgment of life-tenured judges. There were some who saw in Brennan's approach to judging nothing less than the "arrogance cloaked in humility" of which he had accused his critics.[18]

THE CONFUSING WORLD OF DUE PROCESS

Over the years, the debate over the power and obligation of judges to seek not simply the legal or the constitutional but the just had come to center first on one provision of the Constitution, then on another, before finally coming to rest on the Due Process Clause of the Fourteenth Amendment. That clause and, to a lesser extent, its progenitor in the Fifth Amendment, had become, by the end of the nineteenth century, the intellectual and ideological battleground for the clashing factions on the Court.

At the heart of most of the judicial efforts to seek to invoke standards of higher law lay the single most vexing issue of American constitutional law, the principle of federalism. Nearly every questionable interpretation seems to have as its object the diminution of state sovereignty and the enhancement of national

power. That this was to be expected can be seen from the original
design of the Constitution itself. Where the first American constitution, the Articles of Confederation, created an unabashedly confederal form of governance, the new Constitution of 1787 was
designed in large part to correct the political inconveniences posed
by a strictly federal organization. Under the Articles the national
authority was reduced to impotence. The result led those who
dominated the Federal Convention in 1787 to seek ways to com-
pensate. Their solution was not to make the new Constitution
better in a confederal way, but to make it better by making it less
confederal in the first place.[19]

Yet the nationalists at the convention, the Federalists, men like
James   Madison,   Alexander   Hamilton,   James   Wilson,   and
Gouverneur Morris, were resisted by those who remained committed to the idea of small republics united in friendly confederation. Following a long tradition of political theorists, these
Anti-Federalists believed that liberty was threatened by the sort of
big government that seemed implicit in the nationalists' proposed
constitution. These men were not marginal characters; among
their ranks were many of the most significant leaders of the revolutionary period—Patrick Henry, George Mason, and Richard
Henry Lee, among others. They did not share the confidence
their younger colleagues had placed in the new and untried form
of large republic, a republic that was, to their way of thinking, too
far removed from the democratic control of the people, a principle
that was the essence of their older conception of republicanism.

In the end the Constitution that emerged from the convention
was as nationalistic as the Federalists could make it and as confederal as the Anti-Federalists could keep it. It was, as James Madison
would famously describe it in *The Federalist*, "partly federal, and
partly national."[20] That compromise would, in a very short time,
reveal the new notion of federalism as the most difficult part of
the Constitution on which to find consensus. The animosities between the Federalists and the Anti-Federalists had not in truth
been stilled; the fundamental tension simply had been made part
of the Constitution itself. Thus it was inevitable that the proper
relation of states to nation would come to be "our central political
problem."[21]

The most basic fear was that the national government would, as George Mason said at the time, "utterly . . . destroy the state governments."[22] Even though the Federalists could seek to assure the doubters that the Constitution was a balance of confederal and national features, the Anti-Federalists knew better: all bets were hedged in favor of nationalism. The constitutional deck had been stacked. Over time, the Anti-Federalists argued, the states would cease to enjoy anything remotely resembling sovereignty and would be absorbed into one great consolidated republic. There was no doubt in the minds of the Anti-Federalist critics of the Constitution where the problem would manifest itself most clearly: in the federal courts. Consolidation would occur through the interpretations that would be given to the *national* Constitution by the *national* judiciary.

The structure of the new judiciary, the Anti-Federalists said, was such that the judges would be unrestrained in the exercise of their powers. One critic warned that they would be "independent in the fullest sense of the word. There is no power above them, to controul any of their decisions. There is no authority that can remove them, and they cannot be controuled by the laws of the legislature. In short, they are independent of the people, of the legislature, and of every power under heaven." And therein lay the constitutional dilemma: "Men placed in this situation will generally feel themselves independent of heaven itself."[23]

With such institutional independence the judges would be "constitutionally unaccountable for their opinions." Untethered by any textual shackles, they would feel free to "find in the spirit of the constitution, more than was expressed in the letter." This freedom of interpretation would allow the judges enough power to "enable them to mould the government into most any shape they please." The determination of the cases and controversies that would come before them could be decided "as their conscience, their opinions, their caprice, or their politics might dictate."[24] Given the natural national bias one could reasonably expect of such national judges, the great danger would be that they would by their interpretation of the Constitution "melt down the states into one entire government, for every purpose as well internal and local, as external and national."[25]

For the first twelve years of the republic the judiciary seemed to belie the Anti-Federalists' warnings. The first Chief Justice, John Jay, found his job so tedious and insignificant that he eventually resigned in 1795. Under the second Chief Justice, Oliver Ellsworth, the role of the Court did not much change. Then, in 1801, John Marshall of Virginia became the third Chief Justice, a post he would hold until 1836. It was during Marshall's long tenure that the Anti-Federalist warnings began to come true. An ardent nationalist, Marshall set out to put the Federalist stamp on the new republic. Guided by an unfaltering vision of the power and political importance of commerce, Marshall sought to flesh out the terms of the constitutional text with his theory of commercial republicanism. At a minimum that meant a radical expansion of the most nationalistic provisions of the Constitution. The fulfillment of Marshall's vision could come only at the expense of the states.

By the interpretations of the Marshall Court of the Contracts Clause and the Commerce Clause, national power was greatly enhanced, but not without a struggle. In cases such as *Marbury* v. *Madison* (1803) and *Cohens* v. *Virginia* (1821) he secured the power of the Supreme Court to exercise judicial review over Congress and the states. In a long line of cases he established the authority of the Congress to exercise enormous control over commerce despite any protests by the states. So opposed was Marshall's jurisprudence by the descendants of the Anti-Federalists, the Jeffersonians, that he was driven to defend himself, albeit pseudonymously, in the public newspapers of Virginia against Jeffersonian attacks on his opinion in *McCulloch* v. *Maryland* (1819).

In the original Constitution the Contracts Clause was the one provision that offered a way for the Court to invalidate state legislation that threatened private property. The Fifth Amendment, with its Due Process and Takings Clauses, did not apply to the states but only to the federal government.[26] The prohibition that barred states from "impairing the obligation of contracts" afforded the Supreme Court a means to curb what the Justices saw as the excesses of state legislatures and to make certain that the commercial republicanism that they saw as informing the Constitution's underlying political theory would be allowed to prevail. From the time of the Marshall Court until 1889 the Contracts Clause was at issue in nearly 40 percent of the cases before the Court that raised the question of the validity of state legislation; during that time the clause was the reason for no fewer than seventy-five of the decisions that struck down state laws, nearly 50 percent of all such invalidations.[27] The problem was that often the facts of the cases did not make such an interpretation easy; the Court frequently had to stretch and strain to find the means to strike down state legislation it somehow knew was wrong even though it might not at first glance appear to qualify as an "impairment" of contracts.

In the view of the Court, the right to private property was a vested right, one so fundamental, so in the nature of things, as to be always and everywhere beyond the legitimate reach of any government. This was the issue in *Fletcher* v. *Peck* (1810), the first case in which the Supreme Court invalidated a state law on the basis of the Constitution.[28] *Fletcher* involved the validity of the State of Georgia's rescission of a former grant of land. The question was whether the Georgia legislature could constitutionally rescind such grants. The Court held unanimously that it could not.

But there was more. Marshall's opinion went far beyond the original intention of the clause by extending what was in all likelihood a protection for private contracts to include public contracts as well.[29] The decision also conformed, Marshall assured his readers, with "certain great principles of justice, whose authority is universally acknowledged." Echoing Justice Chase's musings in *Calder*, Marshall put it bluntly: It "may well be doubted, whether the nature of society and government does not prescribe some limits to the legislative power; and if any be prescribed, where are they to be found, if the property of an individual, fairly and honestly acquired, may be seized without compensation."[30] Justice Johnson was even more forthright in resting his opinion on something more fundamental than the Constitution. "I do it," he said, "on a general principle, on the reason and nature of things: a principle which will impose laws even on the Diety."[31]

The Court would return to this mystical world over the case of *Terrett* v. *Taylor*. Writing for a unanimous Court, Justice Joseph Story held that Virginia did not have the power to take title to

land that had been held by the Episcopal Church since the lands
in question had become part of the District of Columbia and
hence were under the exclusive jurisdiction of Congress. Yet that
was not enough for Story; the attempted taking violated more
than merely the Constitution—it was at odds with fundamental
justice. The Court based its rationale not only on the Constitution
but

> . . . upon the principles of natural justice, upon the fundamental
> laws of every free government, upon the spirit and the letter of the
> Constitution of the United States, and upon the decisions of most
> respectable tribunals, in resisting such a doctrine.[32]

Story's explicit imprimatur on the idea that the Court could invalidate legislation on the basis of "natural justice" gave the notion no small degree of legitimacy in the eyes of those who
would find the Constitution too restrictive in its explicit terms
and intentions.

The Marshall view of the Contracts Clause was extended in
other cases: *New Jersey* v. *Wilson* (1812),[33] *Trustees of Dartmouth
College* v. *Woodward* (1819),[34] and *Sturges* v. *Crowninshield*
(1819).[35] In most cases none of the Justices saw fit to go beyond
the text and arguable intention of the Contracts Clause as the
basis of the decision. There was no need for recourse to any notion of higher law or natural justice. But in the only case in which
Marshall dissented in all his many years on the Court, *Ogden* v.
Saunders (1827),[36] he once again nudged up against something
outside the Constitution's text as the justification for his inability
to go along with the majority of the Court. In a sense, the *Ogden*
dissent fleshed out the same thought that he had expressed somewhat guardedly in *Fletcher:* Individuals "do not derive from government their right to contract, but bring that right with them
into society; that obligation is not conferred on contracts by positive law, but is intrinsic, and is conferred by the act of the
parties."[37] Marshall's argument that certain of the rights attaching
to contracts are "intrinsic", and that certain rights antedate society
and hence the Constitution, begged the tough question of how a
judge or a justice is to distinguish that which is fundamental and

intrinsic from that which is not. In begging that basic question, Marshall's logic left open the question of what precisely are the limits on a judge's power to try to effect justice. Marshall's allusions in his decisions to the standard of natural justice or higher law are few and far between, which suggests that, whatever his willingness to employ them on occasion, he did indeed recognize the seriousness of the question he never fully confronted. That later and lesser lights who would come after him to serve on the Court would not or could not appreciate the gravity of such a mode of interpretation seems, on reflection, to have been inevitable.

Whatever Marshall's juridical sins as measured against his usual regard for the importance of the written Constitution, his suggestions of a binding higher law in his various Contracts Clause opinions at least had the virtue of being nominally related to the sorts of legislation being struck down by the Court.[38] To the degree to which Marshall and his Court sought to flesh out the contours of the Contracts Clause they endeavored to do so within the general confines of the concerns the clause was originally meant to address. Nothing of the sort can be said for the judicial fate of the Due Process Clause.

The concept of "due process of law" was not, either at the time of the founding or during the creation of the Fourteenth Amendment, a matter of much confusion. Its roots went deep into the soil of the Anglo-American legal tradition, stretching all the way back to the thirty-ninth chapter of Magna Carta in 1215. In that fundamentally feudal document concerned with fundamentally feudal things—Magna Carta was not the great charter of individual liberty in the modern sense that it is often protrayed to be—the barons extracted from a less than willing King John the guarantee that they would be secure from his all too frequently arbitrary commands. In particular, the charter provided:

No free man shall be taken, imprisoned, disseised, outlawed, banished or in any way destroyed, nor will We proceed against or prosecute him, except by the lawful judgment of his peers and by the law of the land.

What, precisely, was meant by "the law of the land" was nothing mystical; it was a phrase intended to bind the King himself to the forms and practices of the common law, the legal customs of the realm. He was no longer free, after Magna Carta, to behave arbitrarily; there was a standard to which his behavior had to conform. The concern was to demand that a set procedure be followed so those who confronted the law would know where they stood and what they could expect.

Sir Edward Coke in his seminal *Institutes on the Law of England* insisted that this provision in Magna Carta of "law of the land" meant simply "by due process of law." Coke's interpretation seems to have been accepted at face value by most commentators who followed in his broad wake, including the great American commentators James Kent, Joseph Story, and Thomas Cooley.[39] But the historical evidence for Coke's view is at best highly doubtful. In fact, it seems clear that the two phrases were never understood to mean the same thing at any time in English legal history. While the notion of "law of the land" was taken with a high degree of political seriousness and was indeed understood as a fundamental principle, "due process of law" never enjoyed such a status. It was always viewed as a rather mundane concept of the law, one that had a rather precise, technical meaning. The word "process" meant simply writs, "those writs which summoned parties to appear in court, as well as those by which execution of judgments was carried out."[40] Indeed, the only place in the Statutes of the Realm where the phrase "due process of law" actually appears is in a statute enacted in the reign of Edward III in 1354:

> That no man of what Estate or Condition that he be, shall be put out of land or Tenement, not taken, not imprisoned, not disinherited, not put to death, without being brought in answer by due process of law.[41]

However, given the importance of Coke's *Institutes* to the learning of the law in the early American republic, it is fair to conclude that, right or wrong, Coke's view was one of great importance to the subsequent development of "due process of law."[42] The question then becomes, what did "due process of law" mean to that generation of American founders?

At a minimum it should be assumed that the phrase "due process of law" as it found its way into the Fifth Amendment to the Constitution meant nothing more than what it had come to mean in the English common law tradition—"the process which the person involved is entitled to receive."[43] Such a view does not carry with it any substantive demand that the process must somehow be suitable or desirable; the phrase "does not purport to create any new procedural rights."[44] Put slightly differently, "the 'due process' imposed is not primarily a requirement that right be done, but that appropriate machinery for doing right be provided."[45] There is no doubt that the meaning of "due process of law" was never understood to be a power of courts to investigate and set aside legislation on substantive grounds; the clause in the Fifth Amendment was never intended to "create a new, federal criterion of justice."[46]

Alexander Hamilton neatly summed up the true meaning of "due process of law" as embraced by his generation. In commenting on the New York Constitution in the New York Assembly on February 6, 1787, Hamilton put it this way:

It is there declared that, no man shall be disenfranchised or deprived of any right, but by *"due process of law"*, or the judgment of his peers. The words *"due process of law"* have a precise technical import, and are only applicable to the process and proceedings of the courts of justice; they can never be referred to an act of legislature.[47]

This view of "due process of law" as a phrase of "precise technical import" was the accepted meaning of the generation who framed and ratified the Constitution and the Bill of Rights. This view would also generally hold sway for the better part of the next century; it was the received tradition. But around the middle of the nineteenth century this common law understanding began to be challenged, first subtly as pertaining to the clause in the Fifth Amendment and then without restraint concerning the clause of the Fourteenth Amendment. So wholesale was the intellectual assault that by 1911 it could be reported that "the most important clause of the United States Constitution judged as a restriction upon the legislative power of the states is the due process of law clause of the Fourteenth Amendment."[48] It is necessary to recall that transformation in order to grasp the full implications of the reasoning in *DeShaney* v. *Winnebago County*.

THE RISE OF SUBSTANTIVE DUE PROCESS

The first flutter of judicial activity—and one can only call it a flutter—concerning the substantive concerns allegedly implied in "due process of law" came long before the Civil War and the constitutional amendments which that conflict spawned. The point of departure was a New York State case, *Wynehamer* v. *New York* (1856).[49] Interestingly, the effort of the New York court was aimed at discrediting the idea that appeals to natural law were sufficient to invalidate legislation. The *Wynehamer* court recognized that the doctrine of fundamental law as broached in such cases as *Calder* and *Fletcher* was too "vague and unstable" a foundation for judicial decisions to rest upon.[50] Something more textually sturdy was necessary lest the courts be accused of simply passing their own predilections off as fundamental law.

In *Wynehamer* the New York Court of Appeals invalidated a state prohibition law because it violated property rights in liquor. The law not only declared liquor to be a nuisance that was to be prohibited but demanded that anyone who owned liquor at the time the law was adopted had to destroy it under the threat of criminal prosecution.[51] To the court's way of thinking such strictures were unreasonable and arbitrary and hence violations of the property rights of those who held such spirits. The demand for the destruction of liquors that were perfectly legal at the time the law was passed was a demand not legitimately within the power of the government: "The legislature cannot make the mere existence of the rights secured the occasion of depriving a person of them even by the forms which belong to 'due process of law.'"[52] The court, not the legislature, would decide whether or not the substantive demands of the law comported with what the court understood to be "due process of law."

This appeal to "due process of law" was intended to expel from the courtroom the mystical and indefinite "theories, alleged to be found in natural reason and inalienable rights." Such appeals as these were "subversive of the just and necessary powers of government."[53] When it comes to the judicial definition of the legislative power, Justice Comstock continued, "where the constitution is silent and there is no clear usurpation of the powers distributed to the other departments," the court would face "great difficulty and great danger" in attempting to articulate limits to that power. In particular, Comstock argued, the court in *Wynehamer* simply rejected the argument

> . . . that the power of the legislature is restricted not only by the express provisions of the written constitution but by limitations implied from the nature and form of our government; that aside from all special restrictions the right to enact such laws is not among the delegated powers of the legislature, and that the act in question is void as against the fundamental principles of liberty and against common reason and natural rights.[54]

Justice Selden was more than willing to second such a view. The "doctrine that there exists in the judiciary some vague, loose and undefined power to annul a law, because in its judgment it is 'contrary to natural equity and justice,' is in conflict with the first principles of government and can never, I think, be maintained."[55] And Justice Hubbard was of precisely the same mind: "I am opposed to the judiciary . . . declaring a statute invalid upon any fanciful theory of higher law or first principles of natural rights outside the constitution."[56]

It would seem that in the old battle between Chase and Iredell in *Calder* Iredell was finally triumphant, at least in the New York Court of Appeals. Stronger condemnations of the Chase view would be hard to imagine than these of Selden, Comstock, and Hubbard. But what the court took away with one hand, it slipped back in with the other. The notion of "due process of law" it had articulated as the means of invalidating the harsh prohibition law was in truth the old natural law reasoning wrapped in an explicit constitutional provision.

Justice A. S. Johnson felt compelled to offer an example of what sorts of evils "due process of law" would actually prevent: "For instance, a law that any man who after the age of fifty years, shall continue to live, shall be punished by imprisonment or fine would be beyond the power of the legislature. It would be so, upon the ground that he cannot be deprived of life, liberty, or property without due process of law."[57] By what clear constitutional meaning such a harsh and unreasonable law would be prohibited, Johnson did not say beyond "due process of law." But to reach such a conclusion is to concede that the judiciary does indeed possess the power to explore the substance of legislation in order to determine if it is reasonable or not. Such exploration and determination under the rubric of "due process of law," however, would be no different if carried out in light of the judicial concern for "the nature and form of our government" or "natural reason and inalienable rights," the very standards the court had just ridiculed.

The opinion in *Wynehamer* as a matter of law was of fleeting significance; only ten years later the same court denounced "the inconsiderate dicta" of *Wynehamer*.[58] But as an indication of where judicial reasoning could head under the guise of defining "due process of law," the case looms large in judicial history. It has proved to have been "a new starting point in the history of due process of law."[59] Moreover, there is no reason to think that Chief Justice Roger Taney was not aware of it when the Supreme Court the next year came to consider the problem of slavery in *Dred Scott* v. *Sandford* (1857).[60] For the association in *Wynehamer* between the vested rights of property and the idea of "due process of law" was reflected in Taney's infamous opinion in the slavery case.

It is perhaps appropriate that the roots of such a constitutional doctrine as substantive due process at the national level stretch back to the most vile of all the decisions ever handed down by the Supreme Court of the United States. For it was in *Dred Scott* that Chief Justice Taney first suggested that there was indeed a substantive element to the meaning of due process of law in the federal Constitution. By Taney's measure there were certain rights so fundamental as to be securely vested in the individual; they were beyond the reach of legislation. In a sense, Taney's effort to protect the rights of slaveholders not to be deprived of their property—slaves like Dred Scott—was a joining of Justice Chase's view in *Calder* with the common law language of due process of law. Taney wrote:

> [T]he rights of property are united with the rights of person, and placed on the same ground by the fifth amendment to the Constitution, which provides that no person shall be deprived of life, liberty, and property, without due process of law. And an act of Congress which deprives a citizen of the United States of his liberty or property, merely because he came himself or brought his property into a particular territory of the United States, and who had committed no offence against the laws, could hardly be dignified with the name of due process of law.

Those actions of the government that would be "dignified with the name of due process of law" were to be those actions the Court, or at least a majority of the Justices, might find to be reasonable. Thus were the seeds of the so-called rule of reason planted in the morally tainted soil of *Dred Scott,* only to be brought to fruition in countless ways in the years to follow.

Taney's initial, somewhat tentative association of vested rights with due process of law in *Dred Scott* would eventually seem tame indeed. The catalyst for unleashing the notion that there was a substantive content to due process would be the Fourteenth Amendment. Although the Court at first refused to infuse the Fourteenth Amendment's clause with the sort of logic that informed the opinion of Taney concerning the Fifth Amendment, once it began to do so there would be no stopping it. In time there would seemingly be no area of public life on which the Court would not rule in the name of guaranteeing "due process of law." It is more than slightly ironic that when *Dred Scott* was overruled by the ratification of the Civil War Amendments, the most doctrinally suspect part of Taney's opinion would come to be incorporated into the new Due Process Clause of the Fourteenth Amendment by the next generation of Justices.

When the Fourteenth Amendment was ratified, its primary pur-

pose was to guarantee the former slaves that their rights would be
no less within the states than their white fellow citizens'. The
Reconstruction Congress had undertaken to pass certain civil
rights laws that were designed to protect the freedmen from the
political reprisals of the less than enthusiastic Southern state legislatures. Yet it seemed likely that the Supreme Court would invalidate any such legislation as being too intrusive; the Civil War may
have ended the noxious institution of slavery, but it had not altered the basic structure of the Constitution. Under the original
Constitution's federal design such intrusions into the domestic affairs of the states seemed to be out of bounds. Thus Congress
amended the Constitution to allow itself to pass legislation to assure all those within the states certain fundamental rights.

Section one of the Fourteenth Amendment spelled out clearly
what the amendment was designed to achieve: "All persons born
or naturalized in the United States, and subject to the jurisdiction thereof, are citizens of the United States and of the State
wherein they reside. No State shall make or enforce any law
which shall abridge the privileges or immunities of citizens of the
United States; nor shall any State deprive any person of life, liberty, or property, without due process of law; nor deny to any
person within its jurisdiction the equal protection of the laws."
Yet the constitutional guts of the amendment lay in its fifth section: "The Congress shall have power to enforce, by appropriate
legislation, the provisions of this article." The purpose of the
Fourteenth Amendment was not to empower the courts to create new rights—after all, it was precisely the Court's interpretive
rambunctiousness that had prompted the need for the amendment in the first place—but rather to empower Congress to
guarantee by legislation—civil rights laws—that the rights the
states already had in place would extend to all citizens regardless
of race or previous condition of servitude. To that extent, the
original federal balance of the Constitution was given a more nationalistic tilt.

Within that context the Due Process Clause was understood to
mean what it had meant for several hundred years of Anglo-
American legal history: that those who were involved in criminal
cases were assured that they would not suffer deprivation of life,

liberty, or property without the processes of the law to which they were entitled. Only by the fulfillment of preexisting procedural re-quirements—the proper writs, and so forth—could the citizen be assured that the actions of the government were not being arbi-trarily imposed. It was not shorthand for a limitless field of natural rights; each of its terms had "a peculiar and definite meaning."[61] At a minimum, it was never understood to empower the Court to revise legislation through the exercise of judicial review.[62]

When the Court first confronted claims raised under the Fourteenth Amendment it limited itself to what it saw as the his-torical intention behind the amendment's language. In *The Slaughterhouse Cases* the Court was asked to strike down a Louisiana law that created a monopoly in the slaughtering busi-ness that had the effect of depriving independent butchers in New Orleans of their livelihood.[63] The Butchers' Benevolent Association claimed that the legislation violated the Thirteenth Amendment and the Privileges or Immunities, Due Process, and Equal Protection clauses of the Fourteenth Amendment. The Court refused to invalidate the law. When it came to the con-struction of the Due Process Clause sought by the butchers, Justice Samuel F. Miller was blunt: It is "sufficient to say that under no construction of that provision that we have ever seen, or any that we deem admissible, can the restraint imposed by the State of Louisiana upon the exercise of their trade by the butch-ers of New Orleans be held to be a deprivation of property within the meaning of that provision."[64] The Court was not unanimous, however. Justices Stephen J. Field and Joseph P. Bradley dissented, with Bradley relying explicitly on the Due Process Clause.

Four years later, in *Munn* v. *Illinois,* the Court again refused to infuse the Due Process Clause with any substantive meaning.[65] In *Munn* the plaintiff, Ira Y. Munn, claimed that an Illinois statute that regulated grain warehouses by requiring a license and by reg-ulating the fees they could charge violated the Due Process Clause. Munn had operated his warehouse without a license and had charged higher fees and was subsequently fined $100. The Court held that when a person "devotes his property to a use in which the public has an interest, he, in effect, grants to the public an interest in that use, and must submit to be controlled by the public for the common good."[66] Once again, the Court ruled over the impassioned libertarian dissent of Justice Field. "If this be sound law," Field argued, "if there be no protection, either in the principles upon which our republican government is founded, or in the prohibitions of the Constitution against such invasion of private rights, all property and all business in the State are held at the mercy of a majority of its legislature."[67] To Field such majoritarian tyranny was the very essence of a deprivation of due process of law.

In 1878 Justice Miller would once again refuse to stretch due process of law to embrace substantive content. In *Davidson* v. *New Orleans* a landowner had claimed that an assessment to pay for the drainage of a swamp was a violation of the Due Process Clause of the Fourteenth Amendment.[68] Miller was not only unwilling to buy such an argument, but he was beginning to suspect that something far larger and more ominous was afoot:

> [T]he docket of this court is crowded with cases in which we are asked to hold that State courts and State legislatures have deprived their own citizens of life, liberty, and property without due process of law. There is here abundant evidence that there exists some strange misconception of the scope of this provision as found in the Fourteenth Amendment. In fact, it would seem, from the character of many of the cases before us, and the arguments made in them, that the clause under consideration is looked upon as a means of bringing to the test of the decision of this court the abstract opinions of every unsuccessful litigant in a State court of the justice of the decision against him, and of the merits of the legislation on which such a decision may be founded.

As time would soon show, Miller was grimly prophetic. But, try as he may, he "was no more successful than Canute in holding back the tides."[69] Yet Miller himself was not without fault. In the next breath, in "a single gratuitous sentence,"[70] he eroded for all intents and purposes the foundation he had just sought to create, affirming that "due process of law" meant nothing more metaphysical than "the modes of proceeding" that were applicable to a particular case in the State courts.[71] He wrote:

It seems to us that a statute which declares in terms, and without more, that the full and exclusive title of a described piece of land, which is now in A., shall be and is hereby vested in B., would, if effectual, deprive A. of his property without due process of law, within the meaning of the constitutional provision.[72]

At a minimum, Miller seemed to be fueling the fires of the "strange misconception" regarding the nature and extent of the Due Process Clause of the Fourteenth Amendment. He most assuredly did nothing to retire that misconception, a misconception that would, in a very short time, come to be controlling law.[73]

A subtle erosion of the Court's ostensibly procedural view of due process of law had been taking place. While such cases as *Munn* and *Davidson* seemed to imply that there were no substantive concerns open to judicial cognizance under the provision, the Court was in truth speaking out of both sides of its mouth. As shown in Miller's oddly schizophrenic opinion in *Davidson,* the Court was sending two equally clear messages. On the one hand, no piece of legislation that violated the Due Process Clause by regulating property had come to light; on the other hand, there was no guarantee that none could ever be found.

In 1886, Chief Justice Morrison Waite, writing in *Stone* v. *Farmers Loan and Trust Co.,*[74] tried to clarify:

[I]t is not to be inferred that this power of limitation or regulation is itself without limit. . . . Under the pretense of regulating fares and freights, the State cannot require a railroad corporation to carry persons or property without reward; neither can it do that which in law amounts to a taking of private property for public use without just compensation, or without due process of law.[75]

The fact that the Due Process Clause was becoming a vehicle for a sort of "extraconstitutional judicial review" was made all too clear in *Mugler* v. *Kansas:*

[N]ot . . . every statute enacted ostensibly for the promotion of [the public welfare] is to be accepted as a legitimate exertion of the police powers of the State. There are, of necessity, limits beyond which legislation cannot rightfully go . . . The courts are not bound by mere forms, nor are they to be misled by mere pretenses. They are at liberty—indeed, are under a solemn duty—to look at the substance of things whenever they enter upon the inquiry whether the legislature has transcended the limits of its authority. If, therefore, a statute purporting to have been enacted to protect the public health, the public morals, or the public safety, has no real or substantial relation to those objects, or is a palpable invasion of rights secured by the fundamental law, it is the duty of the courts to so adjudge, and thereby give effect to the Constitution.[76]

While the Court still refused to employ the doctrine of substantive due process to strike down state legislation, there was no real doubt that the doctrine itself was clearly recognized by the Court. It was simply a matter of time before the Court would be confronted by a law that it believed did violate due process of law. And it would not be long. Times were changing. More important, the Justices on the Supreme Court were changing. Either by death or by choice, seven of the Justices who had participated in *Munn* in 1877 were no longer sitting on the Court by 1890. Only Justices Field and Bradley remained. The new Justices who would join them on the high Court brought with them far greater solicitude for property rights than had those whom they had replaced. The concern for federalism and state sovereignty that had marked the jurisprudence of such Justices as Miller in *The Slaughterhouse Cases* and Waite in *Munn* had given way to a new way of thinking; a far more nationalistic view of the Constitution would now be dominant—at least insofar as the Court's power to keep the state legislatures in line was concerned.[77]

Time for restraint finally ran out in 1890 in the case of *Chicago, Milwaukee, and St. Paul Railway Co.* v. *Minnesota* (1890),[78] in which the Court declared a Minnesota rail rate in violation of the Fourteenth Amendment. Although the question was seemingly one of procedure and thus not a stretch of the provision, Justice Samuel Blatchford's opinion revealed deeper and more troubling currents of thought. The commission that had set the rates was not, by law, subject to judicial review. As such the law clearly deprived "the Company of its right to a judicial investigation, by due process of law, under the forms and with the machinery provided by the wisdom of successive ages for the investigation judicially of the truth of a matter in controversy." But that did not go to the heart of the issue, the reasonableness of the rates set by the commission and objected to by the company involved. Blatchford did not shy away. The question of the reasonableness of rates, he pronounced, "is eminently a question for judicial investigation, requiring due process of law for its determination. If the company is deprived of the power of charging reasonable rates for the use of its property, and such deprivation takes place in the absence of an investigation by judicial machinery, it is deprived of the lawful use of its property, and thus, in substance and effect, of the property itself, without due process of law and in violation of the Constitution of the United States."[79] Still, the Court had never invalidated any statute passed by a legislature, as opposed to a regulatory commission, under due process of law. In 1894 the Court affirmed its power to do so in *Reagan* v. *Farmers' Loan and Trust Co.*,[80] but it did not finally strike down a state law until it voided a Nebraska statute that set intrastate freight rates in *Smyth* v. *Ames* (1898).[81]

As the Court finally worked its way to declaring laws unconstitutional on the basis of the doctrine of substantive due process, there was another movement within the doctrine itself. From the first, the doctrine had been tied to the idea that the states could not deprive a person of his "property" without "due proceess of law." But "property" was a reasonably restrictive notion, even in the hands of a Court bent on pouring new meaning into it. The other provision of the Due Process Clause, however, "liberty" was not so cabined a concept as property; it held forth great promise to judges who hoped to expand ever farther the boundaries of rights against state power. It did not take long for that seemingly simple and straightforward word to become "an especially convenient vehicle into which to pack all kinds of 'rights.' "[82] In particular, the focus was to redefine "liberty" as it was originally used as meaning freedom from restraint—in the sense of incarceration—into a new and broader sense of incorporating all the civil rights of an individual. However illogical[83] or historically suspect,[84] the redefinition had an obvious appeal. It would put things beyond the grasp of the legislatures as the judges might see fit. Thus did the

Due Process Clause extend to substantive rights that went far beyond property; of course, those rights depended upon judicial definition.

By 1897 it was clear that the change in the Court had wrought a fundamental change in the way the Constitution was understood; the idea of due process of law had now been fully infused with a meaning that went far beyond its historic and proper meaning. In *Allgeyer* v. *Louisiana* Justice Rufus W. Peckham summed up the new view without flinching:

> The liberty mentioned in that Amendment means, not only the right of the citizen to be free from the mere physical restraint of his person, as by incarceration, but the term is deemed to embrace the right of the citizen to be free in the enjoyment of all his faculties; to be free to use them in all lawful ways; to live and work where he will; to earn his livelihood by any lawful calling; to pursue any livelihood or avocation, and for that purpose to enter into all contracts which may be proper, necessary and essential to his carrying out to a successful conclusion the purposes above mentioned.[85]

The Due Process Clause was now understood as extending its substantive protections to something called the "liberty of contract." Not only would this judicial construct protect the vested rights of private property, but it could in time be made to extend far beyond any commonsense understanding of property. By 1905 the judicially created doctrine of substantive due process, with its new concern for protecting the "liberty of contract," had come to full flower.

Lochner v. *New York* (1905)[86] opened a significant new era in the history of due process of law. From that time forward there would be no turning back to the original understanding; history was largely banished from constitutional construction when it came to giving definition to the meaning of "due process of law." There would, of course, be occasions when this Justice or that would bewail the egregious departures of the Court in cases with whose outcome he disagreed, but it would become impossible to find any Justice who simply rebuffed the seductive charms of the doctrine in all cases.[87] Yet *Lochner* was not a radical departure from all that had gone before it; it simply confirmed all that had been growing increasingly explicit in the line of cases that stretched from *Munn* to *Allgeyer*.

The lessons of *Lochner*, like those of *Allgeyer*, were to be taught by Justice Peckham. The New York law in question sought to limit the hours bakers could work. To Peckham's way of thinking, such a law was demeaning. Surely bakers were "equal in intelligence and capacity to men in other trades" and were "able to assert their rights and care for themselves."[88] To tamper with the hours free men could work was to deny them the very essence of their liberty. The Supreme Court was not about to allow that. The law violated the "liberty of contract" guaranteed by the Due Process Clause of the Fourteenth Amendment and could not stand. But there was more at stake than merely bakers' rights to contract for work as they might see fit; there was a far broader constitutional principle at risk if such laws should be allowed to stand. Peckham was not pusillanimous:

> It must of course be conceded that there is a limit to the valid exercise of the police power by the state . . . otherwise the Fourteenth Amendment would have no efficacy in the legislatures, and the legislatures of the state would have unbounded power, and it would be enough to say that any piece of legislation was enacted to conserve the morals, the health, or the safety of the people; such legislation would be valid no matter how absolutely without foundation a claim might be. The claim of the police power would be a mere pretext—become another and elusive name for the supreme sovereignty of the state, to be exercised free from constitutional restraint. . . . In every case that comes before this Court, therefore, where legislation of this character is concerned and where the protection of the federal court is sought, the question necessarily arises: Is this a fair, reasonable, and appropriate exercise of the police power of the state, or is it an unreasonable, unnecessary, and arbitrary interference with the right of the individual to his personal liberty?[89]

The Court's decision in *Lochner* did not portend as much mischief as could have been imagined; it did not, in fact, "usher in a reign of terror for social legislation."[90] Yet it did go far in confirming a theory of judging that was at odds with the idea of a written constitution of limited and enumerated powers. The notion that judges are to be guided by what they deem to be reasonable or just in striking down legislation is a theory of judging that goes far beyond the relatively modest role assigned to the courts by the Constitution and by the intentions of the founding generation that lay behind its text. While it may be true that *Lochner* did not unleash a reign of terror on legislation across the board, it did most assuredly unleash a full-scale attack on the idea of limited, popular, constitutional government. Like its even more unseemly ancestor, *Dred Scott, Lochner* helped set in motion the mechanics of government by judiciary. Nothing made that clearer at the time than Justice Oliver Wendell Holmes's impassioned dissent. He wrote:

> This case is decided upon an economic theory which a large part of the country does not entertain. If it were a question whether I agreed with that theory, I should desire to study it further and long before making up my mind. But I do not conceive that to be my duty, because I strongly believe that my agreement or disagreement has nothing to do with the right of a majority to embody their opinions in law. It is settled by various opinions of this court that state constitutions and state laws may regulate life in many ways which we as legislators might think as injudicious, or if you like as tyrannical, as this, and which, equally with this, interfere with the liberty to contract. . . . The 14th Amendment does not enact Mr. Herbert Spencer's Social Statics . . . a Constitution is not intended to embody a particular economic theory, whether of paternalism and the organic relation of the citizen to the state or of *laissez-faire*. It is made for people of fundamentally differing views, and the accident of our finding certain opinions natural and familiar, or novel and even shocking, ought not to conclude our judgment upon the question whether statutes embodying them conflict with the Constitution of the United States.[91]

The inherent problem of the majority opinion in *Lochner*, in Holmes's view, was precisely the same as the problem of Taney's opinion in *Dred Scott*, as Justice Curtis had pointed out in his dissent nearly half a century earlier. When the meaning of the Constitution is made to depend upon nothing more certain than the often fluctuating opinions of those who fill the highest bench, the result can only be arbitrariness. Dress it up as the Court may try, such notions as "vested rights," "liberty of contract," and the more general standard of "reasonableness" are but thin covers for unbounded judicial discretion. Constitutional and, as we have seen, extraconstitutional meaning is left to be buffeted by the winds of political and social opinion that may dominate this age or that.

This inherent arbitrariness was glaringly exposed only three years after *Lochner* in the case of *Muller* v. *Oregon*.[92] Like *Lochner*, *Muller* involved the legally provocative question of whether and to what extent legislatures could regulate the hours of workers. The Oregon law in question differed from that in *Lochner* in that it was aimed at protecting the health and morals not of bakers but of women. In particular, the Oregon law limited the time women could work in certain kinds of jobs—factories and laundries, for instance—to no more than ten hours a day. At the time such laws were considered to be on the cutting edge of progressive thinking. In order to defend the law before the Supreme Court the State of Oregon enlisted the services of a very socially conscious Boston attorney, later an Associate Justice on the Court itself, Louis D. Brandeis.[93]

Brandeis plunged into his task with sociological zeal. Not satisfied to rest his argument simply upon the law—*Lochner*, after all, would be one tough nut to crack—he turned to the still nascent social sciences to make his case. And make it he did. Legal precedents were relegated to a mere two pages while more than a hundred were devoted to statistics on all manner of subjects designed to convince the Court that the Oregon statute was indeed a reasonable exercise of its police power to protect the health and morals of the citizens of Oregon.[94] If constitutional meaning was to hinge upon the Justices' collective view of what was reasonable, then a good lawyer's skill was better used at marshaling the evidence that the law was reasonable in the most abstract sense. Sociology, not law, was the foundation upon which such a jurisprudence of judicial reason would have to rest. The "Brandeis Brief," as it came to be known, did the trick; the Court bought its argument. Justice David Brewer confessed it for the Court:

The legislation and opinions referred to in the margins may not be, technically speaking, authorities, and in them there is little or no discussion of the constitutional question presented to us for determination, yet they are significant of a widespread belief that a woman's physical structure, and the functions she performs in consequence thereof, justify special legislation restricting or qualifying the conditions under which she should be permitted to toil. Constitutional questions, it is true, are not settled by even a consensus of present public opinion, for it is the peculiar value of a written constitution that it places in unchanging form limitations upon legislative action, and thus gives a permanence and stability to popular government which otherwise would be lacking. At the same time, when a question of fact is debated and debatable, and the extent to which a special constitutional limitation goes is affected by the truth in respect to that fact, a widespread and continued belief concerning it is worthy of consideration. We take judicial cognizance of all matters of general knowledge.[95]

The Court strove to distinguish *Muller* from *Lochner* by emphasizing that a "woman's structure" and her realtively weak and defenseless place in society demanded that a state interfere with her "liberty of contract," even though it could not so interfere with that judicially created right when it came to men.[96] Not all such pieces of progressive legislation, either state or national, would be viewed equally. In the same term that the Court handed down *Muller* it handed down *Adair* v. *United States,*[97] in which the Court could not be persuaded that a labor law was reasonable.

As though to underscore the intellectual confusions of the doctrine of substantive due process, the Court in 1917 upheld yet another Oregon law limiting the hours of both men and women to ten and also specifying the rate of overtime pay in certain cases. The Court in *Bunting* v. *Oregon*[98] seemed to suggest that, given that holding and the one in *Muller, Lochner* had been silently banished from the books, unofficially overruled but overruled nonetheless. But only six years later the Court would exhume *Lochner*, shake the juridical dust from it, and bring it back to precedential life. In 1923, in *Adkins* v. *Children's Hospital,*[99] the Court made clear the degree to which constitutional rights derived from the Justices' view of *laissez-faire* economics when it invalidated a District of Columbia minimum wage law on the grounds that it violated the liberty of contract protected by the Fifth Amendment. With *Adkins* the doctrine of *Lochner* was to enjoy a far more vigorous life than it ever had under its own name. With *Adkins* the era of substantive due process reached its clearest and most powerful expression. The logic of individualism that fueled the economic debate over the meaning of "due process of law" was not limited simply to the workplace; its implications were even broader. In *Meyer* v. *Nebraska*[100] and *Pierce* v. *Society of Sisters,*[101] for example, the Court stretched the protection of the Due Process Clause of the Fourteenth Amendment to cover subjects as disparate as the teaching of foreign languages and the rights of parents to educate their children as they thought best. While both *Meyer* and *Pierce* were, at bottom, economic liberties cases, they touched other substantive issues as well. And as time would show, the future of the doctrine of substantive due process as enunciated in *Meyer* and *Pierce* would be secure long after the notion of "liberty of contract" had faded from view.

THE END OF *LAISSEZ-FAIRE*

During the decade of the 1920s and the first half of the 1930s, the Supreme Court created something of a constitutional no man's-land when it came to legislative regulations. The Due Process Clause of the Fifth Amendment cordoned off a field Congress could not traverse, while the clause in the Fourteenth Amendment kept the state legislatures out of the same substantive areas. *Laissez-faire* economic theory and the judicially contrived doctrine of "liberty of contract" succeeded in drastically altering the structure of constitutional government in the United States. But then the libertarian jurisprudence of economic rights was suddenly abandoned by the Court. Beginning with *Nebbia* v. *New York*[102] in 1934 and ending with *West Coast Hotel* v. *Parrish*[103] in 1937, the Supreme Court stepped away from the ideas of "liberty of contract" and *laissez-faire* economics as constituting the core values of American constitutionalism. Not only had the personnel of the Court changed since the days of *Adkins, Meyer,* and *Pierce,* but the confidence in the free market that lay at the heart of *lais-*

sez-faire economic theory and the idea of "liberty of contract" had been shattered by the Depression into which the United States had sunk. The old arguments against regulation and in behalf of rugged economic individualism rang hollow; more seemed to be needed from the government than merely a hands-off, best-of-luck approach.

It was perhaps fitting that the beginning of the end came in New York, where *Lochner* had ushered in the era of substantive due process nearly three decades earlier. The issue in *Nebbia* was one that struck at the very heart of the notion of economic liberty and the free market—price regulation. Aimed at protecting the market from price-cutting, the New York legislature established a board to control both maximum and minimum prices on milk. Even five years earlier it would have been impossible to conceive of the Court as willing to uphold such a law, but uphold it the Court did. While the dairy industry had never been considered an industry cloaked in the public interest and thus subject to the police powers of the state, that would no longer be the case. Justice Owen Roberts wrote for the majority of the Court that such things were not fixed:

> It is clear that there is no closed class of category of businesses affected with a public interest, and the function of courts in the application of the Fifth and Fourteenth Amendments is to determine in each case whether circumstances vindicate the challenged regulation as a reasonable exertion of governmental authority or condemn it as arbitrary or discriminatory. . . . The phrase "affected with a public interest" can, in the nature of things, mean no more than that an industry, for adequate reason, is subject to control for the public good.[104]

The most distressing thing about the logic of the majority in *Nebbia* is that it failed adequately to regroup and truly abandon the philosophical underpinnings of the doctrine of substantive due process. The theory of judging and the view of the nature and extent of judicial power implicit in such cases as *Lochner* were not abandoned; the idea that judicial review is properly propelled by what the judges think reasonable remained in full force and effect. Only the ends changed. Whereas the earlier *laissez-*

faire courts had found economic regulations like that at issue in *Nebbia* to be unreasonable and hence unconstitutional, the new court was inclined to find such laws reasonable and hence constitutional. The foundation of constitutional meaning remained unchanged: It was not the historic Constitution but rather contemporary judicial decisions.

If there was any confusion as to the import of the holding in *Nebbia,* by 1937 that confusion had been dispelled. The Court in *West Coast Hotel* v. *Parrish* voted 5–4 to uphold a Washington State law (which had been passed in 1913) that had established minimum wages for women and minors. The claim raised against the Washington law rested on the Court's precedent of *Adkins.* Not only did the Court, in an opinion written by Chief Justice Charles Evans Hughes, uphold the Washington law, but it went further and explicitly overruled *Adkins.* The "reasonableness of the protective power of the State must be reconsidered," Hughes argued, not simply because the doctrine upon which *Adkins* rested was wrong in some concrete constitutional sense, as if the *Adkins* court had simply erred in its interpretation. It was murkier than that. The real reason came down to the fact that certain "economic conditions [had] supervened." Moreover, "recent economic experience," Hughes continued, had "brought into a strong light" certain sociological facts—in particular the "exploitation" of certain defenseless classes of people, namely women and minors.

Justice George Sutherland in his dissent cut to the heart of the problem:

> It is urged that the question involved should now receive fresh consideration, among other reasons, because of "the economic conditions which have supervened"; but the meaning of the Constitution does not change with the ebb and flow of economic events. We frequently are told in more general words that the Constitution must be construed in the light of the present. If by that it is meant that the Constitution is made up of living words that apply to every new condition which they include, the statement is quite true. But to say, if that be intended, that the words of the Constitution mean today what they did not mean when written—that is, that they do not apply to a situation now to which they would have applied

then—is to rob that instrument of the essential element which continues it in force as the people have made it until they, and not
their official agents, have made it otherwise.

Rising to defend the principles adduced by such predecessors as
John Marshall in *Marbury* and Benjamin Curtis in *Dred Scott,*
Justice Sutherland sought to point out the limits of the judicial
power:

> The judicial function is that of interpretation; it does not include
> the power of amendment under the guise of interpretation. To miss
> the point of difference between the two is to miss all that the
> phrase "supreme law of the land" stands for and to convert what
> was intended as inescapable and enduring mandates into mere
> moral reflections.[105]

The problem with Sutherland's dissent is not that it lacks truth or
even passion; it is that it was written in defense of *his* earlier majority opinion in *Adkins* v. *Children's Hospital.* What he saw in the
Washington minimum wage law as "the product of a naked, arbitrary exercise of power" was in truth none other than a law at
odds with the judicially contrived doctrine of "liberty of contract"
fashioned in *Lochner* and given wider application in *Adkins.* Like
most judges and Justices inclined to accept the "liberty of contract" logic, Justice Sutherland could not see that the judges who
created such a doctrine might themselves be guilty of a "naked
[and] arbitrary exercise of power." Indeed, they might be guilty of
an exercise of power even more naked and more arbitrary than
anything wrought by any legislative body.

But what the Court seemed to give with one hand in *West Coast
Hotel* v. *Parrish,* it slyly began to take back with two other cases
handed down that same term. Time would soon show that the
predilection of the Court for intruding into questions of policy
had not, in fact, faded; the Justices were only in the process of re-
focusing their attentions. *Palko* v. *Connecticut* addressed the question of whether the Due Process Clause of the Fourteenth
Amendment "absorbed" or "incorporated" (the words are used
interchangeably) the Bill of Rights and thus made those provisions

applicable to the states and not merely the national government, as was originally intended. The problem with this doctrine of incorporation is not that the states should somehow as a matter of principle be immune to the dictates of the Bill of Rights. Rather the problem arises from the fact that the Fourteenth Amendment makes no mention that such an incorporation was ever intended; thus to "incorporate" provisions from the Bill of Rights and apply them to the States reduces those rights to judicial fiat.[106]

The significance of *Palko,* however, lay not in its being the first case to suggest the Bill of Rights may apply to the states; the Bill of Rights had first been applied to the States in 1925 in a case called *Gitlow* v. *New York.*[107] In *Gitlow,* without so much as an argument, the Court merely asserted that at least portions of the Bill of Rights affected the states.[108] But a sustained defense of what the Court was doing was left for Justice Benjamin Cardozo in his opinion in *Palko.*

The heart of the *Palko* decision lay in Cardozo's idea that there is, as Henry Abraham has described it, "an honor roll of superior rights," which, in Cardozo's words, are to be considered "of the very essence of ordered liberty." These rights were deemed "superior" insofar as they were distinguished from those without which "justice . . . would not perish." Only those rights "implicit in the concept of ordered liberty [and] so rooted in the traditions and conscience of our people as to be ranked fundamental" were to be considered superior. In particular, Cardozo contended that strictly procedural rights (such as protection against being placed twice in jeopardy for one's life) were of a lower order than such rights as "freedom of thought and speech"—the "matrix, the indispensable condition, of nearly every other form of freedom."

Cardozo established two notions in *Palko.* First, that not all rights spelled out in the Bill of Rights are equal. Any incorporation or absorption would thus have to be done on a case-by-case basis. Second, that the distinction between what rights are to be deemed fundamental and what rights are not is to be drawn by the Court, by what the Justices (or at least a majority of them at any given time) think is reasonable. Those two ideas would become the source of fuel for the next period of substantive due process, a period of judicial activism that continues to this day. Together, these ideas created one doctrine: Rights depend only upon the Court.

The second case, *Carolene Products Co.* v. *United States*, was, on the face of it, just one more decision coming to grips with the new regulatory state that was the New Deal. The substantive issue in question dealt with the power of Congress to prohibit the interstate shipment of "filled milk," in which the natural butterfat had been replaced by vegetable fat. To the Court's way of thinking, it possessed no special competence to judge Congress's motives and thus had to allow the law. The significance of the opinion by Justice Harlan Fiske Stone, however, did not have to do with the substantive issue at hand; embedded in a footnote was a new doctrine of judicial power that would in time come to hold sway. In that footnote, Stone argued that while the Court was willing to defer to congressional regulation in the economic realm, there was another area in which Congress, and by extension the state legislatures, should not expect such deference. As Stone put it:

> It is unnecessary to consider now whether legislation which restricts those political processes which can ordinarily be expected to bring about the repeal of undesirable legislation, is to be subjected to a more exacting judicial scrutiny under the general prohibitions of the Fourteenth Amendment than are other types of legislation. . . . Nor need we enquire whether similar considerations enter into the review of statutes directed at particular religious, . . . national, . . . or racial minorities . . . : whether prejudice against discrete and insular minorities may be a special condition, which tends seriously to curtail the operation of those political processes ordinarily to be relied upon to protect minorities, and which may call for a correspondingly more searching judicial inquiry.[109]

As in the days of old, when economic regulation was subject to the whim of the judges as to whether it was "reasonable" or not, so in the years to come would regulations that touched upon the freedoms of individuals be subject to the same standard. With *Carolene Products* and *Palko,* the Court demonstrated that the doctrine of substantive due process had not in truth been abandoned but merely transformed.[110] It remained to be brought back to life by a Court increasingly concerned with protecting individual civil liberties, but it never lost its essential characteristic: arbitrariness.

THE PRIVACY MUDDLE

In the area of constitutional law, it is fair to say that the leading privacy case of *Griswold* v. *Connecticut*[111] has been to the current generation what earlier cases such as *Dred Scott* and *Lochner* had been to theirs; not only has it come to stand in the eyes of many as a gross perversion of the interpretive authority of the Court, but, by being so seen, has come to scar the politics of the nation. The right to privacy discovered and proclaimed by the Court in *Griswold* v. *Connecticut* had its roots not in constitutional law but in the private law of torts. To the extent that one can point to a fundamental source for the doctrine, it emerged in the first instance not from the courts but from a law review article. That article, by Louis D. Brandeis and Samuel Warren, appeared in the *Harvard Law Review* in 1890.[112]

Brandeis and Warren sought to create a protection against the infliction of emotional distress by having one's private affairs made public. They undertook their task by attempting to stitch together older bits and pieces of doctrine that derived from sources as disparate as defamation, breach of confidence, the invasion of property rights, and the idea of implied contract. The end result was a general cover they called simply the "right to privacy." The article had "little immediate effect on the law."[113] By 1939, however, with the publication of the *Restatement of Torts,* those who advocated judicial recognition of such a right within the common law courts were winning the contest. And by 1960 the idea of such a right to privacy had been accepted in a clear majority of the states. But as late as 1960 the right to privacy had developed only along the lines first suggested by Brandeis and Warren.

At the very time the right to privacy was struggling for acceptance in tort law, the idea that the Fourteenth Amendment was, as

Justice James McReynolds said in *Perry* v. *Butler* in 1916, "intended to preserve and protect fundamental rights long recognized under the common law system" emerged. During the next
decade this idea of a common law constitutionalism would establish itself in the Court's mind, and it is no accident that Justice
McReynolds helped pour the foundation upon which a much later
generation could erect a general right to privacy as a matter of
fundamental constitutional right. Two cases especially would come
to be seen as the forerunners of *Griswold* v. *Connecticut*—*Meyer* v.
Nebraska (1923) and *Pierce* v. *Society of Sisters* (1925).

The question in *Meyer* was whether a state could prohibit the
teaching of foreign languages to children under a certain age—the
eighth grade. The state put forth a simple argument defending the
law on the grounds that the "object of the legislation . . . was to
create an enlightened American citizenship in sympathy with the
principles and ideals of this country, and to prevent children
reared in America from being trained and educated in foreign languages and foreign ideals before they have had an opportunity to
learn the English language and observe American ideals." Meyer
was a teacher who had been prosecuted under the law for teaching
a class in German; he claimed the law violated his rightful freedom
to engage in his chosen profession.

The Court found Meyer's claim persuasive. The "liberty" contained in the Due Process Clause, Justice McReynolds declared,
"denotes not merely freedom from bodily restraint but also the
right of the individual to contract, to engage in any of the common occupations of life, to acquire useful knowledge, to marry, to
establish a home and bring up children, to worship God according
to the dictates of his own conscience, and generally to enjoy those
privileges long recognized at common law as essential to the or-
derly pursuit of happiness by free men."

The issue in *Pierce* v. *Society of Sisters* was closely related to that
in *Meyer.* Oregon had passed the Compulsory Education Act,
which, with few exceptions, required that children be sent to public schools. The law had the practical effect of killing private
schools like those operated by the Society of Sisters. Yet when the
Court looked at the facts of the case the Justices were confronted
with the fact that the Society was a corporation, not an individual,

and thus could not "claim for themselves the liberty which the Fourteenth Amendment guarantees." Still, that would not prove an insurmountable obstacle to a court bent on doing what it saw as the right thing. The real issue, McReynolds noted, was that the plaintiffs were seeking "protection against arbitrary, unreasonable and unlawful interference with their patrons and the consequent destruction of their business and property." In what may have been the first consumer rights case, McReynolds reached his objective this way: "Under the doctrine of *Meyer* v. *Nebraska* . . . we think it entirely plain that the Act . . . unreasonably interferes with the liberty of parents and guardians to direct the upbringing and education of children under their control."

Two years after the Court had handed down both *Pierce* v. *Society of Sisters* and *Gitlow* v. *New York*, it made its first foray into the area that would in time come to dominate the discussion of the right to privacy, reproductive freedom. The case, *Buck* v. *Bell*,[114] involved the involuntary sterilization of Carrie Buck, a patient in Virginia's State Colony of Epileptics and Feeble Minded. The law authorizing such procedures was, Carrie Buck's lawyer argued, "repugnant to the due process of law clause of the Fourteenth Amendment." There was, he insisted in Buck's behalf, a "constitutional right of bodily integrity."

Justice Oliver Wendell Holmes, one of the Court's best-remembered civil libertarians, wrote the opinion rejecting Carrie Buck's claims. The principle that legitimates such public health measures as compulsory vaccination, Holmes argued, "is broad enough to cover cutting the Fallopian tubes." The public interest to be served, an interest well within the powers of the state, was clear: "Three generations of imbeciles are enough."

In time, however, the Court would return to the problem of forced sterilization. In *Skinner* v. *Oklahoma*[115] the Court had to grapple with a state law that required the sterilization of certain classes of prisoners. Justice William O. Douglas argued that the case "touches a sensitive and important area of human rights." Douglas sidestepped Holmes's opinion in *Buck* v. *Bell* (an opinion that has never been overruled) by striking down the Oklahoma law on the basis of the Equal Protection Clause of the Fourteenth Amendment rather than the Due Process Clause.

In 1961 the Court stumbled ever closer to the privacy abyss in
Poe v. *Ullman*,[116] the forerunner of *Griswold;* it involved the constitutionality of the same birth control statute that would be invalidated four years later. The Court, however, refused to reach the
constitutional questions because it found that the way in which
the cases had been brought raised "serious questions" as to
whether they were cases properly before the Court. There were
four dissenters from that opinion by Justice Felix Frankfurter—
Justices Douglas, John Marshall Harlan, Hugo Black, and Potter
Stewart. The opinions of Douglas and Harlan are especially worthy of note.

Douglas's view was sweeping: "Though I believe that 'due
process' as used in the Fourteenth Amendment includes all of the
first eight amendments, I do not think it is restricted and confined
to them." Reflecting the earlier opinions of McReynolds in *Meyer*
and Cardozo in *Palko*, Douglas went further: "Liberty is a conception that sometimes gains content from the emanations of
other guarantees . . . or from experience with the requirements of
a free society." In his view there were rights, fundamental rights,
that had not found expression in the Constitution but nonetheless
deserved judicial protection. One of those "rights" was the right
to privacy in the marital relationship: "This notion of privacy is
not drawn from the blue. It emanates from the totality of the constitutional scheme under which we live." Douglas's dissent in *Poe*
would later be seen to have been the intellectual bridge between
his opinion in *Skinner* and that in *Griswold*.

Justice Harlan made a powerful case for finding a general right
to privacy in the Constitution. "The full scope of the liberty guaranteed by the Due Process Clause," he wrote in his dissent, "cannot be found in or limited by the precise terms of the specific
guarantees elsewhere provided in the Constitution." The proper
foundation for such unenumerated rights, he argued, was not text
but tradition; for Harlan, tradition was "a living thing." When tradition was examined closely, Harlan insisted, what it revealed was
that due process of law "is a rational continuum which, broadly
speaking, includes a freedom from all substantial arbitrary impositions and purposeless restraints."

In 1965 the Connecticut birth control statute that was refused its day in court in *Poe* v. *Ullman* found its way back to the Supreme Court in *Griswold* v. *Connecticut.* In a surprisingly brief opinion by Justice Douglas, the law was struck down. Douglas took his point of departure from his dissent in *Poe* and argued that "specific guarantees in the Bill of Rights have penumbras, formed by emanations from those guarantees that help give them life and substance." The law in question violated no specific constitutional right but rather infringed upon "a relationship lying within the zone of privacy created by several fundamental constitutional guarantees." Douglas wove a right to privacy out of the strands of explicit rights such as the right to be secure from unreasonable searches and seizures and the right to be free from having troops quartered in your home.[117]

Justices Black and Stewart, who had dissented in *Poe* on the grounds that they thought the constitutional issues should have been reached by the Court, vigorously dissented in *Griswold.* The majority opinion, along with the concurrences by Harlan and Justice Arthur Goldberg (who attempted to rest the decision on the Ninth Amendment rather than simply the Due Process Clause) struck Black and Stewart as nothing more than the Court's self-claimed power "to measure constitutionality by our belief that legislation is arbitrary, capricious, or unreasonable, or accomplishes no justifiable purpose, or is offensive to our own notions of 'civilized standards of conduct.'" When it came to the right of privacy in particular, Black considered the Court's action especially innovative.

As Black knew, the effort by the Court to correct the arbitrariness of legislatures by subjecting statutes to the Court's rule of reason would not in fact correct arbitrariness but would only supplant legislative with judicial arbitrariness. That was made clear in the concurring opinions that supported the outcomes in both *Poe* and *Griswold.* In *Poe,* Justice Harlan had been quick to point out that "the right of privacy is most manifestly not absolute. Thus I would not suggest that adultery, homosexuality, fornication, and incest are immune from criminal enquiry, however privately practiced." Similarly, Justice Goldberg in his concurrence in *Griswold* emphasized that "Connecticut does have statutes, the constitutionality of which is beyond doubt, which prohibit adultery and fornication." Why these practices were not encompassed by the right to privacy was not made clear; at least not made clear beyond the obvious fact that they simply were viewed differently by the Justices as a matter of their personal moral judgments.

But the inherent arbitrariness of the right to privacy was demonstrated most powerfully in a 1986 case involving a Georgia statute that made homosexual sodomy between consenting adults illegal. After a series of cases that seemed to stretch the limits of the privacy right ever further, *Bowers* v. *Hardwick* came as something of a constitutional shock. After all, after *Griswold* the Court had never really shied away from extending the privacy right. The right of married couples to have access to contraception had been extended to unmarried couples in *Eisenstadt* v. *Baird* (1972);[118] the right of women to choose an abortion (within certain judicially drawn guidelines) was established in 1973 in *Roe* v. *Wade*;[119] and the rights of advertisers of contraception had been nailed down in *Carey* v. *Population Services International* (1977).[120] And from 1973 on the Court had repeatedly reaffirmed the abortion right.[121] Writing for the majority in *Bowers,* Justice Byron White argued that the right-to-privacy line that had begun in *Griswold* stopped at the issue of homosexuality. For White, the determining factor was that such laws as that of Georgia had "ancient roots." It had long been common to hold that homosexual sodomy was "immoral and unacceptable," and on the basis of that well-known tradition Georgia was entitled to outlaw such behavior. In a sense, White's logic in *Bowers* is but another side to the tradition to which Douglas had appealed in *Griswold,* where he celebrated the fact that the sanctity of the marriage chamber was older than the Constitution and the Bill of Rights and thus deserving of judicial protection. Thus while at one level White's opinion in *Bowers* seems impossible to square with the precedents leading up to it, at another level it squares perfectly: The right to privacy depends not upon any constitutional provision but only upon the will of the Court.

In *The Federalist, No. 78,* Alexander Hamilton had argued that the Court was institutionally capable of exercising the extraordinary power of review precisely because it would exercise neither force nor will but merely judgment. But when it has come to interpreting the seemingly simple and straightforward phrase "due process of law," the Court, nearly from the beginning, has been incapable of resisting the temptation to exercise more than merely its judgment. By infusing the Due Process Clause of both the Fifth and Fourteenth Amendments with an allegedly substantive meaning, by using those clauses as a means of determining whether the statute in question is reasonable and neither arbitrary nor capricious, the Court has departed from its original charge to interpret the law. In the name of the law the Court has endeavored to effect justice; in the name of the law the Court has thus abandoned the very idea of the rule of law and in its place erected the dangerous alternative of rule by men. The price that has been paid is arbitrariness in our constitutional law. Thus did it make sense for Joshua DeShaney's lawyers to take their shot at the Court being willing to extend the meaning of due process of law to include placing positive demands on the States to prevent harm to their citizens. As history had taught, in the confusing world of due process of law, anything goes.

CHAPTER FIVE

CONSTITUTIONAL MORALISM AND THE POLITICS OF ADVICE AND CONSENT

T hat Melody DeShaney might seek constitutional relief for the tragedy that ruined her son's life should come as no surprise. For many Americans, the Constitution is seen as a charter of fundamental justice and the federal courts as arbiters of competing moral claims. Surely what happened to Joshua was an injustice that the courts would remedy, for a larger issue was also at stake. The State of Wisconsin had failed to protect the welfare of an innocent child. And when the government fails to meet its obligation it is up to the courts to correct the problem. Here, then, was not just a private dispute over the welfare of a child but a public policy debate over the obligations of government.

As the courts have assumed a more prominent position in the policy-making process, the issue of judicial selection has acquired enhanced political significance. Simply put, as judges and courts wield more power, the issue of deciding who will become a judge has become politically very important. Con-stitutional moralism has taken its toll on the politics of advice and consent.

Indeed, it was the transformation in the politics of appointing Justices to the Supreme Court that made *DeShaney* v. *Winnebago County* such a significant case in the first place. When *DeShaney* was handed down, it seemed that Ronald Reagan's dedication to the task of returning the courts to their proper constitutional place had paid off. Reagan sought to rein in the activism of the courts by appointing as judges individuals who agreed with his vision of a limited judiciary. Coming after the protracted and painful battles over William Rehnquist to become Chief Justice in 1986 and over Robert Bork to replace Lewis Powell in 1987, *DeShaney* seemed to suggest that the tide was turning and that the Court might be returning to its legal, constitutional, and historical roots. But within a few years, and after several more political skirmishes over judicial selection, it became apparent that the moralism of the modern judiciary would continue.

The political significance of *DeShaney* can be understood only in light of the confirmation wars that took place during the Reagan years and how they affected the Court. To understand those wars, it is necessary to place them in their proper historical perspective. While nominations to the Court historically have often been divisive and hotly contested, the judicial battles that took place during the Reagan years differed in both type and degree. The most immediate impact of this could be seen in the way Reagan's successor, George Bush, approached judicial selection. But the true impact of the changing politics of advice and consent that began during the Reagan years is more subtle; it touches upon the way the role of the Court is understood in American politics and society today.

THE PRESIDENT, THE SENATE, AND THE IDEA OF ADVICE AND CONSENT

Interestingly, the issue of selecting judges occasioned relatively little debate during the convention in Philadelphia that produced the Constitution in 1787. It was an important issue, surely, but it was discussed within the context of a greater debate that took place during the entire convention. That was a debate over the proper extent of executive power.

The delegates to the Philadelphia Convention seemed to coalesce around two different approaches to executive power. Many of those in attendance were quite wary of a powerful executive. They feared the development of executive tyranny and pointed to the experience of the colonies under King George III as evidence that such a fear was well founded. That group of delegates, among them some of the more respected citizens in the country, argued that the selection of judges should be a legislative responsibility. Not only would that help to curb executive power, but the legislature was better suited for such a task. It would bring to the appointment process a sense of the opinions, interests, needs, and desires of the people. Moreover, legislators would be in a better position to know the pool of qualified contenders for judicial posts.

One delegate, Luther Martin of Maryland, argued that the Senate should appoint judges because "being from all the States [Senators] would be best informed of characters and most capable of making a fit choice."[1] Another delegate, Roger Sherman, asserted that the Senate "would have more wisdom" and that Senators "would bring to their deliberation a more diffusive knowledge of characters."[2] George Mason, the very influential Virginian who eventually opposed ratification of the Constitution, offered that providing the executive with the power to appoint judges would be "a dangerous prerogative."[3]

Those who favored a strong national executive felt that fears of executive tyranny were somewhat misplaced. Recent experience under the Articles of Confederation had demonstrated that many of the problems of popular government could be traced to legislative tyranny and corruption. They argued that an energetic executive was needed to counter the power of the legislature. And for them, energy in the executive could be secured only by creating an executive branch independent of the legislative branch, rather than subservient to it. From this general premise, those delegates who favored a strong national executive supported the executive appointment of judges. James Wilson, one of the more influential delegates, who was instrumental in the creation of the presidency, argued that "experience showed the impropriety of such appointments by numerous bodies." According to Wilson, "[I]ntrigue, partiality and concealment were the necessary consequences" of lodging the power to appoint judges in the legislature.[4]

James Madison, rightly or wrongly considered by many to be the "father of the Constitution," was genuinely ambivalent about the issue for much of the summer. Initially he favored giving the Senate the authority to appoint judges. He saw the Senate as "numerous enough to be confided in—as not so numerous as to be governed by the motives of the other branch [of the legislature]; and as being sufficiently stable and independent to follow their deliberate judgments."[5] But as the debates continued he came to shift his position. Lodging the power in the Senate alone became somewhat problematical to Madison because of the character of the institution. Since each state was to have two Senators, it might be possible, he reasoned, for judges to be appointed "by a minority of the people, though by a majority of the States," which seemed at odds with the principle of popular government. For that reason, and because the executive "would be considered as a national officer, acting for and sympathizing with every part of the United States," Madison gradually moved to support those arguing for executive selection of judges.[6]

As the summer progressed, the argument for an energetic executive gained the upper hand. The key issue seemed to be responsibility. By providing a single chief executive with the power to appoint judges, it would be possible to hold that executive accountable for his choices. This would have the effect of ensuring that good candidates were chosen for judges since executives would know that bad judges would surely lead to "public censure." In the end Madison spoke glowingly of the compromise that was reached: "the judges . . . be appointed by the Executive with the concurrence of the second branch . . . would unite the advantage of responsibility in the Executive with the security afforded in the second branch against any incautious or corrupt nomination by the Executive."[7] Writing in *The Federalist*, Alexander Hamilton provided the best summary of the need for executive action in judicial appointments. "One man of discernment," he wrote,

> . . . is better fitted to analyze and estimate the peculiar qualities adapted to particular offices, than a body of men of equal, perhaps even superior discernment.
> The sole and undivided responsibility of one man will naturally beget a livelier sense of duty and a more exact regard to reputation. He will on this account feel himself under stronger obligations, and more interested to investigate with care the impartiality the persons who may have the fairest pretensions to them. He will have fewer

personal attachments to gratify than a body of men . . . . [A] single
well directed man by a single understanding, cannot be distracted
and warped by that diversity of views, feelings, and interests,
which frequently distract and warp the resolutions of a collective
body.[8]

Hamilton, no friend of legislative power, recognized a glaring
defect in legislative bodies: "[I]n every exercise of the power of
appointing to offices by an assembly of men we must expect to see
a full display of all the private and party likings and dislikes, par-
tialities and antipathies, attachments and animosities, which are
felt by those who compose the assembly."[9] Simply put, legislative
appointment of judges would "politicise" judicial selection. Rather
than focus on the "intrinsic merit of the candidate," legislators will
tend to strike bargains. Hamilton wrote: "Give us the man we
wish for this office and you shall have the one you wish for that."[10]
It is a process that tends to bring out the less impressive aspects of
men involved in politics. For those reasons, Hamilton concluded
the Constitution was correct to lodge the appointment power in
the executive.

Of course, according to the Constitution, the Senate is a full
partner in the appointment of federal judges. Every individual
nominated to the federal courts must be confirmed by the Senate.
And since the very beginning of the Republic, the Senate has asserted its authority under the Constitution with vigor.

Ironically, Alexander Hamilton anticipated a relatively limited
role for the Senate in the process of advice and consent to judicial
nominees. He seems to have believed that the Senate would
merely check the fitness of a nominee for a judicial post, considering nomination by the President to be tantamount to appointment. The Senate's job, Hamilton thought, was to check any
"spirit of favoritism" in the President and prevent the appointment of "unfit characters from State prejudice, from family connection, from personal attachment, or from a view to
popularity."[11] The Senate could fulfill this function simply by
blocking a nomination. But more important, the very presence of
the collaborative process involved in advice and consent would
provide a political incentive to a President to nominate individuals
of merit. "The possibility of rejection would be a strong motive to

care in proposing," wrote Hamilton. The President "would be both ashamed and afraid to bring forward for the most distinguished or lucrative stations, candidates who had no other merit than that of coming from the same State to which he particularly belonged, or of being in some way or other personally allied to him, or of possessing the necessary insignificance and pliancy to render him obsequious instruments of his pleasure."[12] Hamilton got it wrong.

THE HISTORY OF JUDICIAL SELECTION AND CONFIRMATION

The history of advice and consent to presidential nominations to the federal courts, and the Supreme Court in particular, is very much a political history, rich in confrontation between the Senate and the President. Since the early years of the Republic, the Senate has discharged its constitutional responsibilities with a mixture of restraint and demagoguery, challenging nominees for political as well as jurisprudential reasons.[13]

The Judiciary Act of 1789, passed by the First Congress, established the federal judiciary. The only court required by the Constitution was the Supreme Court, and the Congress set the number of justices at six. President George Washington appointed all six. But even Washington encountered challenges from the Senate. In 1791 Washington nominated John Rutledge of South Carolina as Associate Justice. Rutledge was a man of considerable accomplishment. He had served at the Philadelphia Convention and had helped to write the original drafts of the Constitution. He was a leader in public affairs in his home state and had served in the First Congress of the United States. The Senate confirmed Washington's choice almost without debate. But Rutledge never served, preferring instead to return to South Carolina, where he became Chief Justice of that state's Supreme Court.

In 1795, with the retirement of the first Chief Justice, John Jay, Washington tried again to place Rutledge on the Court, this time as Chief Justice. He gave Rutledge a recess appointment. But when the Senate reconvened it voted to deny the seat to Rutledge, largely because he had antagonized many in the Senate during debate over the Jay treaty. Rutledge therefore had to give up his position as Chief Justice, primarily because of politics.

In 1800 Thomas Jefferson was elected President by the House of Representatives. Jefferson had been a vocal critic of the Federalists who had controlled both the presidency and the Congress since the birth of the Republic. He had been critical of Chief Justice John Marshall as well, referring to him as a "gloomy malignity."[14] His ascent to the presidency presented Jefferson with the chance to remold the federal judiciary along Republican lines. The outgoing President, John Adams, had other thoughts, however, and before Jefferson was sworn in he was able to appoint a number of Federalists to prominent positions in the judiciary (the so-called midnight appointments) as well as to get Congress to pass the Judiciary Act of 1801, which created new circuit court judgeships and stipulated that the next vacancy on the Supreme Court should remain unfilled, effectively reducing the size of the Court to five Justices. Jefferson and the Republicans were outraged. The Republican Congress immediately repealed the Judiciary Act. A challenge to that repeal was filed. Before it could be heard by the Supreme Court, the Court's term was postponed by Congress. In 1803 the Court issued its opinion in *Stuart* v. *Laird,* upholding Congress's authority to repeal the Judiciary Act of 1801.[15] The size of the Court was returned to six Justices, and Jefferson finally had his chance to influence the composition of the federal judiciary.

Jefferson's successor to the presidency, James Madison, had a difficult time securing replacements for two justices who stepped down, William Cushing and Samuel Chase. Eager to find a Republican to help stem the Federalist tide that continued to dominate the courts, Madison failed three times before he was able to appoint Joseph Story in 1811.

Thomas Jefferson was firmly convinced that the thirty-two-year old Salem, Massachusetts, lawyer Joseph Story was a poor choice. Jefferson thought him to be not only "too young" but, far worse, "unquestionably a tory." In light of his friend's vehement resistance, Madison had looked elsewhere—but without success. His first choice, Levi Lincoln, was confirmed by the Senate but for reasons of health declined to serve; his second, Alexander Walcott, was rejected by the Senate as professionally unqualified; and his third choice, John Quincy Adams, refused the appointment in order to continue in his diplomatic post. In desperation, Madison turned to Story, making him the youngest man ever to serve on the Supreme Court.

From Jefferson's Republican point of view, Story proved an even more unfortunate choice than he had imagined. Not only was Story a jurisprudential student of the great Sir William Blackstone, whom Jefferson held in utter contempt as a tory, but he quickly became Marshall's ideological right hand on the Court. Story soon proved himself to be a strong nationalist with glaring Federalist sympathies. His appointment and performance simply enraged Jefferson; he denounced Story as a "pseudo-Republican," a "political chameleon," and "an independent political schemer."[16] But despite Jefferson's assessment, Story went on for thirty-four years to establish himself as one of the most influential Justices ever to sit on the Supreme Court.

As the Jeffersonian Republicans transmogrified into Jacksonian Democrats, the ideological hostility toward the Supreme Court continued unabated. In 1836 President Andrew Jackson created a controversy by nominating Roger Brooke Taney to replace the retiring Justice Gabriel Duval. At the time Jackson and Taney were both embroiled in a bitter political struggle with the Congress over the future of the Bank of the United States. Jackson was opposed to the bank and had instructed Secretary of the Treasury W. J. Duane to remove funds from that bank. Duane refused, citing his responsibilities to manage the funds according to statutes passed by the Congress. Jackson consequently fired Duane, thereby igniting a political firestorm. The Senate passed a resolution censuring the President for his actions. Jackson refused to back down, however, and apponted Taney as Secretary of the Treasury while Congress was in recess. Taney shared Jackson's views regarding the bank and would carry out the President's orders. But he didn't get the chance. As soon as the Congress reconvened, the Senate voted to deny Taney confirmation, and he was forced to resign.

Justice Duval's departure from the Court provided Jackson with a means with which to repay Taney for his loyalty. Again, however, the Congress tried to deny the President the opportunity. The Senate delayed acting on the Taney nomination and passed legislation to reduce the size of the Supreme Court, effectively getting rid of the vacancy Taney was nominated to fill. But the House of Representatives refused to go along with that action.

On July 6, 1835, Chief Justice John Marshall died, leaving Jackson with two seats to fill on the Supreme Court. Still committed to placing Taney on the bench, Jackson nominated Philip Barbour of Virginia to replace Duval and nominated Taney to replace John Marshall. The Senate reacted with predictable agitation. For three months Taney's nomination was debated in the Senate. Three of the most able and influential Senators in the history of that institution—John C. Calhoun, Henry Clay, and Daniel Webster—led the opposition to Taney. But in the end, perhaps out of sheer perseverance on the part of both Jackson and Taney, Taney was confirmed by a vote of 29–15.

During those formative years of the Republic, Presidents tended to choose nominees for the federal courts for reasons that had relatively little to do with their thoughts regarding the Constitution or statutory interpretation. The political loyalties of nominees usually mattered quite a lot. So too did a nominee's residence and citizenship. Every President attempted to balance the courts with appointments that reflected the regions of the nation. As the tension between the North and the South increased, the need to balance the federal bench became ever more pressing. Most nominees had to have acquired a reputation for public service as well. Every President conferred with Congress when selecting nominees. Thomas Jefferson went so far as to invite the members of the House and Senate to suggest names of potential jurists to him. Members of the Senate were always involved in the discussions that produced district and appellate court judgeships. The primary consideration, in addition to overall merit and fitness for service, however, was not an individual's jurisprudence, but the political implications of the nomination.

As America entered the twentieth century, the substantive political issues of the day had markedly changed. An increasingly urban and highly industrial nation faced vexing new problems—minimum wages and hours, regulation of working conditions, the income tax, and child labor, to name but four. But however different the substance, politics was largely business as usual; as the nation struggled to come to moral grips with its commercial self, those chosen to sit in judgment were subjected to close ideological scrutiny. In 1916, when President Woodrow Wilson nominated "The People's Lawyer," Louis Denibitz Brandeis, to the Supreme Court, "all hell broke loose in the financial, legal, and political communities, where many powerful elements had long fought and feared him as a 'radical.'"[17]

Brandeis had long antagonized the most powerful elements in the American legal and business establishment. After amassing a personal fortune as a Boston lawyer, Brandeis had plunged into public affairs, seeking to rectify social and economic inequities through the law. Indicative of his professional skills and personal principles, as a lawyer in 1908 Brandeis wrought a fundamental change in the judicial process. We have already mentioned his famous brief in the case of *Muller* v. *Oregon,* in which Brandeis argued before the Court that Oregon's statute limiting women's working hours in certain kinds of businesses was constitutional and did not violate the then judicially fashionable notion of liberty of contract.[18] His use of sociological evidence (150 pages) to supplement legal precedents (two pages) established a method that continues to this day. By the time of his nomination he had committed an unforgivable sin in the eyes of those who sought to keep government's regulatory paws off business.

In addition to the fear of his alleged radicalism and distrust of his sociological jurisprudence, the political waters were further muddied by the fact that Brandeis was the first Jew to be named to the high Court at a time when anti-Semitism was not unknown in American politics. The opposition to Brandeis was joined by such notables as Elihu Root and William Howard Taft. When the Senate finally voted to confirm on June 1, 1916, by a 47–22 vote, Brandeis was opposed by such leaders as Henry Cabot Lodge of Massachusetts, George Sutherland of Utah, and Warren G. Harding of Ohio; the legendary William E. Borah of Idaho did not vote.

Despite the conservative wrath against Brandeis, such ideological dissents on a President's nominee's have never been the preserve of either the left or the right. When the presidency passed to conservatives in 1921, with the election of Warren G. Harding, and went further right in 1923 and 1929 with the ascent of Calvin Coolidge and Herbert Hoover, respectively, the liberals and Progressives in Congress dug in their heels. Insurgent Republicans, led by George Norris and Robert La Follette, with the support of the Democrats, made a determined effort to block appointments, serving notice that the nomination of conservatives to the Court would be opposed in the Senate.

The celebrated conservative Calvin Coolidge got only one shot at a Supreme Court appointment and chose his friend, Attorney General Harlan Fiske Stone. Stone had impeccable credentials: A solid Republican and former corporation lawyer, he had taught law at Columbia Law School and had become Dean in 1910; in 1924 Coolidge had named him as Attorney General. Stone's nomination in 1925 is historically significant in that he was the first candidate to appear in person before the Senate Judiciary Committee. There Stone faced a grueling interrogation. He handled himself ably, though, and the Judiciary Committee reported the nomination favorably to the Senate. On the floor of the Senate the Stone nomination was attacked head-on by the distinguished George W. Norris of Nebraska. The Senator called Stone a "tool of the House of Morgan" because Stone had served as legal counsel to the firm of J. P. Morgan.[19] But despite such opposition, the Senate confirmed Stone by an overwhelming 71–6 vote.

In 1930 Chief Justice William Howard Taft died, giving President Herbert Hoover his first of three appointments to the Supreme Court. To the surprise of some, Hoover passed by the chance to elevate Justice Stone in favor of Charles Evans Hughes. Hughes's nomination was really the first where the emphasis was not at all on ability and qualifications but dramatically on political philosophy. Even more than Stone, Hughes was portrayed as no friend of the common man and high in the affections of big business.

Senator Borah stood forth and, with an air of Progressive disdain, asked his colleagues in the Senate: "When during the last 16

years has corporate wealth had a contest with the public . . . that
Mr. Hughes had not appeared for organized wealth and against
the public?" Conceding that Hughes was a man of unquestioned
ability and integrity, Borah concluded by attacking him in the only
place he could, in the realm of ideas. "I am only concerned,"
Borah intoned, "with the proposition of placing upon the Court
as Chief Justice one whose views are known upon these vital and
important questions . . . views which ought [not] to be incorporated in and made a permanent part of our legal and economic
system."[20]

Picking up the Progressive pace, Senator Norris drummed even
harder on the nominee. Hughes, Norris declared,

> . . . has not seen who suffers, the man who knows what it is to be
> hungry and not have the necessary money to buy food. His vision is
> circumscribed by yellow gold. . . . I am not willing that there
> should be transferred from that kind of surrounding one who shall
> sit at the head of the greatest judicial tribunal in the world; I am
> not willing to say that that kind of man, regardless of his ability,
> should go on the Supreme Bench.[21]

Hughes was confirmed—as was always expected—but only by a
vote of 52–26. "The Progressive Republicans, led by Norris,
Borah, Nye and La Follette, voted solidly against confirmation
and were joined by about half of a small group of Democratic senators."[22] Ironically, the liberals were off the ideological mark.
Hughes became a rather liberal Chief Justice, frequently siding
with Justices Holmes, Brandeis, Cardozo, and Stone.

In addition to the attack on Hughes, 1930 would prove to be a
hallmark year in the history of political appointments to the
Supreme Court. Judge John J. Parker of the Fourth Circuit Court
of Appeals was the first nominee to be rejected by the Senate in
thirty-six years. Parker's nomination was significant as well because
he was the first nominee to be defeated by means of a carefully orchestrated campaign by well-organized and powerful interest
groups, such as the National Association for the Advancement of
Colored People (NAACP) and the American Federation of Labor.

Parker was a man of solid reputation, both politically and professionally, a man of known ability and integrity. Despite being supported by a considerable portion of the Senate aligned with Hoover and "by the press . . . as well as by a great majority of the bar," Parker was done in by most Democratic Senators and the Progressive Republicans again led by Borah and Norris and emboldened by the vociferous opposition of the interest groups. "The opposition to Judge Parker was based on three contentions: (1) that he favored 'yellow-dog' contracts and was unfriendly to labor; (2) that he was opposed to Negro suffrage and participation in politics; and (3) that the appointment was dictated by political considerations."[23]

William Green, president of the American Federation of Labor, was blunt about his opposition:

> Labor is of the opinion that the appointment and confirmation of Judge Parker means that another injunction judge will become a member of the Supreme Court of the United States. As a result, the power of reaction will be strengthened, and the broad-minded, human, progressive influence so courageously and patriotically exercised by the minority members of the highest judicial tribunal of the land will be weakened. There is the kernel in the nut.[24]

Similarly, Walter White, Secretary of the NAACP, opposed Judge Parker for what White called his "open, shameless flouting of the fourteenth and fifteenth amendments of the Federal constitution." White based his opposition solely on the basis of a comment Parker had made ten years earlier while campaigning for Governor of North Carolina.[25] Responding to Democratic charges leveled at the Republican party concerning the enfrancisement of Negroes, Parker had said: "The participation of the Negro in politics is a source of evil and danger to both races and is not desired by wise men in either race or by the Republican party of North Carolina."[26]

After the nomination was reported adversely out of Committee, the floor debate followed the organized opposition. Senator Borah argued that he was "opposed to the confirmation of Judge Parker because I think he is committed to principles and propositions to which I am very thoroughly opposed. . . . He is particularly identified with this [yellow-dog] kind of a contract. [And] if the Senate decides that Mr. Parker should be confirmed, it is in moral effect a decision of the Senate in favor of the yellow-dog contract."[27]

Senator Norris, in typical fashion, picked up the theme and fleshed out the general opposition from the particular grievance. Since Congress lacked the power to deal legislatively with the problem of yellow-dog contracts, Norris said, "we are down to this one thing. When we are passing on a judge . . . we ought not only to know whether he is a good lawyer, not only whether he is honest—and I admit this nominee possesses both of those qualifications—but we ought to know how he approaches these great questions of human liberty."[28] The final vote was against confirmation. For the first time ever, a nominee was obstructed entirely for political reasons. A watershed had been reached.

Perhaps no President has had as stormy a relationship with the Supreme Court as Franklin Roosevelt. Elected in 1932, and then reelected by an unprecedented mandate in 1936, Roosevelt sent hundreds of pieces of legislation to Congress aimed at dealing with the Depression that gripped the nation. While the Congress passed almost all of Roosevelt's proposals, the Supreme Court, in a number of very close opinions, struck many of them down. In early 1937, frustrated by the Court's rebukes, he sent his famous "Court Packing Bill" to Capitol Hill. Although officially described as a bill that would allow the President to appoint additional federal judges in an attempt to help the courts deal with the crush of business, it was obvious to everyone that the real purpose of the bill was to increase the size of the Supreme Court so that Roosevelt might appoint to it individuals more supportive of his New Deal initiatives. The President's plan never survived scrutiny by the judiciary committee of the Senate, but it did have an impact. Within months the Supreme Court issued three decisions that upheld important New Deal initiatives.

In June 1937 Roosevelt received his first chance to nominate someone to the Supreme Court when Justice William VanDevanter announced his retirement. He chose Senator Hugo Lafayette Black of Alabama. It was a controversial choice. The *New York Times* said that nominating Black was like dropping "salt in the political wounds already rubbed raw by the Court issue."[29] Black was a staunch defender of Roosevelt's New Deal policies, a liberal, and had supported Roosevelt's court-packing plan. But he was also considered by many of his colleagues in the Senate to be unqualified for the Court, too partisan in his outlook and too radical. In addition, his having been a member of the Ku Klux Klan during the 1920s undermined his suitability for the nomination. Although a member of the Senate, Black did not receive the sort of courteous treatment usually accorded to a colleague.

Black's confirmation hearings were stormy and confrontational. When the nomination went to the floor of the Senate, his opponents raised every issue they could to defeat their senatorial brother. Critics argued that he had precious little experience; his only previous judgeship had come as a police court judge years earlier. His supporters tried to defend the nomination on that very ground. Senator Tom Connally noted, for example, that out of the Justices then on the Court, neither Butler nor Sutherland, neither Stone nor Roberts had "ever sat on a bench unless it was in the park" prior to joining the Court.[30] Senator Borah claimed Black was constitutionally disqualified for service on the Court because as a Senator he had voted on a bill increasing the retirement pay for Justices; the Constitution clearly provides: "No Senator or Representative shall, during the Time for which he was elected, be appointed to any civil Office under the Authority of the United States, which shall have been created, or the Emoluments whereof shall have been increased during such time." But in the end Black and Roosevelt prevailed, and he was confirmed by a large margin.

The controversy surrounding Black's appointment did not recede after his confirmation, however. After the vote in the Senate, press reports appeared that emphasized Black's previous membership in the KKK and openly questioned his fitness for the Court. In an unprecedented and never repeated act, Black, before joining the Court, responded to the press reports with a radio address. Associate Justice Black served on the nation's high Court until 1971.

The fact is that all the arguments marshaled against Black were disingenuous. The real issue was his ideological bent and his partisan connection with President Roosevelt. The biggest issue of the day, of course, was the New Deal. Questions abounded regarding the constitutionality of its various legislative components. The old Court had been unwilling to allow the President to play fast and loose with traditional notions of separation of powers and federalism. The ultimate success of the New Deal policies hinged upon their approval as constitutional by the Supreme Court. Hugo Black's confirmation signaled the beginning of the end for the old regime and ushered in a new era of constitutional law. As Roosevelt saw his other appointments fall into place, the Court would move farther and farther away from its traditional role in negating regulatory legislation; with the ascendance of the ideology of Roosevelt on the Court through his appointees, the nature and scope of American government was dramatically changed.

CREATING THE *DESHANEY* COURT

The nine individuals sitting in judgment in the *DeShaney* case had all come to the Court through the same political process that had delivered their predecessors. The judges who had turned back Joshua's and his mother's suit at the federal district and appellate courts were also the products of the process of "advice and consent" established by the Constitution. When the evidence of abuse to Joshua first surfaced in 1982, the Supreme Court differed considerably from the Court that would sit in judgment in 1988. In fact, the 1982 Court would probably have decided in Joshua's favor. But by 1988 the Court had a conservative cast, due primarily to the appointments made by President Reagan. But it was, as well, a Court in transition. The newest member, Associate Justice Anthony Kennedy, had only just arrived on the bench. The most senior member of the Court, Associate Justice William Brennan, was completing his thirty-second year. Sitting on the bench were six Justices with established records who had arrived at the Court long before Reagan became president.

William Brennan was named to the Court by President Eisenhower in 1956. Brennan, along with Thurgood Marshall, appointed by Lyndon Johnson, and Harry Blackmun, appointed by Richard Nixon, provided the liberal thrust to so many of the

Court's decisions—the year preceding Ronald Reagan's election. With that election, and the change in the Court that resulted, Brennan, Marshall, and Blackmun found themselves trying to protect many of the positions they had taken in earlier years.

Justice Byron White was appointed by President Kennedy. A moderate, White, along with Justice John Paul Stevens (who was appointed by Gerald Ford), formed the less ideological center of the *DeShaney* Court.

The leader of the Reagan-era New Court, William Hubbs Rehnquist, holds the dubious distinction of having been confirmed twice by the Senate, each time receiving the highest number of votes against confirmation among all who have been confirmed—until the vote on the confirmation of Clarence Thomas in 1991.

In September 1971 Justices Black and Harlan, two of the giants of the Supreme Court, announced their plans to retire. President Nixon, having only recently completed exhausting confirmation battles with the Senate, sought two nominees who might bring his conservative approach to politics to the bench. He also wanted badly to bring a Southerner to the Court. He named Lewis Powell of Richmond, Virginia, a distinguished attorney and former head of the American Bar Association, to replace Black. Powell danced through his confirmation hearings and was easily confirmed. As a replacement for Harlan, Nixon looked to his own Justice Department and, upon the advice of his Attorney General, John N. Mitchell, he picked his forty-seven-year-old Assistant Attorney General for the Office of Legal Counsel, William Rehnquist.

Rehnquist's credentials were impressive, especially given his relatively young age. An honor graduate from Stanford and Stanford Law School, and a former law clerk to Associate Justice Robert H. Jackson, he had established a strong reputation as an attorney before coming to Washington. At the Department of Justice he was responsibile for crafting some of the more important legal arguments and analyses for the Attorney General and the White House. Rehnquist was an established conservative—far more conservative than Lewis Powell, far more conservative than many who had gone onto the Court. And his conservative politics and jurisprudence came under repeated attack during his confirmation hearings.

For much of the confirmation hearings, Rehnquist was asked to respond to various questions concerning the Constitution and the Court. But some on the judiciary committee were far more interested in the nominee's politics than in his jurisprudence. Having been active in conservative Republican politics in Arizona in the early 1960s, Rehnquist, it was alleged, had been instrumental in designing and implementing the state GOP's "voter intimidation" program. In those days Arizona voters had to demonstrate literacy in order to cast a ballot. Officials from both political parties, in an attempt to limit the support of the opposition, would visit voting precincts on election day and challenge the literacy of voters. It was a common, if controversial, practice then, outlawed now by bans on such voting rights requirements as literacy tests. The rumor had existed for some time that Rehnquist had been active in challenging and intimidating Hispanic voters. It was rumored that he had even been involved in a fracas on election day in 1962.

All of this may seem somewhat tame, considering Justice Black's former membership in Ku Klux Klan. But by 1971 membership on the Supreme Court had taken on increased importance. Moreover, Black had been a member of the Senate and was accorded, therefore, some measure (albeit rather little) of senatorial courtesy. But Rehnquist was the nominee of a Republican President, this was a Democratic Senate, and, moreover, he was relatively unknown, apparently very conservative, and so young that should he be confirmed he might serve on the Court for some time.

Peppered with questions about the alleged voter intimidation, Rehnquist repeatedly denied the rumors. An FBI investigation failed to provide the members of the Senate with compelling evidence. It created a debate and a stage for some on the committee to lecture the nominee about sensitivity to minorities and the importance of the political process, but little else. Another issue that came to the attention of the committee as it was preparing to adjourn did cause some real concern and foreshadowed a debate that was resumed years later when Rehnquist was nominated to be Chief Justice.

Having clerked for Justice Jackson while the Supreme Court was deliberating *Brown* v. *Board of Education*,[31] Rehnquist had been involved in the debate over whether or not the Court should overturn *Plessy* v. *Ferguson*,[32] the case that established the legitimacy of "separate but equal" educational and other public facilities for the races. Rehnquist had written a memo for Justice Jackson urging him not to vote to overturn *Plessy*, and that memo became the object of some speculation toward the end of his confirmation hearings. The Senators wanted to know whether the memo reflected Rehnquist's thoughts at the time or whether the memo was the young clerk's attempt at outlining the sorts of arguments Justice Jackson might want to make should he vote to sustain *Plessy*. Rehnquist was equivocal in his responses and seemed to be trying to evade the Senators' questions. But because the issue surfaced so late in the confirmation process, and because the judiciary committee was chaired at that time by the conservative Senator from Mississippi, James O. Eastland, the *Brown* memo did not derail the nomination. Rehnquist was confirmed in December 1971 by a vote of 68–26.

The Court that would decide the case of *DeShaney* v. *Winnebago County Department of Social Services* was composed of a number of Justices who had survived the rigors of nomination and appointment before Ronald Reagan had come to office in 1981: Brennan, White, Marshall, Blackmun, and Stevens. In addition, of course, three of the Justices on the Court were Reagan appointees, and a fourth had been promoted to Chief Justice by Reagan. These four Justices—Associate Justices O'Connor, Scalia, and Kennedy and Chief Justice Rehnquist—were the products of a process of judicial selection that had undergone considerable transformation. During the Reagan years the politics of judicial selection took on a new character, reflective of both the changes that had taken place in the nature of judicial power and changes that had taken place in the nature of the Senate. By the time the *DeShaney* case reached the Court, the Supreme Court itself and the process that surrounds appointment to the Court had both become the subjects of considerable controversy.

During the 1980s, the nature and extent of judicial power emerged as a critical political issue—in part because Ronald

Reagan and George Bush decided it should be, in part because they confronted a Senate that had not only the constitutional power of advice and consent but its own understanding of judicial power as well. The political brawl between the White House and the Senate over the future of the judiciary had everything to do with the constitutional fate of Joshua's quest for justice.

When President Reagan nominated the Arizona jurist Sandra Day O'Connor for a seat on the Supreme Court he was making good on a campaign promise from the year before. Candidate Reagan had sought to reach out to women during his campaign against Jimmy Carter in 1980 and on one occasion promised that he would, when presented with the opportunity to do so, nominate the first woman to the Supreme Court. So on July 7, 1981, he chose to make political and Supreme Court history by making Judge O'Connor his first nomination to the Supreme Court.

Presenting his nominee to the press, Reagan hailed the fifty-one-year-old state appeals court judge as a "person for all seasons" and asserted that she possessed "those unique qualities of temperament, fairness, intellectual capacity and devotion to the public good which have characterized the 101 'brethren' who have preceded her."[33] In the Senate, majority leader Howard Baker of Tennessee promised the nomination would receive the quick confirmation of the Republican-controlled Senate.

In naming O'Connor, Reagan had made a bold move. Not only was he naming the first woman to the Court, but he was naming someone who did not fit neatly into most people's preconceived notions of what a conservative jurist might look like. True, she was a friend of Barry Goldwater, and she had been a classmate of Associate Justice William Rehnquist at Stanford Law School. But in Arizona O'Connor had favored passage of the failed Equal Rights Amendment. While a state legislator, she had sided with pro-choice groups in some political battles. So while her nomination was greeted by many with surprise, and by some with enthusiasm, there were those in both the liberal and the conservative communities who were disappointed and willing to go on record against her. Almost as soon as she was nominated, the Moral Majority announced plans to oppose the nomination, as did the National Right to Life Committee. Liberal groups, on the other

hand, were nervous. The judge's record in Arizona offered relatively little to indicate how she might vote on issues of national
importance. While they considered the anxiety of some conservative groups to be a good sign, the fact remained that a very conservative President had nominated this person, and that meant
that on most issues she would probably agree at least on the fundamentals of the conservative agenda.

During the days immediately following the nomination, much
of official Washington was consumed with it. In the Senate
Howard Baker scheduled confirmation hearings for early in
September, thus assuring a full complement of Justices by the
Monday in October when the Court would begin the new term.
Senator Jesse Helms of North Carolina groused at the prospect of
anointing O'Connor without challenging her on issues important
to conservatives. But the nominee had an able and influential ally
in the senior Senator from Arizona, Barry Goldwater. Perhaps the
single most influential conservative in the Senate, Goldwater told
O'Connor's critics to "back off" and argued that "a lot of foolish
claptrap" had been circulating about her in the Senate.[34]
Meanwhile, as some conservatives organized to try to challenge
the nomination, Senator Edward Kennedy announced his support
for O'Connor, and Senator Alan Simpson of Wyoming dismissed
most of her opposition by claiming that the support for O'Connor
was much too strong to be defeated.

As the summer of 1981 wore on, the nomination became the
focus of ongoing scrutiny and rumor. As O'Connor met with the
various members of the judiciary committee, she encountered the
warm embrace of some and the polite, somewhat grudging respect
of others. Those groups interested in the direction the Supreme
Court might take with Sandra Day O'Connor sitting on the bench
directed their energies toward determining the would-be Justice's
position on the issues.

That proved to be very difficult. Most of the media found
O'Connor "vague" on the issues, described her record as mixed,
and said it defied convenient labels. In part this was due, no
doubt, to the fact that she was a state appeals court judge, and
therefore had not confronted many of the sorts of issues she might
confront on the Supreme Court. It was also due to the fact that

O'Connor was not a doctrinaire judge. Her record demonstrated that she tended to approach each issue on its own merits and to write opinions that were narrow and closely tailored to the facts presented. Moreover, Sandra Day O'Connor had been a state legislator and politician, someone familiar with the need to make difficult decisions but to also make those decisions palatable to citizens. Her judicial career reflected this; to Judge O'Connor, moderation was no vice.

The opposition to O'Connor was never strong enough to threaten the nomination. In part because of her record, and in part because of the political momentum created by the fact that she was a woman, her critics were reduced to impotence. In the end she was confirmed by the Senate by a vote of 99–0.

President Reagan did not get another chance to nominate someone to the Supreme Court until the middle of his second term in office. In May 1986 Chief Justice Warren E. Burger paid a call to Ronald Reagan to inform him that he wanted to retire from the Court in order to direct the nation's celebration of the bicentennial of the Constitution. His decision came as a complete surprise to the President and to those of his advisers who were involved daily with the issue of selecting federal judges. But it was because the President had a judicial selection system well established within his Department of Justice that the response to Burger's retirement was well organized and swift.

Those closest to the judicial selection process recommended to President Reagan that Associate Justice Rehnquist be nominated for Chief Justice. That was an easy decision. Rehnquist had established his conservative credentials going back to the Nixon years. Replacing Rehnquist as Associate Justice was trickier. Two schools of thought emerged regarding that second nomination. And it was agreed that the President should nominate either Judge Robert Bork or Judge Antonin Scalia, both serving on the Federal Court of Appeals for the District of Columbia Circuit. Bork was already a known figure, a nationally recognized conservative lawyer and jurist, and by most counts Ronald Reagan's favorite judge. All of this worked to his advantage in securing the nomination but might hurt him during the confirmation. The prospect of sending the Senate two very well-known and outspoken conservatives might cost the Administration at least one, if not both of the nominations. Scalia was equally conservative but was less well known and had less of a record on the sorts of legal and jurisprudential issues the Senate might want to focus on. Moreover, Scalia possessed the sort of personality and charm that could manage the trials of confirmation before the Senate, while Bork was notorious for his gruff demeanor and his inability to suffer fools gladly. The fact that Scalia was a first-generation Italian-American carried the day. It made him a very attractive candidate who would be difficult for the Senate to deny confirmation.

There was really never any question that William Rehnquist would receive the most attention in the media and from the Senate, and therefore from the Administration. Rehnquist was a good target. An intellectual, he often came across as distant and cold, uncaring and remote. The fact that he had served on the Court since 1971 was no advantage to his nomination as Chief Justice; he had a record as a Justice that would haunt him. Further, he had been confirmed initially after stormy and somewhat confrontational hearings, and many of the issues that were raised then would resurface during his confirmation hearings to become Chief Justice.

The nominations of Rehnquist and Scalia came at a time when the relationship between the Senate and the Reagan Administration was strained, in part over the issue of judicial selection. Not since the controversy that had surrounded Nixon's two failed nominations of Clement Haynesworth and G. Harrold Carswell had the issue of judicial selection taken on such political significance. By 1986 Reagan had appointed more individuals to the federal courts than any of his predecessors—a fact that was not lost on the Democratic minority in the Senate. With a congressional election coming in November, the Democrats saw the Rehnquist hearings as an opportunity to charge that Reagan was attempting to pack the federal judiciary with judges who adhered to a strict conservative agenda reflecting Reagan's position on a host of issues such as school prayer, abortion, busing, and separation of powers.

Those opposed to the Rehnquist nomination planned their strategy carefully. By focusing on his record on the bench, they would attempt to portray him as a strident conservative who was reduced to the intellectual solitude of "lone dissents" because he stood so far out of the mainstream of American law. He was, they would insist, an extremist. They would then build upon this image of an isolated extremist by pursuing Rehnquist's political and personal history in an attempt to portray him as a man with a long history of opposition to civil rights.

Picking up where Rehnquist's initial confirmation hearings in 1971 had ended, the Democrats on the Judiciary Committee challenged the Justice on his views of the Court's landmark desegregation decision, *Brown* v. *Board of Education*. The memo Rehnquist, then a clerk to Associate Justice Jackson, had written seemed to imply that he was opposed to overturning *Plessy* v. *Ferguson* and ending segregation, and they wanted to know if that was indeed Rehnquist's opinion at the time.

It was the perfect strategy for the Democrats on the committee to pursue. While it was impossible to prove whether or not the memo reflected Rehnquist's personal opinion at that time, his opponents employed the discussion of the memo to undermine support for the nominee.

The Democrats on the committee coupled their focus on the *Brown* memo with recently reinvigorated rumors that Rehnquist had participated in a program of voter harassment and intimidation during the early 1960s. The fact that the rumors had been checked out by the FBI and nothing that would implicate Rehnquist was discovered made no difference. Rehnquist's opponents were able to enhance his image as a conservative ideologue by pointing out that the deed to his summer home in Vermont contained a restrictive covenant barring sale of the property to "anyone of the Hebrew race."

The other issue Rehnquist's opponents used as the hearings came to a close forced the Administration to confront the Democrats head on. Throughout the hearings, Democratic Senators Edward M. Kennedy and Howard Metzenbaum had been arguing that Rehnquist's memos and opinions from his days as Assistant Attorney General for Legal Counsel should be made available to the committee. On the surface it was a strong argument. Those were legal opinions written by a man who now sought to be Chief Justice. They would indeed provide some insight into the man's approach to legal and constitutional questions. Moreover, they were written during a very difficult time in the nation's history and for a very controversial president, Richard Nixon. The Democrats sought all of Rehnquist's memos.

The Administration responded by invoking executive privilege to deny the committee access to the documents. The position of the Justice Department was that those papers represented the confidential, and therefore privileged, deliberations between the President and his attorney and hence were not subject to public disclosure. The argument had merit. A President's advisers might indeed be reluctant to provide candid advice if they felt it might be made public one day. Moreover, the idea of attorney–client privilege is well accepted. Besides, Rehnquist was hardly a stranger to the committee or the Court, and his views on legal and constitutional questions could be clearly determined from his opinions from the bench and the hearings. The Administration knew that the Democrats were on a fishing expedition, hoping to find something in the memos that might be used against the Justice.

The immediate reaction to the invocation of executive privilege was emotional. Kennedy accused the Administration of a coverup and tried to link Rehnquist to an earlier attempt to keep information from Congress during the Watergate era.

In the end, however, the Democrats were unable to paint a portrait of a Chief Justice Rehnquist dark enough to galvanize opposition within the Senate adequate to defeat the nomination. On September 17, 1986, Rehnquist was confirmed by the Senate. In the history of the country, no other successful nominee to the Supreme Court had received as many negative votes.

The very next day Antonin Scalia was confirmed by a unanimous vote. Scalia's confirmation was never in doubt. While the Administration had prepared for the hearings with the same vigor and thoroughness that had attended Rehnquist's struggle, Scalia was never really challenged by the Senators. His character, integrity, and politics were not discussed, in part because the nominee charmed the committee with his wit and style, and in part because virtually everyone on the committee had already decided that Scalia would be confirmed. Most of the questioning focused on legal and constitutional issues, as Senators attempted to determine where the jurist might move the Court. For his part, Scalia was adept at dodging the questions, citing a need to refrain from getting too specific because he might confront the questions on the bench and should maintain the appearance of no bias. After a while Scalia's refusal to be more forthcoming annoyed some on the committee, including one of his more ardent supporters, Arlen Specter of Pennsylvania. Even though they found Scalia frustrating, they still voted for confirmation.

THE BORK FIASCO

The political environment into which the Bork nomination was dropped, a year after the Rehnquist and Scalia hearings, had worsened considerably. By the fall of 1987 the Democrats had regained the control of the Senate and were eager to press this advantage over the Reagan Administration, having endured minority status for six years. On the judiciary committee, chairmanship had been turned over to Joseph Biden of Delaware, who was already running for the Democratic nomination for the presidency in 1988. By the time Judge Bork's hearings began, Congress and the nation had witnessed a summer of controversy surrounding the Iran–Contra affair; President Reagan's prestige had suffered severely. His ability to dictate the flow of political events in Washington was undermined. It was into this political thicket that Robert Bork was nominated to replace retiring Justice Lewis Powell. From the outset, it seemed that the Bork nomination might establish new levels for political rancor.

Robert Heron Bork seemed destined to sit on the Supreme Court of the United States. A man of unquestioned intellectual ability and personal integrity—even his critics agreed on those points—Bork had compiled a truly impressive professional resumé. A graduate of the University of Chicago, both its College and its Law School, Bork had become a practicing attorney with the distinguished firm of Kirkland & Ellis from 1955 to 1962; he left Kirkland & Ellis to begin teaching at Yale Law School. During his time at Yale he served as both the Chancellor Kent Professor and the Alexander M. Bickel Professor of Public Law, published and lectured widely, and moved from his primary interest in antitrust law to constitutional law under the tutelage of his closest friend, Alexander Bickel. Bork had taken leave from Yale to serve as Solicitor General of the United States under Richard Nixon from 1973 to 1977. When he left Yale in 1981 after the deaths of both his friend Bickel and his first wife, Claire, Bork had returned as a partner to Kirkland & Ellis. That was where he was when President Reagan tapped him for the United States Court of Appeals for the District of Columbia Circuit in 1982. Bork was considered by friend and foe alike to be a formidable figure in the world of law.

When Lewis Powell resigned on June 26, Robert Bork had one other qualification that augured well for his being picked to succeed Powell on the high Court. Bob Bork was Ronald Reagan's favorite judge. At a time when the Constitution seemed nearly swamped by the "torrents of theorizing pouring from the law schools" (as Bork had said) Reagan saw in the burly and good-humored judge a brother in the bonds of an older understanding of limited constitutional government. They shared, to Reagan's way of thinking, the faith of the Founding Fathers suffused as it was by doubts about untethered judicial power. As the President succinctly put it when he announced Judge Bork's nomination, they shared the "view that judges' personal preferences and values should not be part of their constitutional interpretations." Finally, in the autumn of his presidency, Ronald Reagan acknowledged what his conservative friends had been urging all along: Bob Bork was a man for all reasons.

But Bork was not nearly as politically untouchable as Scalia. First, he was not just a conservative, he was a vocal and widely published conservative. There was no mistaking where he stood. Unlike other possible nominees, the White House would not be able to hedge its ideological bets on Bork. Second, Bork had had a close brush with political infamy during the Watergate scandal. As Solicitor General in 1973 Bork had fired Special Prosecutor Archibald Cox at the command of President Nixon. This he had done only after Attorney General Elliot Richardson and Deputy Attorney General William Ruckelshaus had resigned rather than do the President's bidding. Bork's complicity with Nixon in the "Saturday Night Massacre" was sure to cause major political obstacles to his being confirmed for the high Court. Though he had been confirmed unanimously for the Court of Appeals, this was a very different situation. This was, after all, for the seat of the swing vote on a closely divided Supreme Court.

White House strategy was to portray Bork as a more moderate jurist, not the conservative ideologue many thought him to be. He was more like Lewis Powell than William Rehnquist. In addition, they sought to soften his image as a gruff, distant academic, sending him around to meet nearly all the Senators and the press, to shake a few hands, and to discuss his views. Bork was made available to discuss his views and positions to a far greater extent than any other nominee in history. But as that strategy was implemented, it became obvious that Robert Bork was his own worst enemy. To many, it appeared that the judge was so concerned with getting on the Supreme Court—a desire that he had harbored all his professional life—that he was willing to say anything and do anything that seemed likely to advance that cause. Judge Bork, it seemed, had concluded that he had no choice but to "give the Senate anything they wanted."

As Bork spent the summer preparing for the hearings, his opponents in the Senate and in the civil rights community organized a massive and well-orchestrated campaign to defeat him. A week after Bork was named, Senator Biden summed up the battle lines with surprising candor. According to the Senator it went well beyond Judge Bork. It was a question of whether the Reagan-Meese agenda was going to be accomplished through the Court and whether Judge Bork had been picked to be the vehicle to accomplish that.[35]

One of Bork's many published opinions, from a 1971 journal article, had attacked the right to privacy. Early in the confirmation debates Chairman Biden decided that the privacy issue would be the focus of his attack on the Judge. It was a shrewd strategy for two reasons. First, as a constitutional rights issue, privacy was a concept at once amorphous and deeply revered. It would be easy enough for Biden to inflame public passions over the subject— usually couching his attack in the terms of bedroom privacy, birth control, and so forth—and it would be nearly impossible for the Judge to argue against it. The Senators would be able to pepper him with dramatic allegations that would easily make it into the evening news reports. The Judge, on the other hand, would be reduced to offering tedious and complex academic dissertations in rebuttal. It was simply a no-win public relations fix for the nominee: He would be damned if he could explain his views, and damned if he couldn't.

The second reason the privacy issue could be such a politically rich vein to mine, from Biden's viewpoint, was that it was a rights issue that cut across racial, ethnic, and ideological lines. *Everyone* was for the right to privacy, *everyone* would be offended by someone who questioned its foundation publicly. Bork's criticism of the right to privacy—that it was a judge-made right that took judges beyond their legitimate role—was too arcane for the general public; the nuances of his views would be lost on the public. While the theoretical and historical questions were many and technical, the public could be counted on to be emotional, not rational, when it came to such a right as privacy. To cast doubts on that right, Biden knew, would put the nominee in a position akin to casting doubt on motherhood and apple pie. A public opinion poll had confirmed that for Biden long before the hearings.

Meanwhile, as Bork's opponents in the Senate organized in anticipation of the hearings, Senator Edward Kennedy helped to coordinate political opposition to the nomination.

In early September Bork's critics got their biggest boost yet. The Standing Committee on the Federal Judiciary of the American Bar Association had completed its evaluation of Judge Bork and, though it found him "Well Qualified"—the highest rating—the vote was split. Four of the fifteen members of the Committee had voted Bork "Unqualified," the lowest possible rating; one other member had voted "Not Opposed," indicating that while he found Bork qualified for the Court, there were others perhaps better qualified.

The result of the Bork review process was to inject a new and basically political standard into the criterion for what constitutes "judicial temperament." For Bork that standard was stretched to include not just fairness and a concern for individual rights but the more amorphous standard of "sensitivity to the concerns of women and minority groups." At bottom such a sensitivity to "concerns" of various groups is a political judgment, not a legal one.

The Democrats' strategy of tripping Bork on his own words and focusing on Bork's views about "the right to privacy" worked brilliantly. As the hearings got under way, Biden began his attack. The next day the *New York Times* reported, "Biden's sweeping invocations of human rights antedating the Constitution were far easier to grasp than Judge Bork's insistent examinations of the purported legal derivations of such rights." While Biden came across as being draped with the flag and the Declaration of Independence, Bork seemed little more than "a dry technician . . . the deadly serious pedagogue." The Democrats' focus on the Judge's writings and his views on privacy blended nicely with their attack on his apparent insensitivity on civil rights. In August 1963, Senator Kennedy pointed out with dramatic irony, when Dr. Martin Luther King was leading his legendary March on Washington, Professor Robert Bork was scribbling away in *The New Republic* that the Civil Rights Bills were expressions of a principle of governmental intrusiveness of "unsurpassed ugliness." Further, Kennedy demanded of the Judge, why hadn't he ever repudiated those early views when, as the Judge now alleged, he had changed his mind? Why had Bork not reentered the great civil rights debates in 1968? In 1972? Why had he waited till 1973, when he was being confirmed as Solicitor General of the United States? Somehow in all the bluster, little notice was given to the fact that Bork had changed his views on the Civil Rights Act, or that several Senators—including Majority Leader Robert Byrd— had first filibustered and then voted against the act.

While they explored the possibilities of undermining the nomination through these strategies, the Democrats continued to pound away at Bork's substantive views as well. Gradually their focus widened to take account of Bork's position on the issues of separation of powers generally and the tension between the President and the Congress in particular. This provided an occasion to discuss the Watergate era and Bork's crucial role in the Justice Department at that time.

By the end of the hearings the Democrats' campaign to paint Bork as a principle-plundering opportunist was nearly a complete success. While being damned on one side for allegedly changing his views, Bork was pounded on the other for *not* changing his views and thus posing a deep threat to "settled law." Senator Kennedy returned to the theme with a vengeance—and with an audiotape of a Bork speech in 1985. Kennedy reminded the beleaguered witness that in 1985 he had confessed in an interview that "when you become a judge I do not think your viewpoint is likely to change greatly." Perhaps even more damaging, as recently as 1987, Kennedy pointed out, Bork was quoted as saying that "an originalist judge would have no problem whatsoever in overruling a non-originalist precedent because that precedent, by the very basis of his judicial philosophy, has no legitimacy."

An academic nuclear volley was unleashed on the nomination in a letter of September 22 to the Committee from "teachers of law . . . concerned with the preservation and enforcement of constitutional rights," which asked the Senate to "withhold its consent to the nomination of Robert H. Bork to be an associate justice of the Supreme Court of the United States." The power of the letter came not so much from its substance as from its signatories. The names of Philip B. Kurland of Chicago and Charles Fairman of Harvard, among others, carried great weight. Kurland, for example, was widely viewed as a conservative in the tradition of Felix Frankfurter and Alexander Bickel. Their willingness to affix their names to such a letter of protest gave it a public respectability it otherwise would not have had.

When the vote finally came on October 23, Robert Heron Bork was defeated, 58–42. It was the largest margin of defeat in history for a nominee to the Supreme Court of the United States.

Ronald Reagan took the defeat personally. In typical Reagan style, after the Judge's defeat he announced he would send the Senate another nominee who would upset Bork's opponents "just as much." Meanwhile, Robert Bork retired, briefly, from the public eye. His was the twenty-seventh nomination in the entire history of the nation to go down to defeat in the Senate, the first since 1970. Robert Bork joined the other five whom the Senate refused to confirm so far this century: John J. Parker in 1930, Abe

Fortas and Homer Thornberry in 1968, Clement Haynesworth in 1969, and G. Harrold Carswell in 1970.

After the short-lived and embarrassing nomination of Douglas Ginsburg, a federal appeals court judge, who withdrew amid a controversy over marijuana use, Reagan selected California circuit court judge Anthony Kennedy as his nominee to replace Lewis Powell.

During the flight from California, Administration officials sat with the nominee-to-be and grilled him from a list of almost three hundred questions. Every possible source of embarrassment was checked. Kennedy was asked about marital fidelity, drugs, escort services, massage parlors, pornography, everything. He was clean, at least by his own account. There was evidently nothing on this man that would tarnish his chances for the Supreme Court.

Kennedy was nominated by President Reagan three days after Douglas Ginsburg withdrew. He was confirmed by the Senate quickly, almost without debate. By then everyone associated with the process of judicial selection was exhausted. Anthony Kennedy, a nearly unknown federal judge who had made no scholarly contribution to the law, was Ronald Reagan's final effort to curb the excesses of judicial power.

With the appointment of Kennedy, Ronald Reagan could rightly claim his imprint upon the Court. This was now the Supreme Court that would decide *DeShaney*. It included seven justices appointed by Republican Presidents, going back to Dwight Eisenhower. Of those, three had been named by Reagan, and Rehnquist had been chosen Chief Justice by him. It had the appearance of a conservative Court that was poised to make real the revolution in law the conservative President had promised. That Court's decision in *DeShaney* seemed to provide additional evidence that such a revolution was under way. But such an assessment would be premature. While George Bush's first nominee to the high Court was confirmed easily, his final appointment to the Supreme Court demonstrated the degree to which the politics of advice and consent remained vitriolic. And the first major decision that was handed down by the Reagan–Bush court left little doubt that the conservative revolution was cut short.

THE BUSH YEARS

When George Bush ascended to the presidency, he established an office for judicial selection within the White House and staffed it with former officials from the Meese Justice Department. By now judicial selection had become an institutionalized process. The Bush Administration inherited a lengthy list of possible nominees for the federal courts from the Reagan Administration, and the transition between the two Administrations had gone smoothly.

Unlike his predecessor, however, George Bush was not particularly interested in the issue of judicial selection. He embraced, generally, the sort of understanding of judicial authority that Reagan espoused. But he did not look to the federal courts as a primary vehicle for advancing conservative positions or ensuring his legacy after leaving office. Moreover, Bush was eager to practice a kind of politics on Capitol Hill different from Reagan's. Till the end, Reagan had been confrontational with Congress. Bush sought a middle course, often seeking compromise, hoping to find some common ground. In the end he abandoned that strategy. But initially, Bush was sincere in his desire to consult and work with Congress rather than challenge it.

When Justice William J. Brennan announced his decision to retire from the Court, it caught the Bush Administration by surprise, but not unprepared. Within hours of receiving Brennan's note, Administration officials were studying the list of possible nominees that they had inherited from the Reagan judicial selection team. One issue above all others guided their efforts at identifying likely candidates: confirmability. The nightmares of the Bork and Ginsburg debacles were still fresh in their memories. The last thing they wanted was to have the President send a nomination to the Senate that might end in another confirmation controversy and undermine the enormous good will that Bush enjoyed early in his tenure. Whoever was recommended to Bush, the nominee had to be someone who would be able to get by the Senate. For this Administration, issues of jurisprudence would take second place to an overriding concern with politics.

The list of potential nominees was shortened considerably by the confirmability criterion. Many of those individuals who had been considered for earlier nominations remained under consideration. But each had one political liability or another. Moreover, these were by now familiar names among those interested in the judicial selection process. Should one of them receive the nomination, there would be, in all likelihood, immediate, well-orchestrated responses by groups opposed to it. Bork's critics had learned a lot from their success in defeating him. Officials within the Bush White House wanted a nominee who would catch the political establishment by surprise—thereby enhancing the chances for success. They also sought a candidate who would remain difficult to defeat after being nominated. Two names reached the top of the list: Edith Jones, on the Fifth Circuit Court of Appeals in Houston, and David Souter, of the First Circuit Court of Appeals in New Hampshire.

Edith Jones was the more attractive of the two candidates for those who had been close to the selection process since the Reagan days. She was bright, young, engaging, and very conservative. In the lingo of the Reagan judge-pickers, she was "solid." Her confirmation would not be secure the way Sandra Day O'Connor's had been, however, because Jones was a controversial judge. Articles had been written about her courtroom demeanor, challenging her judicial temperament and implying she used the bench to lecture liberal litigants and to offer harangues against the feminist movement. But her gender remained an advantage. And she was from Texas, a protégé of James Baker, and a former partner in the distinguished law firm of Baker & Botts. Not insignificantly, she had also once served as general counsel to the Republican Party in Texas.

David Souter was an enigma. He was viewed with some nagging skepticism even by those closest to the selection process. He had only recently been appointed to the Court of Appeals; for six years he had been a judge on the New Hampshire Supreme Court. Indeed, he had not even written an opinion for the Appeals Court. That had its advantages, however. Souter's relatively modest judicial and scholarly record would provide little potential ammunition for any opponents. The fact that Souter was a loner—a bachelor from a rural state who seemed to be something of a throwback, a modest intellectual who had a voracious appetite for books and lived in a cluttered, poorly kept house in the New Hampshire woods—seemed at once both advantageous and a liability. While there was obviously relatively little to attack him on, it could be argued that here was a man who was ill equipped to deal with the sorts of human issues that a Justice on the Supreme Court must pass judgment on.

Jones and Souter were both invited to meet with Bush, but even before those meetings took place, it was apparent that Bush would name Souter. He offered the right combination of characteristics to ensure confirmation. Most important, he had a strong and able advocate in the Senate in his friend and former boss, Warren Rudman. Rudman would steer the confirmation of Souter through the Senate for Bush. Rudman assured the President that Souter was conservative. Souter's name, after all, had been on the list of potential judges that the Reagan Administration had passed on to officials within Bush's White House. John Sununu, Bush's Chief of Staff and former conservative Governor of New Hampshire, seconded Rudman's vote.

Souter's nomination came as a complete surprise. His confirmation went exactly according to plan. Arm in arm with Rudman, the nominee worked the Senate like a pro. During his visits with individual Senators, he left little clue to his views on important issues and appeared the model of modesty and dignity. Nothing of substance to hurt the nomination ever appeared in the media. His confirmation hearings were a political nonevent. In response to Senators' questions, the Harvard-educated Rhodes Scholar gave long dissertations, often alluding to obscure legal theories and theorists. He was adept at sidestepping tough questions. With Rudman's help both before and during the hearings, he was able to direct the flow of events. He was confirmed quickly. The White House strategy had worked.

Only a year later George Bush was handed another chance to define the composition of the Supreme Court. Thurgood Marshall was not expected to retire. Although his health had been poor for years, Marshall was an indefatigable liberal who had always seemed determined to outlast Republican dominance of the presidency. But by the spring of 1991 he recognized the struggle was too much for him and notified the President.

Upon receiving word of Marshall's decision, the judicial selection team was assembled and immediately put forth a short list of potential nominees, which was floated within the Administration and on Capitol Hill. They were by now familiar names that would elicit predictable responses from the various groups that key on judicial appointments. But the list was something of a ruse. There was never any real doubt within the White House that Clarence Thomas would be nominated to replace Thurgood Marshall.

Clarence Thomas was plucked out of relative obscurity early in the Reagan era and groomed for the seat President Bush would finally offer him. A bright, energetic, and ambitious lawyer, Thomas presented a life story that read something like the American dream. Born to a poor black family in rural Georgia, raised by independent and hard-working grandparents who instilled in him a sense of self-discipline, pride, and hard work, Thomas excelled in academics and graduated from Yale Law School. Service on the staff of Missouri's Senator John Danforth brought him to Washington and led to his total immersion in politics. A bright conservative, Thomas stood out among the legions of ambitious and talented men and women who thrived in Washington, D.C., during the Reagan era, and he quickly rose within the conservative ranks. He held an Assistant Secretary position in the Department of Education and then was named by President Reagan to head the Equal Employment Opportunity Commission.

Thomas's tenure at EEOC was not without controversy, for those were controversial times in Washington. He endorsed President Reagan's position on civil rights and affirmative action issues, which critics said contradicted the purposes of his office. Thomas countered that his record in defense of equal employment was outstanding. In 1988 he was appointed by President Reagan to a seat on the Court of Appeals for the District of Columbia. He replaced Robert H. Bork.

In his public presentations and writings, Thomas had expressed an interest in "natural law" and seemed to argue that constitutional interpretation should somehow be tied to an appreciation for it. His opponents would pounce on this and would attempt to portray Thomas as a potential judicial wild card; a judge whose jurisprudence had no firm foundation and who might go off in any of several directions once seated on the Supreme Court. They would also turn to his record as an administrator and argue that while at EEOC Thomas had opposed many of the policies he had been appointed to enforce and promote. They would point out also that Thomas had only limited experience as a judge, far too little for anyone appointed to replace Thurgood Marshall.

For his part, Thomas worked hard preparing for the hearings. For much of the summer he was coached by members of the Administration. His White House handlers trained him to evade Senators' questions and to refer to his humble origins and impressive career as much as possible—the "Pinpoint, Georgia strategy," as it would come to be known. The goal was to deny Thomas's opponents anything substantive to throw at him. While Thomas worked with his "murder boards" and rehearsed for the hearings, he also traveled the corridors of the Senate with his senatorial sponsor and patron, John Danforth, who would be his most valuable asset during the confirmation debate. Administration officials had learned during the Souter confirmation what the value of a Senate sponsor could be. Danforth lobbied his colleagues hard for Thomas.

As the hearings began, members of the Administration felt their strategy would pay off. For several days Thomas worked the Judiciary Committee, following the directions his handlers had given him. He adamantly refused to go on the record concerning specific legal and constitutional issues he might confront as a Justice. He tried to dispel the argument that his "natural law jurisprudence" made his approach to constitutional interpretation shapeless and without focus, while simultaneously seeking to convince the Senators that he had no rigid constitutional idealogy. When members of the committee attempted to pin Thomas down on *Roe* v. *Wade,* he evaded them, awkwardly. The case had been decided during his final year at Yale Law School, yet he asserted that he had not really given it much thought. Indeed, he went so far as to suggest he had never even discussed it.

As the hearings adjourned, it seemed Thomas would be confirmed. His performance had not been stellar, but because he lacked the "paper trail" of a Bork, his opponents had been unable to find ammunition sufficient to derail the confirmation. While Thomas had not come across as well as Souter, he had not shot himself in the foot either. Officials within the White House felt sure their strategy had succeeded.

Within days of the end of the hearings, however, word was leaked to the media that someone had accused Thomas of sexual harassment on the job and that the members of the committee had looked into the allegations but had decided not to pursue them. The truth is that rumors of sexual harassment had floated around the nominee all summer, but the Democratic staff on Capitol Hill had been unable to get anyone to go on the record about it. At one point the FBI interviewed an accuser, Anita Hill, but she was adamant about remaining anonymous and refused to confront Thomas about the issue. As the summer progressed and it appeared Thomas's chances for confirmation had improved, pressure was applied to Hill to go public. She continued to seek a middle course: She wanted the issue exposed, but she did not want to be identified or to confront Thomas directly. After the hearings were adjourned, someone leaked specific information about the accusations to the press, apparently in a last-ditch effort to derail the nomination.

As the story began to take shape, the accusations became public, as did the identity of Hill, a former employee of the EEOC who had worked for Thomas when he was director and now taught law at the University of Oklahoma. Within days after the story broke, both Thomas and the Judiciary Committee came under intense public scrutiny. New hearings were scheduled to focus on the allegations.

For three days in October 1991 the nation looked on as the accuser and the accused responded to questions from the Senate Judiciary Committee. Witnesses were ushered before the committee in an attempt to shed some light on the issue. It came down to a matter of credibility, as Hill and Thomas offered their versions of what had or had not transpired. The topic of sexual harassment and gender discrimination quickly came to dominate the media, eclipsing every other story. The very legitimacy of the Senate came under attack as critics pointed out that only two women served in that chamber and asserted that the members of the Judiciary Committee "just don't get it."

Thomas, departing from the script prepared by his handlers and in a fit of righteous indignation, lectured the members of the committee and accused them of participating in a "high tech lynching for uppity blacks. . . ."

In the end Thomas was confirmed by the narrowest of margins. His accuser returned to Oklahoma. The truth behind the allegations was never confirmed. The reputations of all involved in the episode were severely tarnished. The following November five women were elected to the Senate.

EPILOGUE

During the twelve years of the Reagan and Bush presidencies, more individuals were appointed to the federal courts than during any other period in American political history. Reagan alone appointed three individuals to the Supreme Court, 83 to the courts of appeals, and over 300 to the district courts—a total of 389 judges out of a potential in the federal judiciary of 740, or 52 percent. President Bush appointed more than 190 men and women to the federal appeals and district courts during his tenure in office. Together, Reagan and Bush shaped the federal judiciary. Only Franklin Roosevelt, who appointed close to 75 percent of the judges within the federal system at that time, comes close in influencing the judiciary. More important, during the Reagan and Bush years the most sophisticated system ever devised for identifying and nominating candidates for federal judgeships was created, while the lower federal courts became something of a breeding ground for judicial appointments. Bush, for example, often nominated district court judges to appeals court positions, and Souter and Thomas had served on appeals courts before being nominated for the Supreme Court, as had the Reagan appointees Kennedy and Scalia.

The character of confirmation politics changed, perhaps forever, during the Reagan–Bush years. The history of advice and consent shows that for a significant amount of opposition to be generated to a nominee it is necessary for two factors to be present: First, there must be strong emotional issues that will capture and excite the public; second, those issues must be portrayed in a concrete way that relates clearly and directly to the nominee in a personal, rather than an abstract, way. During Rehnquist's confirmation hearings in 1971 to be an Associate Justice, the issue of his conservatism was used in an abstract and general way; it was not enough to block him. In 1986 the Senate did not take that chance; its ideological opposition to Rehnquist's elevation to become Chief Justice was personalized in the extreme. During the 1986 hearings there was no longer any doubt that a considerable number in the Senate, even a Republican Senate weighing a nomination by a Republican President, were determined to ascertain whether Rehnquist's personal views were generally good and acceptable in a member of the highest court.

By 1987, when Judge Bork's turn came, the opposition had honed its skills to an even sharper edge. The ideological campaign against Bork was undertaken full tilt from day one. The ACLU went so far as to oppose him publicly, even though it had concluded that the 1971 campaign against Rehnquist had been a mistake.

The fact that George Bush's two nominees to the Supreme Court were confirmed—in Clarence Thomas's case, only after a difficult and bitter struggle—says more about the character of the nominations the President made than it does about the character of the opposition they encountered in the Senate. David Souter was chosen because of his potential for confirmation; the lessons of Rehnquist and Bork were enlightening. Clarence Thomas was chosen because Bush and his advisers knew that the Senate would have a difficult time opposing a qualified minority nominee to take Thurgood Marshall's place. The fact that the nomination almost went down to defeat suggests just how fragile that strategy was, as well as the lengths to which the opposition is willing to go to defeat a nomination.

But perhaps the most enduring lesson of the Reagan–Bush appointments is *not* about Senate opposition. Instead, it concerns Justices' motivations. Few Justices can avoid the temptations of extraconstitutional jurisprudence, now that history has opened that Pandora's Box. Even the elaborate system of judicial selection that Reagan and Bush engineered could not guarantee that each individual named to the courts would subscribe to the vision of judicial restraint embraced by the White House. Initially the Court's decision in *DeShaney* suggested that a transformation of the judiciary might very well have come to pass. However, within a year it became apparent that earlier predictions that the Court was "turning right" were premature. Ironically, it was the two Justices who had received the least scrutiny by the Senate and who had been chosen by the White House primarily out of concern for confirmability who undermined the transformation sought by Reagan and Bush.

CHAPTER SIX

HOW GREAT A REVOLUTION?

For the twelve years of their combined presidencies, Ronald Reagan and George Bush dedicated themselves to stemming the tide of judicial activism. Not only at the Supreme Court level but all the way down to the district courts, attention was paid to what potential nominees thought about the nature and extent of the judicial power they might be called upon to exercise. Some of the best minds in their Administrations were devoted to the task of picking judges. In the Reagan years the Office of Legal Policy in the Department of Justice took the lead; for Bush, the task was given over to the White House Counsel's office in the White House itself. It was as close to a scientific process of judicial selection as the country had ever seen. Through careful scrutiny of what a potential judge had written or said, it was believed, the right sort of judges would be brought to fill the federal bench, hence a proper understanding of constitutionalism would be restored to the courts. The judicial excesses associated with the Warren Court would become a thing of the distant past. Few cases gave as strong a sign of the success of the process as *DeShaney* v. *Winnebago County Department of Social Services*. When the decision was handed down during the first month of George Bush's term, everything seemed to be on the right track. But appearances would prove deceiving.

The basic premise of the Reagan and Bush Administrations when it came to judicial selection was that there were clear—dependably clear—juridical differences between an Anthony Kennedy or David Souter on the one hand, and a Harry Blackmun or John Paul Stevens on the other. What was never taken with enough seriousness was the fact that in today's world nominees may have more in common than at first meets the eye.

What may appear to be deeply rooted intellectual or philosophical differences as to the nature and extent of judging may very well in truth be merely ideological differences, more superficial than expected. Judicial philosophies may differ over ends but converge as to means. And what draws them together is a common acceptance of the idea that there is a substantive element to the meaning of due process of law. Indeed, when it comes to substantive due process, there is not a single dissenter on the Supreme Court. Scalia and Rehnquist, no less than Blackmun and Stevens or Souter and Kennedy, continue to reaffirm the doctrine without hesitation.[1] The only interesting question is what this group or that will allow to pass as fulfilling the substantive meaning of due process of law.

Just how short-lived the hopes generated by the Court's opinion in *DeShaney* would be become clear on June 29, 1992. On that day the newly constituted and presumably juridically conservative Court handed down its long-awaited opinion in *Planned Parenthood of Southeastern Pennsylvania* v. *Casey.* The most recent abortion case, it was widely hoped and feared that the Court would use the occasion to overturn *Roe* v. *Wade,* the great doctrinal shadow under which it had been so long laboring. No case had come to mean more to the revolution in constitutional law promised by Reagan and Bush than this 1973 decision. Indeed, *Roe* had ceased to be merely another case in law; it had become nothing less than a metaphor for the politics of the times. Since the Court had handed down *Roe* on a 7–2 vote, it had subsequently nibbled away at it: Later cases had seen the majority willing to uphold the abortion right shrink to 6–3 in *Thornburgh* v. *American College of Obstetricians and Gynecologists* (1986) and finally to 5–4 in *Webster* v. *Reproductive Health Services* (1989). All bets were that *Roe's* time had run out. But in *Casey,* the Court not only failed to overrule *Roe* but it went out of its way to reaffirm the "essential holding" of the case in an opinion written by Justices O'Connor, Kennedy, and Souter.

The deepest significance of the opinion in *Casey* has nothing to do with abortion. Rather, its importance lies in the radical theory of judging put forward by the three so-called advocates of judicial restraint. It is not too much to say that the opinion by O'Connor,

Kennedy, and Souter is far more expansive than anything ever proffered by such dyed-in-the-wool activists as William O. Douglas and William J. Brennan. In its essentials, the *Casey* plurality opinion goes beyond any notion of judging that ever came out of the Warren Court in its heyday. It is, in effect, the radical extension of one of that Court's most troubling opinions, *Cooper* v. *Aaron* (1958), but *Casey* is an opinion that would never have been able to get through the Warren Court itself.

The issue presented to the Court in *Cooper* v. *Aaron* involved the enforcement of its decisions in *Brown* v. *Board of Education of Topeka, Kansas*,[2] of 1954 and 1955, which had ordered that state-supported school systems had to be desegregated with "all deliberate speed." Three days after the desegregation case was handed down, the District School Board of Little Rock, Arkansas, had undertaken to implement a desegregation plan, and that plan had won the approval, as demanded in *Brown*, of the United States District Court. While Little Rock was moving ahead to desegregate its schools, especially Central High School, state authorities were moving to thwart the Court's decree. In November 1956 the State Constitution was amended to command the Arkansas General Assembly to oppose "in every Constitutional manner the un-Constitutional desegregation decisions of May 17, 1954, and May 31, 1955, of the United States Supreme Court." Following the new constitutional dictate, the General Assembly passed laws relieving children from compulsory attendance at racially mixed public schools and establishing a State Sovereignty Commission.

Still, Little Rock persevered and arranged for nine black students to enroll in Central High in September 1957. At this, Governor Orval Faubus dispatched the Arkansas National Guard to surround and place Central High "off limits" to the black students. The Governor had acted on his own initiative; Little Rock had not requested any such action. On September 4 the National Guard "acting pursuant to the Governor's order stood shoulder to shoulder at the school grounds and thereby forcibly prevented the 9 . . . students from entering." At the behest of the U.S. Attorney and the U.S. Attorney General, the District Court granted a preliminary injunction on September 20 enjoining the Governor and the National Guard from preventing the students'

attendance at Central High. The next morning, under the protection of the Little Rock Police Department and the Arkansas State
Police, the students entered the high school. Because of increasing
disturbances and demonstrations near the school, however, they
were removed early. On September 25 the President sent federal
troops to Central High to ensure the peaceful attendance of the
nine black students; the troops remained until November 27.
After that date the federal troops were replaced by federalized
National Guardsmen, who remained in place through the school
year.

Given the confusions wrought by Governor Faubus and his mo-
bilization of the National Guard, and the subsequent confronta-
tions between angry crowds and the troops and police there to
protect the students, the School Board and the Superintendent of
Schools sought to postpone their desegregation program; they
asked the District Court for a two-and-one-half-year respite during which the nine students would be sent back to segregated
schools. The District Court granted the Board's request insofar as
it found that the students' attendance for the past year had been
accompanied by "chaos, bedlam, and turmoil." The students appealed to the Eighth Circuit Court of Appeals; the Court of
Appeals reversed the District Court. The Supreme Court granted
certiorari and convened in Special Term on August 28, 1958, in
order to reach a judgment in time for the opening of the school
year; on September 12 the Court voted unanimously to affirm the
judgment of the Court of Appeals.

The logic of the Court was simple: Decisions of the Supreme
Court of the United States cannot be thwarted by the actions of
state officials. Yet, as clear as the issue was to the Court, it was just
as clear how thin might be the political ice on which it was skat-
ing. The Court could not risk a divided opinion, nor could it
chance going so far that it would further fuel the political confla-
gration that could engulf the rest of the Southern states, where
massive resistance to *Brown* was continuing to grow. In order to
speak with a voice at once consistent and strong, Chief Justice
Warren carefully orchestrated a unanimous opinion, as he had also
done, and for the same reasons, in the original *Brown* decision. In
Cooper he went even farther and at the suggestion of Justice

Frankfurter had all nine Justices affix their names to the opinion of the Court. Warren wanted to leave no room for doubt that his Court was of one mind on this issue.[3] The Court's order to desegregate was to be obeyed, and the rule of law would not yield the moral ground to crude force. However well intentioned the Little Rock officials had been in seeking to delay their desegregation plan, the scheme had to proceed as scheduled. For Little Rock, "all deliberate speed" meant now.

There would have been no objection to the generally sound premise that the decrees of courts of law must be enforced had not Warren taken his Court yet further. It was not enough to leave it at the simple proposition that decrees had to be enforced; Warren sought to expand the grounds on which the power of the Court to see its decrees fulfilled would rest. Asserting that he was only reciting "some basic constitutional propositions which are settled doctrine," the opinion of the Court posited a radical new notion of the status of judicial decisions; the Court in *Cooper* elevated its pronouncements to the same level as the Constitution itself. Thereafter decisions of the Court were to be deemed the supreme law of the land.

> Article VI of the Constitution makes the Constitution the "supreme Law of the Land." In 1803, Chief Justice John Marshall, speaking for a unanimous Court, referring to the Constitution as "the fundamental and paramount law of the nation," declared in the notable case of *Marbury* v. *Madison* . . . that "It is emphatically the province and duty of the judicial department to say what the law is." This decision declared the basic principle that the federal judiciary is supreme in the exposition of the Constitution, and that principle has ever since been respected by this Court and the Country as a permanent and indispensable feature of our constitutional system. It follows that the interpretation of the Fourteenth Amendment enunciated by this Court in the *Brown* case is the supreme law of the land, and Art. VI of the Constitution makes it of binding effect on the States "any Thing in the Constitution or Laws of any State to the Contrary notwithstanding."[4]

The problem began with what Warren saw fit to omit from his summary of Marshall's famous opinion in *Marbury*. In that case,

in which Marshall gave constitutional life to the premises of constitutional review first articulated by Alexander Hamilton in *The
Federalist*,[5] he also, following Hamilton's lead, emphasized that it
was in the existence of a *written* Constitution that America's best
hope lay. Not only did Marshall hold that a written constitution is
"the greatest of improvements on political institutions," but, more
important from the perspective of Warren's opinion in *Cooper*, he
added that such a written constitution was to be understood as "a
rule for courts as well as for legislatures." And while the Constitution itself provided that supremacy in relation to the States
extended to "the Laws of the United States which shall be made in
Pursuance" of the Constitution, it made no mention of the decisions of the federal courts, not even those of the Supreme Court.[6]

By elevating its opinions to the same status as the
Constitution, the Court in *Cooper* transformed the traditional
understanding of the distinction that both common sense and
political theory draw between the Constitution and constitutional
law. Marshall's most basic premises about the nature of constitutional government were silently but surely dismissed from the
Court's calculus. *Cooper* was not the fulfillment of *Marbury* but
rather its perversion.

Such *hubris* as that in *Cooper* is only rarely displayed with such
clarity on the part of the Court. More often than not the Justices
seek to conceal this same understanding by appeals to and invocations of the traditional trappings of constitutional restraint. Yet
explicit or not, the same sentiment had been growing within the
ranks of the Warren Court in its dedication to scrapping precedent after precedent with abandon. Nor would that notion of judicial power disappear when the Warren Court passed into
history. The judicial cat was out of the constitutional bag. Still, it
would take nearly a quarter of a century for the Court once
again to proclaim itself the moral guardian of the republic. When
it did, the proclamation would not be couched in tones of
Warren Court liberalism, but in the rhetoric of the Reagan
Revolution by judges who found themselves so intellectually en-
tangled in precedents that they could not—or would not—free
themselves. The proclamation would come in *Casey*, but the

stage for what would occur in *Casey* was set three years before in *Webster* v. *Reproductive Health Services.*

ABORTION AND THE POLITICS OF JUDICIAL POWER

In 1989 the Court handed down its decision in *Webster* v. *Reproductive Health Services,* a Missouri case that raised the question of how far the states might go in regulating, as opposed to prohibiting, abortion. The issue of whether *Roe* was rightly decided was not, strictly speaking, before the Court.[7] The decision was 5–4 in favor of the Missouri regulations with the predictable liberal bloc of Blackmun, Brennan, Marshall, and Stevens arguing that such regulations impinged on the abortion right and were therefore unconstitutional. Rehnquist and White (the original dissenters in *Roe*) were joined in upholding the regulations by Kennedy, O'Connor, and Scalia. Only Justice Scalia was willing to go so far as to say that *Roe* was beyond the constitutional pale and should be explicitly overruled by the Court. O'Connor, in direct opposition to Scalia, underscored her continuing commitment to the principle inherent in *Roe.* Thus while regulation of abortion was now clearly to be tolerated, the question remained of how much would be too much; at what point would regulation of abortion be seen by the Court as undermining the abortion right itself?

In a plurality opinion, Chief Justice Rehnquist went as far as he was politically able to go within the Court toward getting rid of *Roe.* There is little doubt that had he had the votes he needed he would not have hesitated in overruling the vexatious case; as he would later make clear in his dissent in *Casey,* he had never wavered in his disregard for *Roe.* It was simply bad law. The most he could accomplish in *Webster* was to abandon what to many seemed the essence of *Roe,* a judicially created trimester formula against which abortion regulations had to be measured. It was not an insubstantial achievement on the part of the Chief Justice, but it was a far cry from simply overruling the abortion case.

Justice Blackmun was predictably outraged but unpredictably vitriolic in his unfettered denunciation not only of the opinion but of the Chief Justice himself. To Blackmun the opinion was "deceptive," "callous," and "disingenuous"; all told, it was a "tortured effort." It was nothing less than "a radical reversal of the law of abortion" that aimed at nothing short of the "evisceration" of the right to choose. Not only was the "newly minted standard . . . circular and totally meaningless," but by refusing to confront the deepest issues—the right to privacy posited by *Griswold* v. *Connecticut* and the abortion right itself—the opinion of the Chief Justice was guilty of "cowardice and illegitimacy." Such a "dramatic retrenchment" of the Court's abortion jurisprudence, Blackmun continued, could occur only through the Court's "distorting the statute" at issue and abandoning all "traditional canons of construction and judicial forbearance." As though all that were not blunt enough, he added that in the plurality opinion "[b]ald assertion masquerades as reasoning."[8]

The essence of the split between Blackmun and Rehnquist came down to their diametrically opposed views of the duties of the Court. For Rehnquist the job of the Justices was not "to remove inexorably 'politically divisive' issues from the ambit of the legislative process, whereby the people through their elected representatives deal with matters of concern to them"; rather, the obligation of the Court was simply "to hold true the balance between that which the Constitution puts beyond the reach of the democratic process and that which it does not."[9] When the Court seeks to resolve issues that are inherently questions more of policy than of constitutional principle, such as the trimester formula in abortion law, "the result [is] a web of legal rules that . . . become increasingly intricate, resembling a code of regulations rather than a body of constitutional doctrine."

For Blackmun, echoing his dissent in *DeShaney* just four months before, the obligations of the Court were far greater, far more moral than Rehnquist was willing to concede. In his view, "the critical elements of countless constitutional doctrines nowhere appear in the Constitution's text." Rather, they are to be created and enforced by the Court. Such doctrines as the trimester formula of *Roe* in a way were inseparable from the constitutional rights involved in such cases; they are "judge-made methods measuring the strength and scope of constitutional rights." The results are often intricate, given the "delicate and complicated" areas of concern with which the Court must deal. This is inevitable because "these careful distinctions reflect the process of constitutional adjudication itself, which is often highly fact specific." For Blackmun the issue was simple—"the rules are intricate because we have remained conscientious in our duty to do justice carefully, especially when fundamental rights rise or fall with our decisions." The reason why "fundamental rights rise or fall" with the decisions of the Court is that, in Blackmun's view, there really is no Constitution distinct from constitutional law. He had noted in the *Thornburgh* case that "constitutional rights do not always have easily ascertainable boundaries"; as a result, "to seek and establish those boundaries remains the special responsibility of the Court."

The predictable Blackmun–Rehnquist feud paled in comparison with the debate between two conservatives, O'Connor and Scalia. Quoting from her dissenting opinion in *Akron* v. *Akron Center for Reproductive Health,* O'Connor urged once again a new standard for the constitutionality of abortion regulations—"a regulation imposed on a lawful abortion is not unconstitutional unless it unduly burdens the right to seek an abortion."[10] The standard was to be an "undue burden" test. Precisely what was implied in Justice O'Connor's notion of an "undue burden" was not at all clear on the face of it. Obviously the standard was one so flexible as to be known only to the Court; it lacked the certitude hoped for in principles enunciated by the Court, especially in the most divisive cases. The one thing that was clear was that O'Connor was not willing to see *Roe* overruled.

Scalia was outraged by what he saw as O'Connor's blatant intellectual weakness. The idea that the Court should not reconsider *Roe,* as O'Connor had argued, because of a "fundamental rule of judicial restraint," was a view, fumed Scalia, that "cannot be taken seriously."[11] Indeed, O'Connor herself had repeatedly violated her own rule of avoiding constitutional issues where possible. When it came to *Roe* there was more going on in O'Connor's rationale than judicial restraint, Scalia contended. The result of such vacillation from case to case did a great deal of damage to the proper

role of the Court in American politics and society. Such an "inde-
cisive decision" as that offered by the Court in *Webster*, Scalia
warned, sent the wrong message to the public; it politicized the
Court in the public imagination.

> The outcome of today's case will doubtless be heralded as a tri-
> umph of judicial statesmanship. It is not that unless it is statesman-
> like needlessly to prolong this Court's self-awarded sovereignty
> over a field where it has little proper business since the answer to
> most of the cruel questions posed are political and not juridical—a
> sovereignty which therefore quite properly, but to the great dam-
> age of the Court, makes it the object of the sort of organized pub-
> lic pressure that political institutions in a democracy ought to
> receive.[12]

If, as Scalia seemed to fear, O'Connor's ambiguous formulation
were to find majority favor within the Court, the issue of abortion
would become an even greater ideological quagmire for the
Justices. They could not hope to extricate themselves from the ongoing constitutional confusions spawned by the abortion controversy, because in each and every case it would be up to the Justices
to weigh the circumstances and render a decision. Scalia's main
objection to this was that it was not constitutional law but public
policy-making. And in that, he argued, the Court had no business
dabbling. To do so would be to exhaust its moral capital by seeking to resolve a social issue that was not susceptible to judicial resolution.

Whatever the intellectual infirmities of the Court's decision in
Webster, when it came to the states' power to deal with abortion, it
was a new and more liberal world. *Webster* gave a green light to
the states to try to pass ever more stringent regulations. Pennsylvania did just that. At issue in *Casey* were five provisions of the
Pennsylvania Abortion Control Act of 1982, as amended in 1988
and 1989. The challenged provisions required a twenty-four-hour
waiting period during which the woman would be provided with
information concerning abortion before she could give her informed consent; the informed consent of at least one parent in the
case of a minor seeking an abortion; that a woman seeking an
abortion must sign a statement indicating that she has informed

her husband of the decision to abort; and that those facilities per-
forming abortions be subject to certain reporting requirements.
Five abortion clinics and one physician brought suit in district
court before any of the provisions took effect, seeking an injunction against their enforcement. The District Court issued a preliminary injunction and, after a brief bench trial, declared all
provisions unconstitutional under *Roe* v. *Wade.* On appeal, the
Third Circuit Court of Appeals upheld all the provisions with the
exception of the husband notification requirement. The Supreme
Court granted certiorari in order to provide the lower federal
courts and the courts and legislatures of the several states with
"guidance as they seek to address this subject in conformance with
the Constitution."[13]

Between *Webster* and *Casey* had come a change on the Court itself. Sitting now in the places of the two most ardent liberals,
William Brennan and Thurgood Marshall, were George Bush's
two appointees, David Souter and Clarence Thomas. Having
learned the lessons of the Bork confirmation battle well, neither
had tipped his hand as to how he viewed abortion as a matter of
constitutional law. While most court watchers were fairly certain
that Justice Thomas was opposed to *Roe* and would be willing to
overrule it, few were ready to bet their rent money on how Souter
would vote. Part of the problem with Souter was that he had long
been a state court judge, like Justice O'Connor. Because a great
deal of state court business is a matter of common law adjudication, there is a greater willingness on the part of many state court
judges to abide by precedents while trimming only occasionally at
the margins. As O'Connor had demonstrated, she had taken that
state court predisposition with her to the Supreme Court; it was
likely that Souter had, too. During his first term, the enigmatic
Souter had not been much given to publicly exposing his jurisprudential views.

Thomas, unlike Souter, had not held back during his first term,
the term *Casey* was on the docket. He had unblushingly voted
with Scalia and Rehnquist in most cases that had come down by
the time *Casey* was decided. In two cases Thomas disagreed with
Rehnquist, and in at least one, Thomas had to go it alone, staking
out a position even more juridically conservative than either

Rehnquist or Scalia. In *Hudson* v. *McMillan* Thomas split with
Rehnquist and managed to bring Scalia along with him on the
point that a prisoner beaten by guards had not suffered harm serious enough to trigger the protections of the Cruel and Unusual
Punishment Clause.[14] In particular, Thomas found Justice
O'Connor's opinion for the Court not only "unconvincing" and
"unpersuasive" but at odds with the Court's own precedents; the
jurisprudential implications were "sweeping." O'Connor had
abandoned any pretense of there being an objective standard to be
applied in Cruel and Unusual Punishment cases. Henceforth,
Thomas warned, there would be only the troubling standard of
judicial subjectivity. To Thomas, O'Connor's view derived from
the wrong-headed belief that "the Federal Constitution must address all ills in our society." The effect of the Court's opinion was,
he said, to transform the Eighth Amendment into "a National
Code of Prison Regulation" at the expense of the state courts,
where such a claim might be properly addressed under tort law.[15]

The second case was even more striking. In *Dawson* v. *Delaware*
Thomas went it alone—the solitary dissent from an opinion written by Chief Justice Rehnquist himself.[16] In *Dawson* the Court
overturned a state murder conviction on First Amendment
grounds because at the sentencing phase, in an attempt to convince the jury of Dawson's bad character, the prosecutor had introduced the fact that the murderer had been a member of the
white supremacist Aryan Brotherhood gang while in prison. Such
membership was irrelevant to Dawson's character and should not
have been introduced without more elaborate proof of its relevance to the case at hand, Rehnquist argued. (Dawson was white,
as was his victim.)

Thomas objected insofar as there was no similar restriction on
the sorts of memberships the defendant could introduce to bolster
his image; the Court thus handicapped the prosecutors with no
real reason to be found in the Constitution. What was more,
membership in a racist prison gang struck Thomas as the sort of
thing a jury could properly weigh as to Dawson's character; it said
something about him. Thomas further objected because he could
not see what the First Amendment had to do with the case at all.
Even if there was a real question of relevance, that was properly a

Due Process Clause problem. Thus, to hold as the Court did was to do violence to the Constitution on two fronts. The young conservative simply could not go along.

The questions about how Souter might vote in *Casey* were brought into even sharper focus by emerging questions about where Justice Kennedy might be heading jurisprudentially. At the time of his appointment there was general agreement among those who had pushed his nomination with Reagan and those who had only tolerated it that he would be generally "solid" on most issues. After his first term, some in the press had derisively dubbed him a "Bork without brains," and by most counts that assessment seemed more cruel than inaccurate. After all, here was a man who had been pushed on President Ford in the first instance by Reagan and Meese; he had to be okay. Yet there had been signs that Kennedy was intellectually adrift on the Court. It seemed to some that his course on the Court would be determined by the stronger forces around him. In the notorious flag-burning case of the term before, *Texas* v. *Johnson,* Scalia and Rehnquist had parted company; their split seemed to leave Kennedy spinning.[17] While he joined Scalia in voting to hold unconstitutional the Texas statute that forbade flag desecration, he could not do so with a clear conscience. He had seen fit to write a strange concurring opinion that seemed as much apology as opinion. Kennedy, many began to worry, was up for grabs.

The first flicker of Justice Kennedy's desire to move out of Scalia's shadow began during the same term as *DeShaney* v. *Winnebago County* in the case of *Michael H.* v. *Gerald D.* That case found the Court confronting the claim that California's law mandating that a child born to a married woman living with her husband is presumed to be the child of the marriage violated the Due Process Clause. Michael, the biological father of the child, Victoria, born to Gerald's wife, Carol, claimed a "liberty interest" in maintaining his "established parental relationship with Victoria."[18] In a judgment joined by Rehnquist, O'Connor, Kennedy, and Stevens, the Court upheld the California statute against Michael's challenge. The significance of the majority opinion written by Justice Scalia was his insistence that a "liberty interest" for purposes of the Due Process Clause had to be not only

" 'fundamental' (a concept that, in isolation, is hard to objectify), but also . . . an interest traditionally protected by our society."[19] To demand that such claims of liberties must be "rooted in history and tradition" would serve to curb the Court's ideological wanderlust when it came to the Due Process Clause, Scalia thought.[20]

From his survey of constitutional and legal history, Scalia concluded that the presumption embraced in the California statute was traditionally sound; history precluded the Court from upsetting the law. To Justice Brennan, Scalia's "exclusively historical analysis portends a significant and unfortunate departure from our prior cases and from sound constitutional decisionmaking."[21] Brennan found tradition to be no less "malleable" a standard than any other the Court had relied on in the past; it was illusory to think that tradition and history placed "a discernible border around the Constitution."[22] Better than any misplaced reliance on "natural parents" and "unitary families," Brennan dissented, it would be far more agreeable to constitutional law and common sense to measure whether "parenthood" was a liberty interest properly falling within the ambit of the Due Process Clause. Scalia's opinion, Brennan concluded, constituted nothing less than a "reworking of our interpretive approach."[23]

Scalia sought to rebut Brennan's standard by pointing to its inherent arbitrariness:

> We do not understand why, having rejected our focus upon the societal tradition regarding the natural father's rights vis-à-vis a child whose mother is married to another man, Justice Brennan would choose to focus instead upon "parenthood." Why should the relevant category not be even more general—perhaps "family relationships"; or "personal relationships"; or even "emotional attachments in general"?

Then Scalia drove an intellectual wedge between his view of the process of interpretation and that shared by O'Connor and Kennedy:

> Though the dissent has no basis for the level of generality it would select, we do: We refer to the most specific level at which a relevant

tradition protecting, or denying protection to, the asserted right can be identified. If for example, there were no societal tradition, either way, regarding the rights of the natural father of a child adulterously conceived, we would have to consult, and (if possible) reason from, the traditions regarding natural fathers in general. But there is such a more specific tradition [dealing with children adulterously conceived], and it unqualifiedly denies protection to such a parent.[24]

It is essential for a judge to consult "the most specific tradition available" in order to keep the judge reined in from (in the words of Chancellor Kent) "roaming at large in the trackless field of his own imagination." General standards are inherently vague and provide only "imprecise guidance" to a judge; "they permit judges to dictate rather than discern society's views." This was hardly a radical proposition; it was simple common sense, Scalia insisted: A "rule of law that binds neither by text nor by any particular, identifiable tradition is no rule of law at all."[25] To ignore the necessity of specificity in tradition is to encourage arbitrariness in judging—nothing more, nothing less.

Justice O'Connor, joined by Justice Kennedy, could not tolerate the shackles of history Scalia had forged; they dissented only from footnote 6. Not only was Scalia's theory of historical analysis "somewhat inconsistent with our past decisions in this area," O'Connor wrote, but there might need to be a greater flexibility when it comes to choosing the "relevant traditions" upon which to rest a constitutional decision than being limited to "the most specific level." O'Connor and Kennedy did not wish to foreclose a more liberal approach to constitutional adjudication than that which would be allowed by such "a single mode of historical analysis."[26] In a quiet, almost unobtrusive way, Justice Kennedy had tipped his hand. But not until the joint opinion in *Casey* would it become clear exactly what the implications were of Kennedy's joining ranks with O'Connor (and with Brennan and the dissenters on this point) in *Michael H.*

There was yet another worry about Kennedy for those who sought to leave a transformed judiciary as the greatest legacy of Reagan and Bush. He had, by many and frequent reports, become a constant monitor of his image in the press. Unlike Justice

Thomas, who apparently gave up newspapers and the news shows once on the Court, Kennedy not only did not do so, but kept up with how he was viewed in the public prints. No doubt being branded a "Bork without brains" did not do much for his self-esteem, and for a public man reputation is all too often everything. Nor was it likely to help keep him tied to the conservatives on the Court when the clerks at the Court dubbed him "Nini," the diminutive of Justice Scalia's nickname, "Nino." Thus Reagan's last pick for the high court looked as though he might very well bend with the winds of popular opinion, however he might see fit to measure them. So taken with bolstering his image was Kennedy that he arranged to allow a reporter from the *California Lawyer* to spend the day with him at the Court—the day *Casey* was to be announced. In the article that appeared in October 1992, "Crossing the Rubicon," the worst fears of those who had pinned so many hopes on the Reagan–Bush Court were confirmed. The reporter noted in his lead, "Anthony Kennedy couldn't have picked a more dramatic moment to declare his independence on the Court."[27] Few on either side of the ideological gulf that was *Roe* v. *Wade* would have argued with that assessment.

There was little doubt that Kennedy recognized the stakes involved in his movement away from Scalia and Rehnquist and into the arms of O'Connor and Souter. Standing before his chambers window, looking down on the friends and foes of *Roe* v. *Wade* who had gathered to await the Court's judgment in *Casey,* Kennedy shared with the reporter in tow an astonishing sentiment. "Sometimes you don't know if you're Caesar about to cross the Rubicon, or Captain Queeg cutting your own tow line."[28] By the end of the day there would be little doubt in the minds of Kennedy's conservative critics: He was no Caesar. Indeed, for some the name Brutus came to mind.

The doubts about just how "solid" Kennedy was had been exacerbated a few weeks before when in the second biggest case of the term, the school prayer case of *Lee* v. *Weisman,* Kennedy had written the opinion—over the dissents of Scalia and Rehnquist—striking down a Rhode Island law allowing nonsectarian prayer at a high school graduation ceremony.[29] Not only had his sudden switch shocked those who thought they could count on him to be consistent with his own earlier church–state decisions, but he had earned himself a new nickname from the clerks for his efforts—"Flipper."[30] *Casey*, however, went beyond anything those who doubted him had come to fear from Kennedy. Little did they know that he had embarked on some sort of personal moral journey, coming to rest finally as a great admirer of Thurgood Marshall, a Justice whom Kennedy had come to celebrate for his "willingness to raise the moral issues which all decent societies must explore and attempt to resolve, whether through the courts or some other means."[31] With his participation in the opinion in *Casey*, it seemed, the important distinction between "the courts" and "some other means" had been abandoned.

The line between courts and the other political means of resolving what Scalia had called in *Webster* the "cruel questions" raised by the abortion issue had been obliterated in the joint opinion of O'Connor, Souter, and Kennedy in two ways: First, by seeking to infuse the notion of due process of law with an even greater substantive meaning; second, by enlarging and thus redefining the principle of *stare decisis*, the ancient common law doctrine that settled law should not be lightly changed. The end result was a new conception of judging, one that was willing to proclaim that under the Constitution it was up to the Court to clear a moral path through the often tangled political underbrush of American society—and up to the American people to follow. "The root of American governmental power is revealed most clearly in the instance of the power conferred by the Constitution upon the judiciary and specifically upon this Court."[32] Rising to heights of philosophical rapture, the opinion concluded with this remarkable revision of American constitutionalism:

> Like the character of an individual, the legitimacy of the Court must be earned over time. So, indeed, must be the character of a nation of people who aspire to live according to the rule of law. Their belief in themselves as such a people is not readily separable from their understanding of the Court invested with the authority to decide their constitutional cases and speak before all others for their constitutional ideals. If the Court's legitimacy should be undermined, then, so would the country be in its very ability to see it-

self through its constitutional ideals. The Court's concern with legitimacy is not for the sake of the Court but for the sake of the Nation to which it is responsible.[33]

The essence of this stunning power of the Court to define the constitutional ideals of the people lay in the Court's self-claimed power to define the meaning of "liberty" as used in the Due Process Clause of the Fourteenth Amendment. The view presented by the joint opinion in *Casey* was as expansive as anything ever offered by the Court:

> Constitutional protection of the woman's decision to terminate her pregnancy derives from the Due Process Clause of the Fourteenth Amendment. . . . Although a literal reading of the Clause might suggest that it governs only the procedures by which a State may deprive persons of liberty, for at least 105 years, at least since *Mugler* v. *Kansas* . . . the Clause has been understood to contain a substantive component as well.

Echoing Justice Douglas's novel opinion in *Griswold* v. *Connecticut*, the Court went on:

> Neither the Bill of Rights nor the specific practices of States at the time of the adoption of the Fourteenth Amendment marks the outer limits of the substantive sphere of liberty which the Fourteenth Amendment protects.

Thus the Court's moral duty was clear to O'Connor, Souter, and Kennedy:

> The inescapable fact is that adjudication of substantive due process claims may call upon the Court in interpreting the Constitution to exercise that same capacity which by tradition courts have always exercised: reasoned judgment. Its boundaries are not susceptible of expression as a general rule.[34]

With text and intention banished from the Court's constitutional calculations, all that is left in this notion of judging is the

Court's own "reasoned judgment." But with neither constitutional text nor intention a part of the calculation, there is no standard by which to judge how "reasoned" the judgment of the Court is; the justices must simply be taken at their word, and the "thoughtful part of the nation"—those, apparently, who agree with the outcome—will be all the vindication their decision requires.[35] The conclusions reached by the "reasoned judgment" of the joint opinion as to the meaning of liberty under the Due Process Clause of the Fourteenth Amendment was nothing less than a metaphysical extravaganza: "At the heart of liberty is the right to define one's own concept of existence, of meaning, of the universe, and of the mystery of human life."[36]

At the heart of this theory of judging resides the belief that constitutional meaning is fluid and changes with the times, or, as the Court put it, "changed circumstances may impose new obligations."[37] But given the importance of stability in the law, it is essential that the Court change constitutional meaning only once it is made clear by "history's demonstration" that the facts upon which a constitutional interpretation rests were indeed false. Thus a line of cases including *Lochner* v. *New York* and *Adkins* v. *Children's Hospital,* in which the Court created and expanded the doctrine of "liberty of contract," were properly overruled by the Court in *West Coast Hotel* v. *Parrish* not because they rested upon a flawed theory of what the Constitution demanded, but merely because they "rested on fundamentally false factual assumptions about the capacity of a relatively unregulated market to satisfy minimal levels of human welfare."[38] Such mistaken factual assumptions "not only justified but required the new choice of constitutional principle that *West Coast Hotel* announced."[39]

When it came to *Roe* v. *Wade,* there had been no such demonstrable proof that changed circumstances demanded a new constitutional decision. The joint opinion put it bluntly: "After considering the fundamental constitutional questions resolved by *Roe,* principles of institutional integrity, and the rule of *stare decisis,* we are led to conclude this: the essential holding of *Roe* v. *Wade* should be retained and once again reaffirmed."[40] The reasons were few and simple: "No evolution of legal principle has left *Roe's* doctrinal footings weaker than they were in 1973. No development of constitutional law since the case was decided implicitly or explicitly left *Roe* behind as a mere survivor of obsolete constitutional thinking."[41] It is not enough that the central holding of *Roe* has "engendered disapproval"; there are more important social considerations the Court felt obliged to take into account:

> An entire generation has come of age free to assume *Roe*'s concept of liberty in defining the capacity of women to act in society, and to make reproductive decisions; no erosion of principle going to liberty or personal autonomy has left *Roe's* central holding a doctrinal remnant; *Roe* portends no developments at odds with other precedent for the analysis of personal liberty; and no changes of fact have rendered viability more or less appropriate as the point at which the balance of interests tips.[42]

Whether a constitutional precedent stands or falls when viewed again by the Court is determined by "a series of prudential and pragmatic considerations designed to test the consistency of overruling a prior decision with the ideal of the rule of law, and to gauge the respective costs of reaffirming and overruling a prior case."[43] Mere "unprincipled emotional reactions" on the part of the public to a decision are not enough to nudge the Court toward abandoning one of its precedents; there can be no "surrender to political pressure."[44] There must be a good and sufficient reason for the Court to reconsider its earlier work, for "to overrule under fire in the absence of the most compelling reason to reexamine a watershed decision would subvert the Court's legitimacy beyond any serious question."[45] Even though there may be many voices raised in opposition to this decision or that, it is essential that the Court not be moved; it must remain "steadfast" in its commitment to what it has said before as a reward to all those citizens whose commitment to the ideal of the rule of law is "tested by following" those decisions of which they disapprove.[46] Such is the price the Court is willing to pay in order to fulfill its moral duty to posit the truths which the people are duty bound to accept as a matter of blind faith in the Court.

At stake was the power of the Court to perform its necessary functions. To overrule *Roe* would, the Court reasoned, bring it near the brink of disrepute:

> [O]verruling *Roe's* central holding would not only reach an unjustifiable result under principles of *stare decisis,* but would seriously weaken the Court's capacity to exercise the judicial power and to function as the Supreme Court of a Nation dedicated to the rule of law.

The reason was simple, to O'Connor, Souter, and Kennedy:

> [T]he Court's legitimacy depends on making legally principled decisions under circumstances in which their principled character is sufficiently plausible to be accepted by the Nation. . . . People understand that some of the Constitution's language is hard to fathom and that the Court's Justices are sometimes able to perceive significant facts or to understand principles of law that eluded their predecessors and that justify departures from existing decisions. [But] there is . . . a point beyond which frequent overruling would overtax the country's belief in the Court's good faith. . . . There is a limit to the amount of error that can plausibly be imputed to prior courts. . . . The legitimacy of the Court would fade with the frequency of its vacillation.[47]

To overrule *Roe* after so many years would only confuse an already constitutionally befuddled public, a public that had been taught to expect the Court not merely to interpret the law and the Constitution but, in Justice Blackmun's phrase from *Webster,* "to do justice." The point of departure for O'Connor, Souter, and Kennedy was but a simple aphorism that summed up their view of their own power: "Liberty finds no refuge in a jurisprudence of doubt."[48] Lest such an aphorism be thought simplistic, the authors of the joint opinion sought to wrap their astonishing view of constitutional review in the comfortable layers of common law logic. "Our Constitution," O'Connor, Souter, and Kennedy concluded, "is a covenant running from the first generation of Americans to us and then to future generations. It is a coherent succession. Each generation must learn anew that the Constitution's written

terms embody ideas and aspirations that must survive more ages
than one." So the Constitution is not a document understood to
enjoy a textual permanence unless and until changed by the
process of formal amendment; rather, it is a collection of judicial
decisions that have sought to declare the constitutional ideals of
the people for the people and to keep the ideals thus declared in
force for a reasonable length of time—until, that is, a new Court
in a new age can adduce evidence to persuade the people that
such earlier decrees must now yield to new thinking.

As to the issues at hand in *Casey,* O'Connor, Souter, and
Kennedy were willing to uphold all the Pennsylvania regulations
except the spousal notification requirement insofar as it violated
the new test for constitutionality of abortion regulations—Justice
O'Connor's long-sought "undue burden" test. As they put it:
"Only where state regulation imposes an undue burden on a
woman's ability to make this decision does the power of the State
reach into the heart of the liberty protected by the Due Process
Clause. . . . In our view, the undue burden standard is the appropriate means of reconciling the State's interest with the woman's
constitutionally protected liberty."[49]

Blackmun and Stevens predictably concurred with the portions
of the opinion that underscored the Court's commitment to *Roe's*
"central holding" but parted company over which regulations
should actually be allowed to pass constitutional muster under the
"undue burden" test. But Blackmun went further, once again
launching a very personal attack on Chief Justice Rehnquist, who
had, in his dissent, come out forthrightly for overruling *Roe* v.
Wade.[50] To Blackmun's way of thinking, the Chief Justice's understanding of individual rights was "stunted," "cramped," and "narrow," as was his notion of *stare decisis.* Against such a neanderthal
vision of liberty, Blackmun could praise the opinion of O'Connor,
Souter, and Kennedy as nothing less than "an act of personal
courage and constitutional principle." The most shocking aspects
of Blackmun's opinion were, on the one hand, its self-serving tone
and, on the other, its radical politicization of the nomination
process in anticipation of the next vacancy on the Court—presumably his own.

In *Webster* Blackmun had dramatically warned that the plurality opinion by Rehnquist "cas[t] into darkness the hopes and visions of every woman in the country who had come to believe that the Constitution guaranteed her right to exercise some control over her unique ability to bear children."[51] Given the vote in *Webster,* the situation was bleak indeed, in Blackmun's estimation: "All that remained between the promise of *Roe* and the darkness of the plurality was a single, flickering flame."[52] At first blush it was not clear exactly what the aging Justice had in mind by "a single, flickering flame." By the end of his opinion in *Casey* it was very clear: Harry Blackmun was that "single, flickering flame":

> In one sense, the Court's approach is worlds apart from that of the Chief Justice and Justice Scalia. And yet, in another sense, the distance between the two approaches is short—the distance is but a single vote.
>
> I am 83 years old. I cannot remain on this Court forever, and when I do step down, the confirmation process for my successor well may focus on the issue before us today. That, I regret, may be exactly where the choice between the two worlds will be made.[53]

What had so raised Blackmun's ire was Rehnquist's blunt and unapologetic rejection of *Roe:* "We believe that *Roe* was wrongly decided, and that it can and should be overruled consistently with our traditional approach to *stare decisis* in constitutional cases."[54] Oddly enough, there was a certain agreement between Blackmun and Rehnquist, however. In Rehnquist's view, as well as in Blackmun's, the opinion by O'Connor, Souter, and Kennedy had posited a "newly-minted" theory of *stare decisis,* which, while keeping the form of *Roe* v. *Wade,* had all but drained that case of its meaning. But in Rehnquist's view the honorable thing for the Court to do would be admit that and push *Roe* completely from the pages of the *United States Reports.* Rather than admit that the Court got it wrong in *Roe* as a matter of constitutional interpretation, the opinion by O'Connor, Souter, and Kennedy undertook to create an elaborate but creaking structure of *stare decisis* that they thought would give them the best of both worlds—keep *Roe* on the books and thus buy a bit of public peace, and allow the states to regulate abortion up to the point of abolishing it.[55] To Rehnquist, the joint opinion's jerry-rigged scheme of *stare decisis* was "truly novel" and simply contrary to history.[56]

Particularly troubling to Rehnquist was the notion in the joint opinion that somehow the louder the public criticism of one of the Court's decisions, the more firmly entrenched that decision ought to be. The mere fact that the Court had thought it had successfully "call[ed] the contending sides of a national controversy to end their national division by accepting a common mandate rooted in the Constitution" was not to be thought sufficient to stifle future reactions to the opinion, reactions rooted in the belief that the Court, in fact, got it wrong.[57] Just because a decision was "intensely divisive," there was no reason to place it beyond the realm of reconsideration. Not only was such a view novel, it was dangerous. Rehnquist's rejection of this notion echoed Abraham Lincoln's reaction to *Dred Scott* v. *Sandford* more than a century before.

> We believe . . . in obedience to, and respect for the judicial department of government. We think its decisions on Constitutional questions, when fully settled, should control, not only the particular cases decided, but the general policy of the country, subject to be disturbed only by amendments of the Constitution as provided in that instrument itself. But we think the Dred Scott decision is erroneous. We know the court that made it, has often over-ruled its own decisions and we shall do what we can to have it over-rule this. We offer no *resistance* to it.[58]

To argue otherwise, as the joint opinion did, Rehnquist believed, was incorrectly to impute to the Court a political transcendence that was at odds with the republican theory of politics embedded in the Constitution. "Strong and often misguided criticism of a decision should not render the decision immune from reconsideration, lest a fetish for legitimacy penalize freedom of expression."[59]

> Our constitutional watch does not cease merely because we have spoken before on an issue; when it becomes clear that a prior constitutional interpretation is unsound we are obliged to reexamine the question. . . . The Judicial Branch derives its legitimacy, not

from following public opinion, but from deciding by its best constitutional lights whether legislative enactments of the popular branches of government comport with the Constitution. The doctrine of *stare decisis* is an adjunct of this duty, and should be no more subject to the vagaries of public opinion than is the basic constitutional task.[60]

The argument of the joint opinion was nothing more than a ruse—"just as the Court should not respond to . . . protest by retreating from the decision simply to allay the concerns of the protesters, it should likewise not respond by determining to adhere to the decision at all costs lest it *seem* to be retreating under fire."[61]

As for the abortion right itself, in Rehnquist's view the Court had erred in *Roe* by reaching too far and making the right to abortion fundamental as were the rights protected in such cases as *Pierce* v. *Society of Sisters, Meyer* v. *Nebraska,* and *Griswold* v. *Connecticut.* By seeking to replace the existing standard with the new "undue burden" test, the joint opinion only perpetuated the original error and doomed the Court to continue "to impart its own preferences on the States in the form of a complex abortion code."[62] In Rehnquist's view, this is a power the Court clearly "lacks . . . under the Constitution."[63] For this reason, Rehnquist argued, all the provisions of the Pennsylvania code should be upheld as consistent with the Constitution. But that is not to say that they are consistent simply because the Court should approve of such regulations: "Our task is, as always, to decide only whether the challenged provisions of a law comport with the United States Constitution. If, as we believe, these do, their wisdom as a matter of public policy is for the people of Pennsylvania to decide."[64]

This was the essence of Justice Scalia's opinion as well, an opinion joined by Rehnquist, White, and Thomas. The notion that the Court was charged with the task of declaring the constitutional ideals of the people and then demanding that they follow the Justices wherever they might lead was nothing less than a "Nietzschean vision."[65] The theory of judging laid down by O'Connor, Kennedy, and Souter was an unapologetic dismissal of any reliance on text and tradition, Scalia argued, because "the Court does not want to be fettered by any such limitations on its preferences."[66] Putting the substantive issue of abortion to one

side, Scalia saw beneath the facts presented in *Casey* the true import of the joint opinion: "a new mode of constitutional adjudication that relies not upon text and traditional practice to determine
the   law,   but   upon   what   the   Court   calls   'reasoned
judgment' . . . which turns out to be nothing but philosophical
predilection and moral intuition."[67]

At the bottom of Scalia's mocking dissent lay the debate between
him and O'Connor and Kennedy in *Michael H. v. Gerald D.*[68] It was
a question of the role of tradition in constitutional adjudication.
For Scalia, tradition was essential in order to keep the judge tied to
something deeper, something more neutral and objective than his
own personal predilections. While the authors of the joint opinion
confessed that they found such an approach "tempting," that was
not enough to persuade them to harness their powers.[69] It was precisely this dismissal of text and tradition as anchors to judicial opinion that had led to the sad spectacle of public protests being
launched against the Court over the abortion question. After all,
Scalia noted, "[t]exts and traditions are facts to study, not convic-
tions to demonstrate about."[70] As in *Michael H.*, Scalia remained
convinced of "the utter bankruptcy of constitutional analysis deprived of tradition as a validating factor."[71]

It was the absence of any standard outside the judge himself
that made the "undue burden" test announced by O'Connor,
Souter, and Kennedy so dangerous to constitutional adjudication.
By Scalia's reckoning, the standard that regulations must not pose
an "undue burden" on the abortion right "is inherently manipula-
ble."[72] The fact is, Scalia insisted, that the "ultimately standardless
nature of the 'undue burden' inquiry is a reflection of the underlying fact that the concept has no principled or coherent legal
basis."[73] If the purpose of the authors of the joint opinion was, as
they said, to give "guidance" as to how to weigh regulations dealing with abortion, they had sadly—and egregiously—missed their
mark.[74] When it came to the lower federal courts especially, the
opinion offered no guidance at all. The "undue burden" standard,
Scalia warned, would be "as doubtful in application as it is unprincipled in origin."[75] The "inherently standardless" nature of the
"undue burden" test would simply encourage the judge "to give
effect to his personal predilection about abortion."[76] This was not

clarity but confusion. Poking at what he saw as the intellectually soft underbelly of the joint opinion, Scalia pulled no punches: "Reason finds no refuge in this jurisprudence of confusion."[77]

As with Rehnquist, Scalia was "appalled" by the *hubris* displayed by O'Connor, Souter, and Kennedy in their newly woven theory of *stare decisis*.[78] [T]he "notion that we would decide a case differently from the way we otherwise would have in order to show that we can stand firm against public disapproval is frightening."

> It is a bad enough idea, even in the head of someone like me, who believes that the text of the Constitution, and our traditions, say what they say and there is no fiddling with them. But when it is in the mind of a Court that believes the Constitution has an evolving meaning, . . . that the Ninth Amendment's reference to "othe[r]" rights is not a disclaimer, but a charter for action, . . . and that the function of this Court is to "speak before all others for [the people's] constitutional ideals" unrestrained by meaningful text or tradition—then the notion that the Court must adhere to a decision for as long as the decision faces "great opposition" and the Court is "under fire" acquires a character of almost czarist arrogance.[79]

This "new mode of constitutional adjudication" called into question in a most fundamental way the very legitimacy the authors of the joint opinion insisted they were trying to shore up. By seeking to be the initial, if not indeed the sole expounders of the constitutional ideals of the people, the Court in fact supplanted the democratic foundations of American constitutionalism with an unfettered paternalism. In its effort to extricate itself from the mire of abortion, and to settle the divisions of the country with its authoritative decree, the Court's intellectual thrashing only served to have it sucked more deeply into the pit. The "undue burden" test, administered as it would have to be on a case-by-case basis in light of the Court's "reasoned judgment," was nothing more nor less than a "verbal shell game."[80] And while it was meant to "conceal raw judicial policy choices concerning what is 'appropriate' abortion legislation," it would in fact expose the Court ever more to public scrutiny and contempt. After all, Scalia admonished, "the American people are not fools."[81] If constitutional adjudication is going to be merely a matter of policy choices and value judgments, the people have every right to demonstrate and "to protest that we do not implement *their* values instead of *ours*."[82]

For Scalia, the issue was simple: The Court "should get out of this area, where we have no right to be, and where we do neither ourselves nor the country any good by remaining."[83] By the dim light of the joint opinion, the Court could only be doomed to continue its "wanderings in this forsaken wilderness."[84] His point of departure and arrival as a matter of constitutional construction came simply to this: "The States may, if they wish, permit abortion-on-demand, but the Constitution does not require them to do so."[85] The analogy between what the Court was willing to do in *Casey* and what the Taney Court had done in *Dred Scott* v. *Sandford* was to Scalia too obvious to leave unremarked. The theory of judging "contrived" by O'Connor, Souter, and Kennedy called to Scalia's mind the dissent of that earlier age, that of Justice Benjamin Curtis:

> [W]hen a strict interpretation of the Constitution, according to the fixed rules which govern the interpretation of laws, is abandoned, and the theoretical opinions of individuals are allowed to control its meaning, we have no longer a Constitution; we are under the government of individual men, who for the time being have power to declare what the Constitution is, according to their own views of what it ought to mean.[86]

Like Taney and his Court 135 years before, the joint opinion had simply pushed personal predilection off on an unsuspecting public as "reasoned judgment." But the rhetoric could not change the reality. For Scalia and his fellow dissenters in *Casey* the lesson was clear: "The Imperial Judiciary lives."[87]

A CHILL WIND BLOWS

The aftermath of *Planned Parenthood of Southeastern Pennsylvania* v. *Casey* was clear. All that had been so vigorously fought for by Reagan and Bush, all that had been achieved, was suddenly lost. It seemed clear that restricting the reach of a morally overconfident judiciary and restoring the written Constitution to its place of prominence over constitutional law were not in the cards. To those who had thought the revolution in law fomented by Reagan and Bush would succeed (to borrow, with some tinge of irony, the words of Justice Blackmun's dissent in *Webster*), "the signs are evident and very ominous, and a chill wind blows."[88]

The idea that it is the legitimate role of the Supreme Court to seek to give political expression to the moral sentiments presumed to be held by the people, rather than be bound by what Blackmun had derided in his dissent in *DeShaney* v. *Winnebago County* as the "sterile formalism" of written law, had been given new life by the joint opinion by O'Connor, Souter, and Kennedy. Presumed to be primarily the handiwork of Justice Souter (insofar as to reach the opinion they did in *Casey* both O'Connor and Kennedy had to abandon views they had only recently expressed), the joint opinion revealed starkly the power of politics over the direction of the Court, and thereby over the meaning of the Constitution. Had the Bork nomination not been defeated, it is likely that neither Kennedy nor Souter would have been elevated to the Supreme Court. But the Bork nomination did go down in defeat, and because it did conceptions of the nature and extent of judicial power under the Constitution were drastically changed.

The argument "to do justice" is a powerful one; it is hard to argue against it as a matter of constitutional law. It is too easy to denigrate those who try as cold and too detached from the realities of life. The only way to counter the claims of the new constitutional moralists is by citing chapter and verse of the law, be that the law of the Constitution or mere statutes. The result is a one-sided public debate where rhetorically flamboyant claims of justice are met with the deadening recounting of the technical minutiae of the law. It is no contest.

The 1988–89 term of the Court closed with great promise. It was the term that had seen not only *DeShaney* v. *Winnebago County* handed down, but similar decisions in *Webster* v. *Reproductive Health Services* and *Michael H.* v. *Gerald D.* It seemed that there was indeed a revolution afoot, that constitutionalism might be set for a dramatic revival. But then it began to fade almost as quickly as it had begun; the Court was soon back to business as usual. In the end it would be the joint opinion in *Casey* in 1992 that would come to be understood as the truly revolutionary statement by the Court. Judicial activism under the guise of interpreting the Due Process Clauses of the Constitution would henceforth have no real limits. The Court would not allow text or tradition or intention to get in its way of seeking to fulfill its self-proclaimed duty "to do justice."

JUDICIAL SUPREMACY AND THE DECLINE OF POPULAR GOVERNMENT

The facts surrounding the fate of Joshua DeShaney were indisputable and compelling. It is impossible to know of his tragedy and not be moved. Here was a young, innocent life destroyed by a man, his father, lacking any apparent sense of guilt or grief. The State of Wisconsin was, for all intents and purposes, an accomplice. Officials associated with the child welfare system and the child abuse rescue effort may have tried earnestly to act according to well-established rules and procedures, but they failed miserably at accomplishing their true task—protecting the welfare of a child abused by a "parent who became a predator." Justice was not served by the Supreme Court's stinging denial of Joshua's constitutional claim.

But that is the point. As the majority in *DeShaney* noted in the Court's opinion, Joshua's was an "undeniably tragic case." But the tragic circumstances that constituted the facts in the case ran up against the limits of the law and the Constitution, at least in the opinion of six of the Justices. Chief Justice Rehnquist addressed the apparent tension between justice and the Constitution in the closing paragraphs of his majority opinion.

> Judges and lawyers, like other humans, are moved by natural sympathy in a case like this to find a way for Joshua and his mother to receive adequate compensation for the grievous harm inflicted upon them. But before yielding to that impulse, it is well to remember once again that the harm was inflicted not by the State of Wisconsin, but by Joshua's father.

... The people of Wisconsin may well prefer a system of liability
which would place upon the State and its officials the responsibility
for failure to act in situations such as the present one. They may
create such a system, if they do not have it already, by changing the
tort law of the State in accordance with the regular law-making
process. But they should not have it thrust upon them by this
Court's expansion of the Due Process Clause of the Fourteenth
Amendment.[1]

At bottom, the majority on the Court did identify with the minority's sense of shock and injustice at what had happened to
Joshua. For the majority, however, the Constitution did not speak
to the issue, no matter how "unjust" that might seem. The Due
Process Clause of the Fourteenth Amendment, Rehnquist argued,
limits actions by the state. "Its purpose was to protect the people
from the State, not to ensure that the State protected them from
each other." The State of Wisconsin's failure to protect Joshua
from his father simply did not constitute a violation of the Due
Process Clause.

For the minority on the Court, the majority position reflected a
dry and uncaring formalism—a rigid, unbending application of the
law—that was blind to the inherent and compelling injustice that
had transpired. Justice Blackmun was particularly distraught over
Joshua's fate and adamant that the Court get beyond the
Constitution in order to ensure that justice be served. According
to Blackmun, the majority was retreating "into a sterile formalism
which prevents it from recognizing either the facts of the case before it or the legal norms that should apply to those facts."[2] The
majority, then, might be technically correct in their reading of the
Fourteenth Amendment, Blackmun reasoned, but it was a reading
that was at odds with the norms and standards of justice.
Blackmun argued that "such formalistic reasoning has no place in
the interpretation of the broad and stirring clauses of the
Fourteenth Amendment" and argued that his was a more "sympathetic reading" which "comports with dictates of fundamental justice and recognizes that compassion need not be exiled from the
province of judging."[3] For Blackmun, compassion and justice are
an important part of judging. The law and the Constitution

should not be permitted to get in the way of doing the right thing—the moral thing. For Blackmun, this is the job of a judge—to exercise compassion in the quest for justice.

> We will make mistakes if we go forward, but doing nothing can be the worst mistake. What is required is moral ambition. Until our composite sketch becomes a true portrait of humanity, we must live with our uncertainty; we will grope, we will struggle, and our compassion may be our only guide and comfort.[4]

There were, to be sure, other arguments that separated the majority and the minority on the Court in *DeShaney*. There was the debate over the degree to which the Wisconsin officials might be considered almost accomplices in the abuse of Joshua because of the way they had handled the case. There was the exchange between Rehnquist and Brennan over the thin distinction between a state's action or failure to take action when circumstances would seem to warrant it. But underlying all of these disputes was a more fundamental debate over the role of the Court and the place of the law and the Constitution in society.

For the majority—at least in *DeShaney*—the Constitution is a limiting document, a document that outlines the powers and the limitations on the powers of government, and the job of the judge is to seek to determine those powers and limits. The judge, as he seeks to resolve issues, is constrained by the limits of the law and the Constitution as well. He is an instrument of the law. For the minority, the Constitution is a vehicle to achieve social good and just ends, empowering the judge to apply his or her sense of morality to the specifics of the case being confronted. The Constitution embodies the moral vision of a just society, and it is the job of the judge to help to make that vision a reality.

It is this fundamental debate that framed the foundation for both the majority and the minority in *DeShaney* and that had been lurking in the background during most of the judicial skirmishes that took place during the Reagan years and continued under George Bush. At times the debate was clothed in the garb of *Roe v. Wade*, or *Planned Parenthood v. Casey*, or *DeShaney v. Winnebago County Social Services*. It was the central, if unsaid, issue dur-

ing the confirmation struggles during the Reagan–Bush years. It is
the debate that helped to galvanize the opposition to William
Rehnquist and led to the defeat of Robert Bork. Anthony
Kennedy and David Souter were able to survive, in part because of
the political contexts in which they came to power and in part because their positions in the debate were not fixed when they
sought confirmation. With *Casey,* those positions are well established. Clarence Thomas's triumph ironically can be traced to the
role of race in law and politics, as much as anything else. His position on the debate of law versus justice was well understood; his
race secured his victory, in spite of that.

The question that confronts the Court and the American people as the era of Republican dominance of our national executive
and judicial institutions comes to a close is, How did it get to this
point? What was once a debate about how to interpret the law and
the Constitution has become a debate over whether or not judges
should let the law or the Constitution get in the way of doing the
right thing. A concern that judges interpret law and be bound by
it has run up against the demand that justice be done and that
judges do it. A scrupulous regard for the intellectual, legal, and
political underpinnings of judicial decisions has been nudged aside
by a seemingly overwhelming preoccupation with results.

Not very long ago, the debate was about the scope of judicial
power. The question was whether or not judges should refrain
from imposing their will over and above that of elected legislators.
Today it is expected that judges shall do that, and that they must.
Because legislatures have become notorious for their inability to
grapple with difficult issues and to resolve tough questions, judges
will have to. We expect judges to "fill the void left by legislative or
congressional inaction."[5] We expect judges to take the place of
representative and policy-making institutions. A once healthy regard for democratic decision-making and representation has run
up against a distrust of democracy coupled with a hopeful embrace
of judicial power to provide just resolutions to society's most
pressing problems.

This fundamental shift in our politics is the result of other subtle, slowly evolving changes in the political and legal landscape
that took place during the 1960s and 1970s and culminated in the

judicial controversies of the 1980s. Our understanding of the relationship of law, politics, and society and our ability to manage the tension between law and justice has changed because our governing institutions have changed.

Accompanying those changes in our political, legal, and social institutions, and in part because of those changes, is the erosion of the popular esteem and confidence those institutions once enjoyed. Americans today are uncomfortable with their politics. A generation of citizens taught to expect justice from the courts can't help but be disappointed when the courts fail to deliver, even though that was never their purpose. As an institution, the Congress of the United States is held in very low esteem. Most citizens feel their government is distant, inefficient, uncaring, and broke. As for the legal profession, while its influence is greater now than ever, as a profession it is held suspect by many who have come to depend upon it, not because of any inherent flaw in the character of lawyers or the legal process, but because people are uneasy with a system of laws and procedures that has become so technical and obscure that only highly trained and highly paid "experts" can manipulate it. And citizens' discomfort has increased as their stake in the operations of the legal system has increased. Many have come to view lawyers the way they view auto mechanics: We entrust our welfare to them because they have the specialized training, but we remain a bit leery, unsure of just what they did to correct the problem and whether or not we got our money's worth. It is a profession we have come to depend upon but not to trust.

These changes in our institutions, then, have produced important changes in the way most Americans view the roles and importance of those institutions. We have come to expect more from our courts than ever before. We have come to expect justice. When it isn't delivered, we are disappointed. Years of congressional decline have contributed to a popular embrace of courts as a viable policy-making alternative and have produced a disaffected citizenry who feels democracy is in decline, and that representative government—at least as practiced in Washington—isn't working. We don't trust politicians, so we turn to the courts. And yet we don't really trust lawyers. It is a recipe for political breakdown.

THE TRANSFORMATION OF JUDICIAL POWER

The onset of this transformation of American law, politics, and society was signaled by the Supreme Court when it handed down its unanimous opinion in 1954 in *Brown* v. *Board of Education*.[6] It is perhaps the single most important decision rendered by the Court in this century. With it, the practice of segregating school-children according to race was declared unconstitutional. A civil rights revolution was introduced, and that revolution continues to this day.

While few would question the importance or the validity of *Brown* today, the fact is that it was very controversial when it was handed down. The controversy is easily explained. Much of the country, almost all of the South, was segregated. *Brown* meant that had to change, and many citizens resented it and sought to undermine the Court's decision, as well as the many civil rights di-cisions that followed it. But *Brown* caused controversy as well because it represented a new activism on the part of the Supreme Court. Nowhere was the controversy more heated than on the Court itself.

By the spring of 1954 Chief Justice Earl Warren had been able to put together a near unanimous Court in favor of over-turning *Plessy* v. *Ferguson*[7] and ending the practice of segrega-tion in public education. Only one member of Court, Associate Justice Robert H. Jackson, stood in his way. Jackson was no fan of segregation, but he was troubled by the direction the Court seemed to be taking. In a series of memos he wrote while recu-perating from a heart attack at Washington's Doctors' Hospital, Jackson conveyed to Chief Justice Warren the nature of his con-cerns.

Jackson was well aware of the monumental importance of the *Brown* case. "The plain fact," he wrote, "is that the questions of constitutional interpretation and of the limitations on responsible use of judicial power in a federal system implicit in these cases are as far reaching as any that have been before the Court since its es-tablishment."[8] For that reason, Jackson had instructed his clerks to conduct an exhaustive analysis to determine whether or not segre-gation according to race might be at odds with the language or intent behind the Fourteenth Amendment's Equal Protection Clause. However, after analyzing the debates in the Congress that produced that amendment, the debates during the ratification of the amendment, commentary in the various states at that time, earlier court decisions, and social customs and practices since the Fourteenth Amendment had become a part of the Constitution in 1868, Jackson had to admit grudgingly that "I simply cannot find in the conventional materials of constitutional interpretation . . . justification for saying segregated schools violate the 14th Amendment."

Jackson's analysis did suggest to him that desegregation could still be ordered; however, the language of the Fourteenth Amendment seemed to him to imply that such an order would have to come from Congress. According to Jackson, "there can be no doubt that [the Fourteenth Amendment] gives Congress a wide discretion to enact legislation on that subject binding on all states and school districts." Here was the nub of the issue, then. The Constitution, in Jackson's view, was silent on segregation even though he and everyone else on the Court felt segregation was wrong, if not immoral. However, the Constitution did seem to leave room for the Congress to do something about that. Jackson felt the real issue confronting the Court was "how far this court should leave this subject to be dealt with by legislation."

There were obvious problems with any interpretation of the Constitution that would leave it up to Congress to resolve the issue of segregation. It was a divided institution, reflecting a nation divided on the issue. It was impractical to expect the Congress to pass a law ending segregation at any time in the near future. There was also a question of the constitutionality of such a law should Congress pass one. Some argued that the last section of the Fourteenth Amendment was not a grant of power to Congress to act but a statement limiting the powers of the states. But what really troubled Jackson was the degree to which judicial action in the face of congressional inaction represented real problems as well.

Jackson felt the courts were ill suited to introducing social reform. "The futility of effective reform of our society by judicial decree," he wrote, "is demonstrated by the history of this very matter." Moreover, he felt the fact that judicial decrees are not self-executing and must depend for their effectiveness upon the degree to which they are viewed as legitimate by the public meant that any court-ordered desegregation was likely to "result in a failure that brings the court into contempt and the judicial process into discredit." Even should the order be obeyed, Jackson feared that the Court's decision would lead to "two generations of litigation." He foresaw years of controversy and worried that the courts would be forced to involve themselves in the management of school systems and the direction of educational policy—an extension of judicial authority that seemed to him "manifestly beyond judicial power or function." Finally, in response to his brethren who argued that the Court had to act because the Congress wouldn't, Jackson was straightforward: "That assumes nothing less than that we must act because our representative system failed. The premise is not a sound basis for judicial action."

Justice Jackson was on the horns of a judicial dilemma. He wanted to end segregation but didn't feel the courts had the authority to do it. For him it was a question as much of judicial power as of constitutional interpretation, a question of law versus justice. "Decision in these cases would be simple if our personal opinion that school segregation is morally, economically or politically indefensible made it legally so," he wrote Chief Justice Warren. But according to Jackson, the job of a judge was to interpret the law and the Constitution, not to enact his own moral theory.

In the end, of course, Justice Jackson found a way to resolve the dilemma. In conversations with Warren and his clerks, Jackson became convinced that his position on the question was not as important as the unanimous vote to overturn *Plessy*. In addition, he gradually came to subscribe to the argument, pressed by one of Warren's clerks, that Congress lacked the authority under the Fourteenth Amendment to desegregate schools. Facing all of this, and in moral agreement with his colleagues regarding the offensiveness of segregation, Jackson sent Warren his final thoughts on the *Brown* question, suggesting that he would join the Court. His rationale for overturning *Plessy* would be rooted in an appreciation for the effect time and change have upon social custom and circumstance:

> It is neither novel nor radical that statues once held constitutional may become invalid by reason of changing conditions, and those held to be good in one state of facts may be held to be bad in another.

On May 17, 1954, an ailing Justice Jackson left his hospital room and traveled to the Supreme Court in order to sit with his colleagues when Chief Justice Warren announced the Court's decision in *Brown*. A few months later he passed away after suffering another heart attack. Had Jackson lived, he no doubt would have been troubled by the degree to which his own reservations about the exercise of judicial power introduced by *Brown* had been vindicated.

The point of all of this is not to question the validity of the Court's opinion in *Brown*. Justice Jackson's arguments have weight and should not be dismissed. But *Brown* is a seminal case that transformed American society. It has achieved a level of legitimacy that rightly or wrongly makes it above question. But that is also its lasting legacy. While the decision in *Brown* was controversial at the time—for many of the reasons Justice Jackson cited—the essential moral rightness of the decision is what has established the importance and legitimacy of *Brown* over time. Generations of law students and students of politics have come to revere *Brown* and the courage of Earl Warren and the Warren Court for overcoming political and social obstacles and striking down legalized segregation. The trouble with this is that it was a moral victory that exacted a high constitutional price. With *Brown,* the Supreme Court exercised raw political power when Congress would not. The fact that today most Americans would agree that it was power exercised for a good cause should not detract from the fact that it was power the Court, according to the Constitution, arguably did not possess. *Brown* was the first example of the triumph of political ends over judicial means. It has acquired its legitimacy today not because of the force of the argument presented by the Court but because of the essential moral rightness of the decision itself. Because we agree with what the Court did, we will not debate whether or not the Court had the authority to do it. The problem with this, of course, is that the reasoning that goes into a court decision is the standard by which the legitimacy of that decision ought to be judged.

The *Brown* decision ushered in an era of Supreme Court activism under Chief Justice Earl Warren that introduced unprecedented change in American politics and law. In a series of important decisions, the Warren Court rewrote the laws governing political redistricting, civil rights, criminal justice, federalism, and the First Amendment. The exercise of judicial power under the Constitution was transformed, as the Court became a powerful engine for the reform of social and political institutions. That judicial transformation continued under Warren's successor, Warren Burger. Although appointed by Richard Nixon, a moderate-conservative President, Burger inherited a spirited activist Court and shared many of his colleagues' sympathies. The judicial activism of the Burger Court may not have been as vibrant, but it continued the legacy of judicial policy-making inherited from Burger's predecessor. When Ronald Reagan was given the chance to place his imprimatur upon the Court by naming Burger's replacement, it was this legacy of activism that he sought to counter. His appointment of William Rehnquist reflected his desire to rein in the federal judiciary, and his comments about the Court were reminiscent of those written by Justice Jackson as he had engaged in 1954 in the deliberations leading up to *Brown*. Reagan tried to revive the debate over the limits of judicial power and the proper exercise of that power in the interpretation of laws and the Constitution and in the resolution of cases and controversies. The Court's decision in *Planned Parenthood* v. *Casey*, written by Justices appointed by Reagan and Bush, says volumes about the relative ineffectiveness of President Reagan's efforts at returning the judiciary to its constitutional roots. *Casey* as well testifies to the ongoing legitimacy afforded a court that seeks to promote its particular view of justice over the rule of law.

THE TRANSFORMATION OF
LEGISLATIVE POWER

While the Court assumed a more active role in American political and legal life, the Congress of the United States was undergoing changes that are still taking place. Gradually the Congress has been transformed from a representative and deliberative policy-making institution into an institution where deliberation has become little more than brokering among interested groups and individuals, and representation has become little more than responding to constituent desires and complaints. Congress was designed to provide representation. But for the Framers of the Constitution, representation meant something other than responding to public opinion polls or constituent mail.

Representation is essentially a matter of style and focus. It is a function of how an individual or group goes about advancing the opinions or interests of some other individual or group. Edmund Burke provided a useful illustration in his *Speech to the Electors of Bristol:*

> Parliament is not a *congress* of ambassadors from different and hostile interests; which interests each must maintain, as an agent and advocate, against other agents and advocates; but parliament is a *deliberative* assembly of *one* nation, with *one* interest, that of the whole; where, not local purposes, not local prejudices ought to guide, but the general good, resulting from the general reason of the whole.[9]

Burke made an important distinction between the focus or constituency of the representative and the way the representative should endeavor to promote the interests of the constituency. Should a representative approach his task as an agent for his particular constituency and, therefore, attempt to enter into "hostile" negotiations with the representatives of other constituencies? Or should he approach his task with the attitude of a free agent, not so much to promote the interests of his constituency as to promote those interests that his constituency has in common with others and, therefore, enter into deliberations with other representatives who are also seeking to provide for the common interests? Burke's opinion was clear: Because it was a national assembly representing a single nation, the purpose of Parliament was the latter.

For the Framers of the Constitution, defining the style and focus of representation in the national legislature was no simple task. During the Philadelphia Convention an exchange between James Madison and Elbridge Gerry brought the issue of representation clearly into focus. Madison and Gerry disagreed about the very purpose of representation. For Gerry the issue seemed quite clear: A representative, including a delegate to the Convention, had a duty to do what the people want, or at least to take popular opinion into consideration. Madison, on the other hand, argued that the responsibilities of a representative went beyond mirroring public opinion. The job of the representative was to provide for good government, and that, in Madison's opinion, required time for elected officials to acquire "knowledge of the various interests" that were unfamiliar to them.[10] Determining the opinions of the people was a difficult task, Madison reasoned. Hence, representation is better accomplished when elected officials make decisions and then submit them during elections to the citizens for support, trusting that the majority would approve a decision that was in the true interest of society. For Madison, then, having members run on their record made sense.

Madison envisioned a legislature in which members would exercise discretion in order to act in the best interests of the nation. Representatives were not to be delegates acting only on the mandate of their states or districts. They should be free agents. The test of a representative's popularity, and thus of the representative character of the chamber, would rest not so much on the extent to which his votes mirrored public opinion as on whether the citizens, after due consideration, endorsed his decisions by returning him to public office. What Madison sought, then, was surely a popular legislature, but not one that merely provided a response to public opinion. It was to be a legislature that truly represented the public interest or, as he would later write in *The Federalist No. 10*, one that acted to "refine and enlarge the public views."[11]

As the discussions concerning representation continued during the summer of 1787, especially as the delegates focused on the second chamber, the Senate, it became clear that most agreed with Madison's notion that members of the national legislature would have a responsibility to go beyond popular opinion when casting a vote. What began to emerge during the discussions was a notion of the national legislature as both a deliberative and a representative assembly, a place where the interests and opinions of a multitude of particular constituencies would be brought together, and where decisions would be reached by elected representatives interested in seeking the common ground among those interests and opinions.

What also emerged during the Philadelphia debates was the understanding that the House and the Senate were to be two very different institutions. The House was to be the "most democratical" branch of the government, reflecting public sentiment more directly than the Senate because it would be elected every two years by the citizens themselves. The Senate, in addition to being a representative institution, would have other important functions to fulfill in the national legislature. According to James Madison, "The use of the Senate is to consist in its proceeding with more coolness, with more system, & with more wisdom, than the popular branch," the House of Representatives.[12] The second chamber of the national legislature, according to Madison, would provide both representation and deliberation as it simultaneously acted to "check" the first chamber.

The Senate was understood to be a very different assembly from the House of Representatives—representing different constituents, composed of a different character of individuals, and operating under different conditions. As the institution began to take shape during the debates, Madison outlined the purposes that the chamber would serve in the new government:

[F]irst [it is] to protect the people agst. their rulers: secondly to protect the people agst. the transient impressions into which they themselves might be led. A people deliberating in a temperate moment, and with the experience of other nations before them, on the plan of Govt. most likely to secure their happiness, would first be aware, that those chargd. with the public happiness, might betray

their trust. An obvious precaution agst. this danger wd. be to divide the trust between different bodies of men, who might watch &
check each other. . . . It wd. next occur to such a people, that they
themselves were liable to temporary errors, thro' want of information as to their true interest, and that men chosen for a short term,
& employed but a small portion of that in public affairs, might err
from the same cause. This reflection wd. naturally suggest that the
Govt. be so constituted, as that one of its branches might have an
[opportunity] of acquiring a competent knowledge of the public
interests.[13]

As Roger Sherman so aptly put it, "[W]e establish two branches
in order to get more wisdom."[14] In Edmund Randolph's opinion,
the second branch would exist to "controul the democratic branch
of the Natl. Legislature."[15] The Senate would provide "a stable &
firm Govt. organized in the republican form," according to
Madison.[16]

The delegates at the Constitutional Convention seemed to
reach some consensus on the importance of a senate and how it
was to help provide for good government. The Senate would contribute to good government by providing a different forum for
representation. But its most significant contribution would be to
provide a way for the "cool and deliberate sense of the community" to prevail over the passions that might, from time to time,
come to animate the public sentiments. The Senate, then, was understood from the beginning to be a deliberative body that would
act with a measure of independence greater than that of the
House of Representatives. The notion of representation at play in
the Senate was to be more akin to Burke's "free agent" than his
"delegate."

Representation was understood by the Framers of the
Constitution to be something more than a mere convenience—
something more than a suitable substitute for democracy in a
country of such size and population that democracy was not feasi-
ble. It was more than what William Paterson of New Jersey described as "an expedient by which an assembly of certain
[individuals] chosen by the people is substituted in place of the in-
convenient meeting of the people themselves."[17] Representation in
the new national legislature would constitute something other

than merely measuring and responding to public opinion. It was understood to be a way of dealing with the problems of public opinion, a method of blunting the "defects of democracy."

Indeed, the Congress created by the Framers in Philadelphia was, by design, very different from the Congress that existed under the Articles of Confederation. Under the new Constitution, Congress would provide a different kind of representation and would operate according to different principles. While the Congress of the Articles might best be understood to have been an assembly of delegates, the new national legislature would provide a distinctive blend of representational styles. In the House, where the terms of service were short and the relationship of the representative to his constituency direct, the Framers expected and hoped that the "interests and rights of every class" would be protected. The Senate, with its smaller size, longer terms, and different method of election, was to provide "the States, in their political character" with representation to counter the tendency of the first chamber to enact faulty legislation. Together, both chambers of the bicameral national legislature would provide for a blend of delegation and trusteeship—a form of representation that would combine a heavy reliance on citizen opinion with a healthy regard for the exercise of discretion and judgment by those individuals elected to serve in the legislature. Representation would be combined with deliberation in order to provide for the public interest.

According to Madison, writing in *The Federalist,* the function of the legislature in representative government was

> . . . to refine and enlarge the public views by passing them through the medium of a chosen body of citizens, whose wisdom may best discern the true interest of their country and whose patriotism and love of justice will be least likely to sacrifice it to temporary or partial considerations.[18]

The virtue of government under the Constitution, then, was that it provided the people with a check upon the government and also upon themselves. Because they were to be representatives elected to a national legislature and separated from the great mass

of the people, the elected representatives could understand the
views, opinions, interests, and concerns of the people with a sense
of perspective. To a point, the elected official could come to understand the public interest by distancing himself from public
opinion. Because he remained an elected official, that distance
could never, in reality, become too great, and his understanding of
the interests of the people could never stray too far from the people's own understanding. Yet, to Madison, some distance was critical in order to promote the public good.

Thus representatives could be expected to act as delegates in
some respects. At the same time, deliberation ensured by the nature of the legislature and the legislative process would render the
elected official more than simply a delegate. In Madison's view,
the very nature of the elected official's position would require him
to go beyond the concerns of his constituents in order to act on
the concerns of society. In this way, he explained, "[I]t may well
happen that the public voice, pronounced by the representatives
of the people, will be more consonant to the public good than if
pronounced by the people themselves."[19]

Originally, the Senate had a special obligation—a "senatorial
trust"—which would require a "greater extent of information and
stability of character."[20] Thus it was decided that qualifications for
membership in the Senate should differ from qualification for
membership in the House. The same reasoning partially explained
why the members of the Senate were to be chosen by the state
legislatures. In Madison's view, the process would afford the selection of more eminent individuals, while also "giving to the State
governments such an agency in the formation of the federal government as must secure the authority of the former."[21] But the
truly distinctive character of the Senate could be found in its responsibility to represent the interests of the states. The Senate
emerged from *The Federalist No. 62* as the chamber expected to
ensure that the federal nature of the republic continued to be recognized:

> If indeed it be right that among a people thoroughly incorporated
> into one nation every district ought to have a *proportional* share in
> the government and that among independent and sovereign States,

bound together by a simple league, the parties, however unequal in size, ought to have an *equal* share in the common councils, it does not appear to be without some reason that in a compound republic, partaking both of the national and federal character, the government ought to be founded on a mixture of the principles of proportional and equal representation.[22]

Madison admitted that the equal representation of the states in the Senate was the product as much of compromise as of political principle. In his view, however, the compromise did not detract from the Senate's role of representing each state as a sovereign body. The Senate, according to Madison, would reflect a "constitutional recognition of the portion of sovereignty remaining in the individual states" and would act as a mechanism for preserving that sovereignty.[23]

The Senate was designed to provide other advantages as well. It would, for example, be "an additional impediment against improper acts of legislation."[24] Because legislation was to receive the concurrent support of both chambers before it could be considered by the President and become law, the Senate offered a check against poor legislation. Madison found this to be a most salutary prospect that "may be more convenient in practice than it appears to many in contemplation."[25]

The true value of the Senate, Madison argued, was in the protection it would provide against the "inconveniences which a republic must suffer."[26] Madison believed, for example, that it was not uncommon for elected officials to "forget their obligations to their constituents and prove unfaithful to their important trust."[27] A Senate would provide a check on such official corruption by doubling the "security to the people by requiring the concurrence of two distinct bodies in schemes of usurpation or perfidy, where the ambition or corruption of one would otherwise be sufficient."[28] In addition, the Senate could check another problem of popular government—the tendency inherent in all assemblies of the people to "yield to the impulse of sudden and violent passions, and to be seduced by factious leaders into intemperate and pernicious resolutions."[29] The Senate would contribute to good government by providing another source of information in the legislative process. The six-year terms for members would contribute to stability in government, helping to counteract the defects of "mutability" and maintaining the confidence of the people.

In Madison's opinion, this "select and stable member of the government"—the Senate—could fulfill an important function in international relations by providing other nations with a sense of the "national character" of the United States. A sense of national character could be found only in an assembly with a number

> . . . so small that a sensible degree of the praise and blame of public measures may be the portion of each individual; or in an assembly so durably invested with public trust that the pride and consequence of its members may be sensibly incorporated with the reputation and prosperity of the community.[30]

The Senate satisfied both conditions and was well suited to determine the "opinion of the world" and to obtain "the respect and confidence" of other nations.

The Senate would cure another defect of republican government, particularly republican government in which elections take place with frequency. In Madison's opinion, responsible government depended on two sorts of measures: those that have an immediate and particular effect, and those that have effects of a more enduring nature, the success of which are dependent on a series of "well-chosen and well-connected measures, which have a gradual and perhaps unobserved operation."[31] If the government were composed exclusively of representatives chosen for terms of short duration—as are members of the House of Representatives—it would be very difficult to adopt those long-term measures. As Madison said, it would be difficult to provide "more than one or two links in a chain of measures, on which the general welfare may essentially depend."[32] The Senate provided an antidote to this affliction, thereby helping to ensure responsible republican government.

Ideally, then, the Senate was to occupy a position of public trust. It would provide a forum for the representation of the interests of the states and would function as a check on both the House of Representatives and the people themselves. By its character, it would provide a perspective radically different from that of the House, and its character would be particularly well suited for the representation of the union in international affairs and for the resolution of long-term issues relating to the public welfare. The Senate was to be the "respectable body of citizens" necessary to ensure that representative government would remain responsible government and that responsible government would not deteriorate into irresponsible government, corrupt government, or tyrannical government.

The Congress that responded to the policy initiatives of the Reagan and Bush Administrations, and in particular the Senate that confirmed their nominees to the federal courts, differed considerably from the institutions envisioned by the Framers of the Constitution. In part, both the House and the Senate have changed in ways that were anticipated by the Framers. Both are larger institutions, befitting a larger nation than the one composed of thirteen relatively rural states. The size of the House has forced it to adopt businesslike rules and procedures that make deliberation all but impossible on the floor itself and encourage decision-making in committees and subcommittees and within party caucuses. The Senate remains small compared to the House of Representatives, and it conducts its business in a far more leisurely way than the House. The rules and procedures of the Senate reflect a concern that the interests of each member be respected and that deliberation of issues be encouraged.

Perhaps the single most significant change in the Senate is the method by which individuals are chosen to be Senators. The Seventeenth Amendment to the Constitution, ratified in 1913, requires that Senators be elected by the citizens of the states. At the very least, this change in the way Senators are selected has brought with it a change in the purpose of that institution within the federal system embraced by the Constitution. The Senate can no longer be considered an institution that exists, at least in part, as a forum for the protection of state sovereignty. Senators are no longer advocates for the states as states. They are representatives of the people who reside in the states.

That is important. The Framers were well aware of the way a method of selecting public officials will shape how those officials define their responsibilities. A popularly elected Senate is a very different institution from a Senate composed of men and women chosen by state legislatures. It is a more democratic institution, a less federal institution, and an institution that, by design, will tend to mirror public opinion much the same way the House of Representative does. Add to this the other trappings of the modern Congress—the increased access to proceedings, televised sessions and committee and subcommittee meetings, and the increased level of popular access to and knowledge of the Congress—and the institution takes on the appearance of a very popular forum. It is an institution very much aware of and responsive to public opinion, making it more difficult than ever for members of Congress to engage in the sort of deliberation that the institution was created to foster. We have a very democratic national legislature and are experiencing the troubles that accompany what one delegate to the Constitutional Convention referred to as the "excesses of democracy."[33]

The decline in the deliberative character of Congress is best illustrated by the members themselves, who understand their job primarily to be taking care of constituents. The modern Congress thrives on constituent casework; its members survive by "bringing home the bacon" to their districts. Both of these activities help to provide members with campaign advantages for reelection. More important, they are low-risk activities. When a member is forced to take a position on an issue, he risks alienating some of his support. By focusing on casework and pork barrel politics, he can court voters without angering them. Members of both the House and the Senate engage in this sort of behavior and have developed elaborate organizational rules and procedures that facilitate such conduct. The size of congressional staffs, the advent of computers and high-tech communications, and the size of the federal budget all testify to the degree to which taking care of the folks back home has become the job of the Congress. The relatively low turnover rate in Congress provides ample evidence of the degree to which such conduct succeeds.

The Congress's reluctance to engage in serious and meaningful deliberation of public policy issues has affected the character and influence of the judiciary. The courts, as noted previously, have sought to "fill the void left by Congress" when possible, thus increasing the presence and scope of judicial power as the legislature abdicates its responsibilities. But, just as troubling, when members of Congress do write legislation they engage in a sort of "political sleight-of-hand" by crafting legislation that is purposely vague, thus avoiding the sorts of difficult political decisions they would have to make in order to write public laws with precision. This usually means that it is left to the courts to give the law and public policy their meaning. Congress then will respond to what the courts say a law means by revising the statute or policy in question and then wait for the courts to respond to those revisions. Legislative imprecision leads to poor public policy and public confusion while elevating the courts and judges to the level of partners in the policy-making process. The extended civil rights debates over the Supreme Court's decisions in a number of cases decided during the Reagan and Bush years—*Ward's Cove* v. *Antonio, Patterson* v. *McLean Credit Union,* and *City of Richmond* v. *Croson*[34]—illustrated this growing congressional tendency. Indeed, with the Court inclined to tighten the judicial process, Congress was forced to take a more precise stand in favor of loosening the process by new legislation. Congress's ambiguity began to come back to haunt it.

The lack of serious deliberation in Congress has had an effect upon the unique role the Senate was designed to play vis-à-vis the executive branch as well. It was because of the deliberative character of the Senate that the obligation to ratify treaties and offer advice and consent on nominees to executive and judicial offices was placed there. In order to determine adequately whether or not to ratify a treaty, a member of the Senate must attempt to become familiar with all the issues related to that treaty. Moreover, he must attempt to consider the relationship of that treaty to the interests of the nation as a whole, not merely his constituents or his state. In other words, a Senator is exercising a fiduciary responsibility when engaged in deliberation over treaty ratification—he is engaged in the sort of obligation envisioned by the Framers when they spoke of the senatorial trust.

Similarly, when the Senate is engaged in debate over a nomination to the federal judiciary, it is attempting to determine how that nominee might serve in that very important job. Ideally, Senators might want to become familiar with the way a nominee's mind works, his vision of the Constitution, his approach to constitutional and statutory interpretation, how he might approach issues relating to such principles as separation of powers and federalism, and so forth. The deliberations surrounding the decision to confirm or deny confirmation to a nominee to the federal courts ideally should reflect the Senate at work as a deliberative institution attempting to carry out its fiduciary responsibilities.

The character of modern confirmation politics mirrors the character of the contemporary Senate, an institution that bears little resemblance to the institution developed by the Framers. As a representative institution it defines its mission much as the House does—responding to voters and interest groups. Deliberation within the Senate has become more a matter of calculating electoral costs and benefits of a vote than of serious discussion of the pros and cons of a bill. Issues are evaluated by Senators in terms of the support they represent among relevant groups rather than the substantive merits or demerits they embody. Real deliberation has been set aside, and in its place are logrolling, bargaining, the trading of legislative favors, responding to public opinion polls, and brokering among interested groups. Predictably, therefore, when a nominee to the federal courts appears before the Senate for purposes of confirmation, what matters most to the Senators is what groups have lined up in favor of and opposed to the nominee and the nominee's position on those issues that are important to those interests that support the Senators. Because of this, questions of constitutional law and interpretation are reduced to quizzes on the pressing legal policy issues of the day. It isn't the nominee's jurisprudence, it's how he will vote on *Roe* v. *Wade*. It isn't how the nominee might approach statutory construction but whether he supports *Miranda,* or the death penalty, or school prayer. All the members of the Senate are interested in is how a nominee will vote if confirmed, not why he will vote the way he will. Nominees are evaluated by the Senate according to policy criteria put forth by interest groups that are important to members of the Senate. Confirmation debates have become little more than rhetorical squabbles over who will vote what way on what issue if appointed to the bench. There is very little serious discussion about the most important part of judging: how a judge makes up his mind. But then, this is to be expected when results-oriented jurisprudence has become the order of the day.

With regard to confirmation debates, deliberation has been transformed into little more than interest group advocacy. Because the judiciary has become such a factor in contemporary policy-making, judges have come to be seen as important policy-makers. Interest groups, which have always attempted to lobby the political process, more recently have had to seek ways to influence the judiciary. Traditionally groups have sought to advance their causes through litigation. They continue, of course, to pursue that strategy. In addition, however, by focusing their efforts on the selection of judges, interest groups can move beyond a strategy aimed at winning in court; they can attempt to mold the judiciary so that winning is easier.

Such was the approach to confirmation politics that came to full flower during the presidencies of Ronald Reagan and George Bush and produced the sort of political theater that surrounded the nominations of Robert Bork and Clarence Thomas. The stakes are higher than ever when an individual is nominated to the federal courts. Interest groups, recognizing this, will do whatever it takes to influence the confirmation process. Whereas in the past groups concentrated their efforts on lobbying Senators for support of or opposition to a nominee, the character of the contemporary Senate—an institution more interested in pleasing public opinion than in "refining and enlarging" it—suggests it makes some sense to approach each confirmation battle with a campaign plan. Putting together a strategy aimed at swaying public opinion can produce immediate returns within the Senate.

THE TRANSFORMATION OF THE LEGAL PROFESSION

Along with the rise of government by judiciary and the decline of congressional responsibility the nation has seen the advent of the litigious society and the increasing importance of the legal profession in this country. On the surface this makes some sense. After all, if legislatures are not making difficult decisions and judges are, it might be expected that citizens will press their interests in courtrooms rather than legislative salons. The legal profession itself has campaigned hard for the public's business as well. The practice of law today is a very big business in which millions of dollars are spent in advertising to attract clients and literally billions of dollars are at stake in contingency fees and settlements. Once upon a time, suing in court was considered a last resort. Today it is a cost of doing business. All of this has produced an explosion in litigation that has jammed the courtrooms, made an administrative mess of our judicial system, and costs the American people billions of dollars while encouraging antagonisms in society. That situation has shifted more and more influence to attorneys and judges, robbed citizens of their privacy, not to mention their money, and yet failed to resolve most of the disputes the system was created to settle. It is a cycle that seems unending: sue more, spend more, go to trial more, but settle nothing.[35]

Perhaps no single aspect of the legal profession has had as great an impact on molding the profession today as the advent of the class action and public interest law suit. Class actions were initially hailed as a way of decreasing court costs. Their popularity, however, has contributed to the problems plaguing the legal system. A series of legal reforms in the 1960s and 1970s made it easier for lawyers to organize actions involving large numbers of people. That, coupled with relaxed standards for demonstrating a significant chance of winning in court and the introduction of contingency fees, has produced a revolution in class action litigation.

The advent of public interest litigation represented the coming together of law and politics in the most direct sense.[36] Traditionally, litigation concerned two individuals or interests. The controversy was about events that had occurred in the past, and the relief or compensation awarded was related to the harm caused. Lawsuits were self-contained, with the effect of the judgment limited to the parties at suit. Most important, lawsuits were initiated by the two parties; the judge was something of a neutral moderator. The public interest model changed this tremendously. "The trial judge has increasingly become the creator and manager of complex forms of ongoing relief, which have widespread effects on persons not before the court and require the judge's continuing involvement in administration and implementation."[37] In countless cases dealing with such policy disputes as school desegregation, prison overcrowding, employment practices, and urban services delivery, judges have been called upon to write and administer public policy. In an attempt to apply broad national policy to specific circumstances, judges have been given vast authority to exercise discretion in fashioning decrees that have the effect of deepening the judge's participation in a dispute.

The increase in public interest litigation was accompanied by an increase in reliance upon standards of equity in the resolution of those cases. Equity offers a remedy when the law does an injustice. Laws are, after all, general statements. There will always be instances in which a faithful application of a law might yield an outcome that is in conflict with the general purposes of that law. Equity provides a means for minimizing injustices of that sort. Traditionally, equity was not about going beyond the law but about remedying deficiencies, inadequacies, or inequities in the law. Equity, traditionally, was ancillary to or supportive of law. It requires the exercise of discretion by judges who must know both the law and the facts of the cases being confronted. But the judicial activism that accompanied the expansion in public interest litigation encouraged judges to fashion relief based upon their own sense of equity and fairness, with little regard for the constraints of the law or the limits of judicial authority.

Surely judges have done some real good with the exercise of the equity powers. But they have also created a fair amount of havoc. While few today will question the wisdom of striking down legal segregation, fewer still can look upon all the progeny of *Brown* as exemplars of social justice. There is room for debate over the degree to which Boston was made a better city and Boston schools better schools by Judge Arthur Garrity's decade-long sojourn as a public school administrator.

Given the way law is studied and practiced in this country, it should come as no surprise that law has become a primary tool of social reform and that judges are directing the use of that tool. In law school students are taught to be advocates and to learn law by reading cases—the opinions of judges. Judges gradually acquire the aura of arbiters of victory or defeat, therefore, since they are the individuals who will determine, in many instances, the fate of an attorney's argument. Students are taught that a judge will rely upon the law, procedure, and precedent in carrying out his duties. In a way, judges become the arbiters of truth for lawyers. It might be understandable, then, that as the legal profession increases in influence in the country, judges might be entrusted with the sorts of responsibilities that citizens no longer feel they can entrust to prison wardens, school administrators, or members of Congress.

There would perhaps be nothing wrong with this if judges were trained for the sorts of duties they have acquired today. But they lack such preparation. What they do not lack, however, is a personal sense of right and wrong. Judges were once lawyers. As lawyers, they were trained as advocates—to stake out a position and to find a way for it to prevail. It is unrealistic to assume that former lawyers who become judges will be able to cast aside the mentality of an advocate and assume the duties of the dispassionate seeker of the truth. The "results-oriented jurisprudence" that dominates the legal process and encourages judges to impose their sense of justice upon society can be traced to the way lawyers are trained and how the legal profession operates in this country.

THE DECLINE IN POPULAR GOVERNMENT

Those three transforming changes in our fundamental institutions—the advent of government by judiciary, the abdication of congressional responsibility, and the creation of the litigious society—came together to form the backdrop for the judicial wars that took place during the Reagan and Bush years. Those wars in turn helped to shape the Court that decided the fate of young Joshua's plea for constitutional relief.

But the changes that have shaped our law, politics, and society have altered the way individuals within society understand their relationship to the government as well. A generation of Americans has been taught that the courts afford a forum not merely for the vindication of rights but for the transformation of society. Citizens look to the courts and the legal process for moral, political, and economic leadership in this country, as well as the settlement of cases and controversies. We have come to rely upon the courts to make the difficult decisions that lie at the very heart of popular government. We lack confidence in the ability of elected representatives to deliberate on those issues. And we lack confidence in our own ability to resolve our own most pressing problems.

The decay of citizenship and a decline in popular government may prove to be the most lasting legacy of the sweeping changes outlined here. A society that relies upon courts and judges to make the important political and moral decisions is a society that has lost touch with what self-government is about. It is a society in which citizenship has little or no meaning.

It is ironic that a generation of Americans who have experienced and participated in such sweeping change finds itself at odds with the very institutions it has altered. But the disaffection many feel toward those institutions can be traced to the misplaced optimism many felt about the ability of courts to establish justice and the naïve confidence many had in the ability of legislatures to solve social problems. Our political institutions—the courts and the Congress—are a disappointment to us primarily because we have expected too much of them. By raising the stakes in the judicial process and asking for more than the rule of law, we have forgotten that the truly important questions that confront a democracy must be debated by the citizens themselves. The true test of a democracy is its ability to deliberate the moral issues. By asking courts to do that for us, citizens have abdicated their most important obligation as citizens. And in so doing, they have in their own way contributed to the decline in popular government that is so strikingly evident in the way the Congress goes about its business. The only way to revitalize representation and deliberation in that institution is to reacquaint citizens with the importance of both to the health of a democratic society. But that will be difficult as long

as citizens seek to resolve their differences through judicial con-
frontations rather than political compromise.

Joshua remains in an institution. He has no idea what has happened to him. He has no understanding of the world beyond his
room. The federal courts have already agreed to hear arguments
on cases similar to his. The Supreme Court will no doubt be asked
to return to the questions his case presented. It will be a different
Court, reflecting the politics of a new President. But it will confront the same questions. How that Court addresses those questions and how Americans then react will shape the relationship
between law and justice in this country, as well as color the character of our democracy.

NOTES

CHAPTER 2. JOSHUA'S QUEST FOR JUSTICE AND THE LOGIC OF THE LAW

1. Sections 2–4 of the Amendment dealt with such matters as the debts incurred during the rebellion, the provisions for representation of the former rebel states, and the disability of any of those who had "engaged in insurrection or rebellion" to hold office under the United States except by a vote of two-thirds of each house of Congress to remove such disability.

2. The complaint argued at great length as follows: "[T]he civil rights of Joshua DeShaney have been violated, and he has been utterly deprived of his civil rights, including without limitation his right to ordered liberty; his right to freedom from physical attack and abuse; his right to personal safety, health and security in his person; his right to live and to exist; his right to live and exist as a normal human being; his right to a family or child–parent relationship with his mother and the other members of his extended family; his right to privacy; his right to engage in the common activities and occupations of life; his right to grow and develop; his right to maintain personal relationships, to marry and to have children; his right to freedom from bodily restraint; his right to contract; his right to learn, become educated according to his abilities and acquire wisdom and knowledge; his right to live in a place and manner of his choosing; his right to hearings, notice, confrontation, representation and the due process of law; his rights and privileges under the common law; and other and diverse rights and privileges, all as secured by the Constitution of the United States, and particularly the First, Fourth, Fifth, Eighth and Fourteenth Amendments thereto, and by the provisions of the 42 United States Code 1983, 1985, and 1988."

3. *Estelle* v. *Gamble*, 429 U.S. 97, 105 (1976).

4. *Youngberg* v. *Romeo*, 457 U.S. 307, 322 (1982).

5. Ibid., at 319.

6. Ibid., at 322.

7. *Estate of Bailey by Oare* v. *County of York*, 768 F.2d 503 (3d Cir. 1985).

8. As described by Judge Posner in *DeShaney* v. *Winnebago County Department of Social Services*, 812 F.2d 298 (7th Cir. 1987), 303.

9. Ibid., at 298, 301.

10. Ibid.

11. Ibid.

12. Ibid., at 303; 302.

13. Ibid., at 303. Citations omitted.

14. Ibid., at 304.

15. Ibid., at 303.

16. Ibid., at 304.

17. Henry J. Abraham, *The Judiciary: The Supreme Court in the Governmental Process*, 8th ed. (Dubuque: Wm. C. Brown Publishers, 1991), pp. 22–23.

18. *Monroe* v. *Pape*, 365 U.S. 167 (1961).

19. Ibid., at 187.

20. Ibid., at 236.

21. Ibid., at 242.

22. Ibid., at 252.

23. Ibid., at 244.

24. *Monell* v. *New York City Department of Social Services*, 436 U.S. 658, 690 (1978).

25. Ibid., at 694.

26. Ibid., at 724.

27. *Procunier* v. *Navarette*, 434 U.S. 555 (1978).

28. *Baker* v. *McCollan*, 443 U.S. 137 (1979).

29. Ibid., at 139–40.

30. Ibid., at 144.

31. Ibid., at 145.

32. Ibid., at 146.

33. *Parratt* v. *Taylor*, 451 U.S. 527 (1981).

34. Ibid., at 537.

35. Ibid., at 543.

36. "Whoever, under the color of any law, statute, ordinance, regulation, or custom, *willfully* subjects any inhabitant of any State, Territory, or District to the deprivation of any rights, privileges, or immunities secured or protected by the Constitution or laws of the United States . . . shall be fined not more than $1,000 or imprisoned not more than one year, or both; and if death results

shall be subject to imprisonment for any term of years or life." 18 U.S.C. 242. Emphasis added.

37. Ibid., at 534 and 535.
38. Ibid., at 546.
39. Ibid., at 548.
40. Ibid., at 549. Justice Stewart in his concurrence also expressed his concern as to the trivial nature of the complaint: "To hold that this kind of loss is a deprivation of property within the meaning of the Fourteenth Amendment seems not only to trivialize, but grossly to distort the meaning and intent of the Constitution." Ibid., at 545.
41. *Daniels* v. *Williams,* 474 U.S. 327, 328.
42. Ibid., at 331–32.
43. *Davidson* v. *Cannon,* 474 U.S. 344 (1986).
44. Ibid., at 345 n.
45. 752 F.2d 826, 829 (1984).
46. Ibid., at 347–48.
47. *Poe* v. *Ullman,* 367 U.S. 497, 543 (1961). *Poe,* of course, was the forerunner of the case wherein the Court discovered the unenumerated right to privacy, *Griswold* v. *Connecticut,* which, in turn, was the basis upon which Blackmun's infamous opinion in *Roe* v. *Wade,* finding a right to abortion in the Constitution, rested. As cited by Blackmun in *McCollan,* 443 U.S. 137, 147–48.
48. 451 U.S. 527, 545.
49. Ibid.
50. 474 U.S. 344, 353.
51. Ibid., at 358–59.
52. Ibid., at 357.
53. Ibid., at 349.
54. Ibid., at 350.
55. Ibid., at 355.
56. Quoting *Mitchum* v. *Foster,* 407 U.S. 225, 242 (1972).
57. N.J. Stat. Ann., Section 59:5-2 (b) (4) (West 1982), as cited at 474 U.S. 344, 358.
58. 474 U.S. 344, 360.
59. The other organization included the ACLU of Wisconsin, Legal Services for Children, the Juvenile Law Center, Bay Area Coalition Against Child Abuse, and the National Woman Abuse Prevention Project.
60. 649 F.2d 134, 141 (1981) (2d Cir.).
61. 747 F.2d 185, 194 (1984) (4th Cir.).

62. 747 F.2d 185, 195.
63. 686 F.2d 616 (1982) (7th Cir.).
64. Ibid., at 618.
65. Ibid.
66. *Martinez* v. *California*, 444 U.S. 277 (1980).
67. Section 845.8 (a) of the Cal. Gov't Code Ann. (West Supp. 1979) provides: "Neither a public entity or a public employee is liable for: (a) Any injury resulting from determining whether to parole or release a prisoner or from determining the terms and conditions of his parole or release or from determining whether to revoke his parole or release."
68. 444 U.S. 277, 281.
69. 768 F.2d 503, 511.
70. Ibid.
71. 818 F.2d 791 (11th Cir. 1987).
72. Ibid., at 794–95.
73. Ibid., at 798.
74. *Reply Brief for the Petitioners,* p. 10.
75. 474 U.S. 327, 334 n.3.
76. 474 U.S. 327, 337.
77. 686 F.2d 616, 618.
78. Brief, pp. 7, 50.
79. Ibid., at 13–14.
80. Ibid., at 47.
81. Ibid., at 52.
82. 457 U.S. 922, 936–37 (1982). Emphasis supplied in the brief for Winnebago County.
83. 474 U.S. at 331.
84. Respondents' brief, pp. 31–32.
85. Section 48.981 (4) of the Wisconsin Statutes provides:

    IMMUNITY FROM LIABILITY. Any person or institution participating in good faith in the making of a report, conducting an investigation, ordering or taking of photographs or ordering or performing medical examinations of a child under this section shall have immunity from any liability, civil or criminal, that results by reason of the action. For the purpose of any proceeding, civil or criminal, the good faith of any person reporting under this section shall be presumed. The immunity provided under this subsection does not apply to liability for abusing or neglecting a child.

86. Brief for National Association of Counties, et al., p. 5.
87. Brief for the State Attorneys General, p. 9.

88. Brief for the National Association of Counties, pp. 17, 19.
89. Ibid., p. 5.
90. Ibid., p. 6.
91. Brief for the State Attorneys General, p. 6.
92. Brief for the National School Boards Association, p. 42.
93. Ibid., pp. 45–46.
94. Ibid., p. 19.
95. Ibid., p. 26.
96. Brief for the United States, pp. 6–7, 9–10. Emphasis in original.
97. Ibid., pp. 12, 15.
98. Ibid., pp. 13, 15.
99. Ibid., pp. 16–17.
100. Ibid., p. 17.

CHAPTER 4.   DOING JUSTICE IN THE NAME OF THE LAW

1. U. S. 386, 388 (1798).
2. Ibid., at 398–99.
3. William H. Rehnquist, "The Notion of a Living Constitution," *Texas Law Review* 54 (1976): 693; 694; 697; 699.
4. Ibid., p. 699.
5. Ibid., p. 704.
6. Ibid., pp. 705–6.
7. William J. Brennan, "The Constitution of the United States: Contemporary Ratification," *U.C. Davis Law Review* 19 (1985): 2–14, p. 2. This speech has been reprinted many times and in many places. It was first delivered on October 12, 1985, at Georgetown University as part of its Text and Teaching Symposium. It was originally celebrated in the media as a response to a speech by Attorney General Edwin Meese III to the American Bar Association in July 1985, wherein the Attorney General voiced a call for a return to what he called a "Jurisprudence of Original Intention." But in fact, in his Georgetown Speech Justice Brennan reiterated many notions he had been articulating in various places over a rather long period of years. Thus the speech was a "response" to Attorney General Meese only in the sense that Meese represented a tradition against which Brennan had long argued.
8. Ibid., p. 4.
9. Ibid., p. 5.
10. Ibid., p. 6.
11. Ibid., p. 8.
12. Ibid., p. 4.

13. Ibid., p. 8.
14. Ibid., p. 8.
15. Ibid., p. 9.
16. Ibid., p. 4.
17. Ibid., p. 7.
18. Lino A. Graglia, "How the Constitution Disappeared," *Commentary* (February 1986).
19. See Martin Diamond, *"The Federalists* View of Federalism" in George C. S. Benson (ed.), *Essays on Federalism* (Claremont, CA: Institute for Studies in Federalism, 1961).
20. Jacob Cooke, ed., *The Federalist* (Middletown, Conn.: Wesleyan University Press, 1961), no. 39, p. 257.
21. Felix Frankfurter and James Landis, *The Business of the Supreme Court* (New York: Macmillan, 1925), p. 2.
22. Jonathan Elliot, ed., *The Debates in the Several State Conventions on the Adoption of the Federal Constitution*, 5 vols. (Philadelphia: J.B. Lippincott, 1896), 3: 52.
23. Herbert J. Storing, ed., *The Complete Anti-Federalist*, 7 vols. (Chicago: University of Chicago Press, 1981), 2:9.189.
24. Ibid., 9.196; 9.134–44; 8.195.
25. Ibid., 9.139–42.
26. *Barron* v. *Baltimore*, 7 Peters 243 (1833).
27. C. Herman Pritchett, *The American Constitution* 3d. ed. (New York: McGraw-Hill, 1977), p. 512. See Benjamin F. Wright, *The Contract Clause of the Constitution* (Cambridge: Harvard University Press, 1938), p. 95.
28. 10 U.S. 87 (1810). The classic history is C. Peter Magrath, *Yazoo: The Case of Fletcher v. Peck* (New York: Norton, 1967).
29. See Stephen R. Boyd, "The Contract Clause and the Evolution of American Federalism," *William and Mary Quarterly*, 44: 3 (July 1987), pp. 529–48.
30. 10 U.S. 87, 133, 135 (1810).
31. Ibid., p.143.
32. 13 U.S. 43, 52 (1815).
33. 11 U.S. 164 (1812).
34. 17 U.S. 518 (1819).
35. 17 U.S. 122 (1819).
36. 25 U.S. 213 (1827).
37. Ibid., p. 346.
38. Marshall did not take the idea of a written constitution lightly. In *Marbury* he argued that the written constitution constituted nothing less than "the greatest improvement on political institu-

tions" and that "the framers of the Constitution contemplated that instrument as a rule for the government of *courts,* as well as for the legislature." 5 U.S. 137, 178; 180 (1803).

39. Keith Jurow, "Untimely Thoughts: A Reconsideration of the Origins of Due Process of Law," *American Journal of Legal History* 19 (1975): 265.

40. Jurow, "Untimely Thoughts," p. 272.

41. Edw. III, ch. 3 (1354), as quoted in Jurow, "Untimely Thoughts," p. 266.

42. See Charles M. Hough, "Due Process of Law—Today," *Harvard Law Review* 32 (1919):218–33.

43. Robert P. Reeder, "The Due Process Clauses and the Substance of Individual Rights," *University of Pennsylvania Law Review* 58 (1910): 204.

44. Ibid., p. 204.

45. Hough, "Due Process of Law—Today," p. 219.

46. Raoul Berger, *Government by Judiciary* (Cambridge: Harvard University Press, 1977), p. 211.

47. Harold C. Syrett, ed., *The Papers of Alexander Hamilton,* 26 vols. (New York: Columbia University Press, 1961–79), IV:35.

48. Edward S. Corwin, "The Doctrine of Due Process of Law Before the Civil War," in Richard Loss, ed., *Corwin on the Constitution,* 3 vols. (Ithaca, N.Y.: Cornell University Press, 1981–8), II:149–79, p. 149. This article originally appeared in *Harvard Law Review* 24 (1911):366, 460.

49. 13 N.Y. 378 (1856).

50. Francis W. Bird, "The Evolution of Due Process of Law in the Decisions of the United States Supreme Court," *Columbia Law Review* 13 (1913):37–50, p.46.

51. The New York law "forbade all owners of intoxicating liquors to sell them under any conditions save for medicinal purposes, forbade them further to store such liquors when not designed for sale in any place but a dwelling house, made the violation of these prohibitions a misdemeanor, and denounced the offending liquors as nuisances and ordained their destruction by summary process." Corwin, "Due Process Before Civil War," p. 170.

52. A.S. Johnson, J., 13 N.Y. at 420.

53. Ibid., at 391.

54. Ibid.

55. Ibid., at 430.

56. Ibid., at 453.

57. Ibid.

58. *Metropolitan Board of Excise* v. *Barrie,* 34 N.Y. 657, 668 (1866).

59. Corwin, "Due Process Before Civil War," p. 170.

60. 19 Howard 393 (1857).

61. Charles Shattuck, "The True Meaning of the Term 'Liberty' in Those Clauses in the Federal and State Constitutions Which Protect 'Life, Liberty, and Property'" *Harvard Law Review* 4 (1891): 375.

62. Raoul Berger, " 'Law of the Land' Reconsidered," *Northwestern Univ. Law Reveiw* 74 (1979): 30.

63. 83 U.S. 36 (1873).

64. Ibid., at 81.

65. 94 U.S. 113 (1877).

66. 94 U.S. 77, 84 (1877).

67. 94 U.S. 77, 89 (1877).

68. 1296 U.S. 97 (1878).

69. Pritchett, *American Constitution,* p. 520. See also David P. Currie, *The Constitution in the Supreme Court: The First Hundred Years, 1789–1888,* pp. 373–75.

70. Currie, *Constitution in Supreme Court 1789–1888,* p. 374.

71. 96 U.S. at 105.

72. Ibid., p. 120.

73. "Without giving the faintest semblance of an explanation and in the same opinion in which he appeared to say due process went only to procedure, Miller had seemed to announce that due process required the legislature to have an acceptable substantive reason for depriving a person of property." Currie, *Constitution in Supreme Court 1789–1888,* p. 375. Perhaps Miller's resistance to the idea of substantive due process was only half-hearted. In *Loan Association* v. *Topeka* (1874) he had reached back to the old natural law tradition: "There are limitations on power which grow out of the essential nature of all free governments. Implied reservations on individual rights, without which the social compact could not exist, and which are respected by all governments entitled to the name." 87 U.S. 655, 663 (1875).

74. 116 U.S. 307 (1886). At issue was the power of the states to create a railway commission with authority to revise rates. Was this a violation of due process of law?

75. Ibid., at 331.

76. 123 U.S. 623, 661 (1887).

77. "The conservatives of the seventies had been concerned with the protection of the old established state–federal relations against the upheavals of the Civil War and the onslaught of Radical reconstruction. The conservatism of the new judges . . . was concerned primar-

ily with protecting the property rights and vested interests of big business and with the defense of the prevailing economic and social order against agrarian and dissident reformers." Alfred H. Kelly and Winfred A. Harbison, *The American Constitution: Its Origins and Development*, 5th ed. (New York: Norton, 1976), p. 485.

78. 134 U.S. 418 (1890).

79. Ibid., at 458.

80. 154 U.S. 362 (1894).

81. 169 U.S. 466 (1898).

82. Charles Warren, "The New 'Liberty' Under the Fourteenth Amendment," *Harvard Law Review* 39 (1926): 439.

83. "It is as unreasonable to say that 'liberty' in this connection, in-cludes all civil rights, as it is to say that the term 'life' includes them or that the term 'property' includes them" Shattuck, "True Meaning of Term 'Liberty,'" p. 375.

84. "There is no basis in the pre-1787 historical materials for the proposition that 'due process of law' comprehended judicial power to test legislation for reasonableness." Berger, "'Law of the Land' Reconsidered," p. 29.

85. 165 U.S. 578 (1897).

86. 198 U.S. 45 (1905).

87. See, for example, the opinion of Justice Antonin Scalia in *Michael H.* v. *Gerald D.*, 491 U.S. 110 (1989).

88. 198 U.S. 45, 57.

89. Ibid., at 56.

90. David P. Currie, *The Constitution in the Supreme Court: The Second Century 1888–1986* (Chicago: University of Chicago Press, 1990), pp. 49–50.

91. Ibid., pp. 75–76.

92. 208 U.S. 412 (1908).

93. Brandeis was never one to view the line between law and politics with much deference, even after he ascended to the Supreme Court. See Bruce Allen Murphy, *The Brandeis/Frankfurter Connection: The Secret Political Activities of Two Supreme Court Justices* (New York: Oxford University Press, 1982).

94. Kelly and Harbison, *American Constitution*, pp. 496–97.

95. 208 U.S. 412, 420 (1908).

96. Kelly and Harbison, *American Constitution*, pp. 497–98.

97. 208 U.S. 161 (1908). At issue was a law passed by Congress mak-ing it a misdemeanor for any employer who was involved in inter-state commerce to extract from his employees guarantees not to join a union. The court found the law violates the due process guarantee of the Constitution.

 98. 243 U.S. 426 (1917).
 99. 261 U.S. 525 (1923).
100. 262 U.S. 390 (1923).
101. 268 U.S. 510 (1925).
102. 291 U.S. 502 (1934).
103. 300 U.S. 379 (1937).
104. 291 U.S. 502, 536 (1934).
105. 300 U.S. 379, 402–3; 404 (1937).
106. Chief Justice John Marshall was the first to address the question of the applicability of the Bill of Rights to the states. While Marshall was concerned simply with the applicability of those amendments on their own ground, not having the Fourteenth Amendment to worry about, his logic nevertheless seems equally compelling even *after* the Fourteenth Amendment was added to the Constitution. In the case of *Barron* v. *Baltimore* (his last constitutional opinion) Marshall put it this way:

> The Constitution was ordained and established by the people of the United States for themselves, for their government, and not for the government of the individual states . . . Had the framers of these amendments intended them to be limitations on the powers of the state governments they would have imitated the framers of the original Constitution, and have expressed that intention . . . Had Congress engaged in the extraordinary occupation of improving the Constitution of the several states by affording the people additional protection from the exercise of power by their own governments in matters which concerned themselves alone, they would have declared this purpose in plain and intelligible language.

Marshall's logic did not fade with the adoption of the Fourteenth Amendment; not until the Court handed down *Gitlow* in 1925 did the incorporationist view prevail, although it had been repeatedly—in at least twenty cases—pushed on the court throughout those sixty years. All along the Court had held to the Marshall view as having established a doctrine that had been "held over and over again," that was "elementary," "well established," and "so frequently held as to not warrant the citation of many authorities." See Warren, "The New Liberty Under the Fourteenth Amendment," *Harvard Law Review* 39 (1926): p. 436.
107. 268 U.S. 652 (1925).
108. Writing in the immediate wake of *Gitlow*, Charles Warren warned

that "if the doctrine of the *Gitlow* case is to be carried to its logical and inevitable conclusion . . . the simple word 'liberty' will have become a tremendous engine for attack on State legislation—an engine which could not have been conceived possible by the framers of the first Ten Amendments or by the framers of the Fourteenth Amendment itself." Ibid. p. 462.

109. 304 U.S. 144, 152 n.4.
110. For a more expansive discussion of the role of *Palko* and *Carolene Products* in the transformation of American rights, see Gary L. McDowell, "Rights Without Roots," *The Wilson Quarterly* (Winter 1991), pp. 71–79.
111. *Griswold* v. *Connecticut*, 381 U.S. 479, 484 (1965).
112. Louis D. Brandeis and Samuel Warren, "The Right to Privacy," *Harvard Law Review* 4 (1890):193.
113. William Prosser, "Privacy," *California Law Review* 48(1960):383.
114. 274 U.S. 200 (1927).
115. 316 U.S. 535 (1942).
116. 367 U.S. 497 (1961).
117. John Marshall Harlan joined the majority but concurred as to how the Due Process Clause "stands . . . on its own bottom" and did not need all the mystical talk about emanations and penumbras.
118. *Eisenstadt* v. *Baird*, 405 U.S. 438 (1972).
119. *Roe* v. *Wade*, 410 U.S. 113 (1973).
120. *Carey* v. *Population Services International*, 431 U.S. 678 (1977).
121. *Planned Parenthood of Central Missouri* v. *Danforth* (1976); *Bellotti* v. *Baird* (1979); and *Thornburgh* v. *American College of Obstetricians and Gynecologists* (1986).

CHAPTER 5. CONSTITUTIONAL MORALISM AND THE POLITICS OF ADVICE AND CONSENT

1.James McClellan and M. E. Bradford, eds., *Jonathan Elliot's Debates in the Several State Conventions on the Adoption of the Federal Convention*, "Debates on the Federal Convention of 1787," as reported by James Madison (Richmond: James River Press, 1989), 3:301; hereafter cited as *Madison's Notes*.
2.Ibid., p. 302.
3.Ibid., p. 330.
4.Ibid., p. 67.
5.Ibid., p. 68.
6.Ibid., p. 328.
7.Ibid., p. 302.

8. Alexander Hamilton, James Madison, and John Jay, *The Federalist Papers,* ed. Clinton Rossiter (New York: New American Library, 1961), no. 76, p. 455.

9. Ibid., p. 456.

10. Ibid.

11. Ibid., p. 457.

12. Ibid.

13. Much of the material presented here is recounted in fuller detail in Henry Abraham's excellent work, *Justices and Presidents: A Political History of Appointments to the Supreme Court,* 3d ed. (New York: Oxford University Press, 1991).

14. *See* Henry Abraham, *The Judicial Process: An Introductory Analysis of the Courts of the United States, England and France,* 2d ed. (New York: Oxford University Press, 1968), p. 310; cited in Abraham, *Justices and Presidents,* p. 74.

15. *Stuart* v. *Laird,* 1 Cranch 299 (1803).

16. Cited in Abraham, *Justices and Presidents,* p. 81.

17. Ibid., pp. 169–70.

18. *Muller* v. *Oregon,* 208 U.S. 412 (1908).

19. Abraham, *Justices and Presidents,* p. 184.

20. J. P. Harris, *The Advice and Consent of the Senate* (Los Angeles: University of California Press, 1953), pp. 125–26.

21. Ibid., p. 125.

22. Ibid., p. 126.

23. Ibid., p. 128.

24. Ibid.

25. Ibid., 129.

26. Ibid.

27. Ibid., p. 130.

28. Ibid.

29. Ibid., p. 306.

30. Ibid., p. 308.

31. *Brown* v. *Board of Education,* 347 U.S. 483 (1954).

32. *Plessy* v. *Ferguson,* 163 U.S. 537 (1896).

33. *New York Times,* July 8, 1981.

34. *New York Times,* July 10, 1981.

35. *New York Times,* July 29, 1987, p. 24.

CHAPTER 6.   HOW GREAT A REVOLUTION?

1. Rehnquist noted in his dissent in *Casey:* "In construing the phrase 'liberty' incorporated in the Due Process Clause of the

Fourteenth Amendment, we have recognized that its meaning extends beyond freedom from physical restraint." *Planned Parenthood of Southeastern Pennsylvania* v. *Casey,* 112 S. Ct. 2791 (1992), at 2804. Similarly, Scalia in *Michael H.* acknowledged the same tradition: "It is an established part of our jurisprudence that the term 'liberty' in the Due Process Clause extends beyond freedom from physical restraint. See, e.g. *Pierce* v. *Society of Sisters* [and] *Meyer* v. *Nebraska.*"

2. *Cooper* v. *Aaron,* 358 U.S. 1 (1958); *Brown* v. *Board of Education of Topeka,* Kansas, 347 U.S. 483 (1954); Brown II, 349 U.S. 294 (1955).

3. Warren was apparently outraged that Frankfurter would weaken the united front he himself had suggested by adding a concurring opinion. See G. Edward White, *Earl Warren: A Public Life* (New York: Oxford University Press, 1982), pp. 183–84.

4. 358 U.S. 1, 18.

5. See, generally, *The Federalist,* no. 81.

6. There were sound political and legal reasons why court decisions ought not to be included in the Supremacy Clause of the Constitution:

> Among the other problems that such a conclusion raises is that of the immutability of constitutional decisions. If *Plessy* v. *Ferguson* was the law of the land imposed on one and sundry . . . it was, as many have contended, binding on the Supreme Court as well. If a Supreme Court opinion remains the law of the land until it is overruled, it becomes difficult to raise the question so that it might be subject to reconsideration. More, if Supreme Court decisions are the law of the land, there are frightening conclusions to be reached from [the] derelicts of constitutional law. . . . A Supreme Court opinon, whatever its merits, cannot seriously be treated as the equivalent of a statute for the purposes of the Supremacy Clause. Nor have they been so treated, however highly the Supreme Court itself may regard some of them.

> Philip B. Kurland, *Politics, The Constitution and the Warren Court* (Chicago: University of Chicago Press, 1970), pp. 185–86.

7. While both the Solicitor General of the United States and the appellants sought to have *Roe* reconsidered, the Court refused, Chief Justice Rehnquist remarking simply that the facts presented

"affords us no occasion to revisit the holding in *Roe*." 492 U.S. 490 (1989), at 521.

8. 492 U.S. 490, at 538; 558; 545; 544; 538; 554; 559–60; 544; 546.
9. Ibid., at 521.
10. 462 U.S. 416, 453 (1983).
11. 492 U.S. 490, 532.
12. Ibid.
13. 112 S. Ct. 2791 (1992), at 2804.
14. 117 L. Ed. 2d 156 (1992).
15. Ibid., at 177, 178, 179.
16. 117 L. Ed. 2d 309 (1992).
17. 491 U.S. 397 (1989).
18. 491 U.S. 110, 121 (1989).
19. 491 U.S. 110, 122.
20. Ibid., 123.
21. Ibid., 137.
22. Ibid.
23. Ibid., 141.
24. Ibid., 127–28, n.6.
25. Ibid.
26. Ibid., 132.
27. Terry Carter, "Crossing the Rubicon," *California Lawyer* (October 1992), p. 39.
28. Ibid., p. 39.
29. 112 S. Ct. 2649 (1992).
30. Terry Carter, "Crossing the Rubicon," p. 104.
31. Ibid., p. 40.
32. 112 S. Ct. 2791 (1992), at 2814.
33. Ibid., at 2816.
34. Ibid., at 2804; 2805; 2806.
35. Ibid., at 2813.
36. Ibid., at 2807.
37. Ibid., at 2813.
38. Ibid., at 2812.
39. Ibid.
40. Ibid., at 2804.
41. Ibid., at 2810.
42. Ibid., at 2812.
43. Ibid., at 2808.
44. Ibid., at 2815.
45. Ibid.
46. Ibid.

47. Ibid.
48. Ibid., at 2803.
49. Ibid., at 2819; 2820.
50. Oddly, Blackmun's wrath seemed to have been reserved for Rehnquist; Scalia, as forthright in his opposition to *Roe* as Rehnquist, was largely spared the assault. This is odd at least insofar as Scalia's dissent in *Casey* was every bit as hostile to *Roe* as was that of the Chief Justice, and it was Scalia, after all, who in *Webster* had chastised Rehnquist for being too weak-kneed.
51. 492 U.S. 490, at 557.
52. 112 S.Ct. 2791 (1992), at 2844.
53. Ibid., at 2854, 2855.
54. Ibid.
55. Ibid., at 2862.
56. Ibid., at 2863.
57. Ibid.
58. Abraham Lincoln, "Speech of June 26, 1857 at Springfield, Ill.," in Roy P. Basler, ed., *The Collected Works of Abraham Lincoln*, 9 vols. (New Brunswick, N.J.: Rutgers, 1953), 2:401.
59. Ibid., at 2866.
60. Ibid., at 2861; 2865.
61. Ibid., at 2863.
62. Ibid, at 2866.
63. Ibid., at 2856.
64. Ibid., at 2873.
65. Ibid., at 2882.
66. Ibid., at 2874.
67. Ibid., at 2884.
68. 492 U.S. 110 (1989).
69. 112 S. Ct. 2791 (1992), at 2805.
70. Ibid., at 2884.
71. Ibid., at 2874, n.1.
72. Ibid., at 2877.
73. Ibid., at 2878.
74. Ibid., at 2804.
75. Ibid., at 2876.
76. Ibid., at 2880.
77. Ibid.
78. Ibid., at 2883.
79. Ibid., at 2884.
80. Ibid., at 2878.
81. Ibid., at 2884.

82.   Ibid., at 2885.
83.   Ibid.
84.   Ibid., at 2877, n.4.
85.   Ibid., at 2873.
86.   *Dred Scott* v. *Sandford*, 19 How. 393, 621 (1857) (Curtis, J., dissenting).
87.   112 S. Ct. 2791 (1992), at 2882.
88.   492 U.S. 490, 560.

EPILOGUE: JUDICIAL SUPREMACY AND THE DECLINE OF POPULAR GOVERNMENT

1.   *DeShaney, A minor, by his guardian ad Litem, et al.,* v. *Winnebago County Department of Social Services, et al.,* 489 U.S 189 (1988), at 202; 203.
2.   489 U.S. 189 (1988), at 212.
3.   Ibid., at 213.
4.   489 U.S. 189 (1988) at 213. Blackmun is quoting C. F. A. Stone, *Law, Psychiatry, and Morality,* 262 (184).
5.   When asked during his confirmation hearings whether the courts might have an obligation to act when Congress does not, David Souter said they must sometimes "fill the void."
6.   *Brown* v. *Board of Education,* 347 U.S. 483 (1954).
7.   *Plessy* v. *Ferguson,* 163 U.S. 537 (1896).
8.   The material cited here comes from working papers of Associate Justice Robert H. Jackson labeled *Segregation Cases* and used in conference at Doctors' Hospital with Chief Justice Warren, p. 4.
9.   E. Burke, Speech to the Electors of Bristol (November 3, 1774), p. 165, reprinted in *The Works of Edmund Burke* (1925); 2:159. For an interesting analysis of Burke and his theory of representation applied to Congress, *see* Heinz Eulau, John C. Wahlke, William Buchanan and LeRoy C. Ferguson, "The Role of the Representative: Some Empirical Observations on the Theory of Edmund Burke," *American Political Science Review* 53 (1959):742.
10.   *See* James Madison, *Notes of Debates in the Federal Convention of 1787,* ed. Adrianne Koch (Athens: Ohio University Press, 1966), p. 106; cited hereinafter as *Madison's Notes.*
11.   Alexander Hamilton, James Madison, and John Jay, *The Federalist Papers,* ed. Clinton Rossiter (New York: New American

Library, 1961), no. 10, p. 82; cited hereinafter as *Federalist Papers.*

12. *Madison's Notes,* p. 83.
13. Ibid., pp. 193–94.
14. Ibid., p. 114.
15. Ibid., p. 110.
16. Ibid., p. 111.
17. Ibid., p. 259.
18. *Federalist Papers,* no. 10, p. 77.
19. Ibid.
20. Ibid., no. 62, p. 376.
21. Ibid., p. 377.
22. Ibid.
23. Ibid., p. 378.
24. Ibid.
25. Ibid.
26. Ibid.
27. Ibid.
28. Ibid., pp. 378–79.
29. Ibid., p. 379.
30. Ibid., no. 63, p. 384.
31. Ibid., p. 383.
32. Ibid.
33. *Madison's Notes,* p. 39, where Elbridge Gerry says, "The evils we experience flow from the excess of democracy. The people do not want virtue, but are the dupe of pretended patriots."
34. 109 S. Ct. 2115 (1989); 109 S. Ct. 2363 (1989); 488 U.S. 469.
35. For an interesting treatment on the topic, *see* Walter K. Olson, *The Litigation Explosion* (New York: Truman Talley Books, 1991).
36. The classic argument for public law litigation was made by Abram Chayes, "The Role of the Judge in Public Law Litigation," *Harvard Law Review,* 89 (1976): 1281.
37. Ibid., p. 1284.

ACKNOWLEDGMENTS

Many people provided assistance and insight during the preparation of this book. Our colleagues in the academy were helpful in their support of our arguments, their criticisms and comments, and their actions. We thank especially Ralph Rossum, Henry Abraham, Mary Ann Glendon, Abigail Thernstrom, Jim McClellan, Gary Gilden, and Raoul Berger. The faculty in the department of political science at Dickinson College and at The Dickinson School of Law provided a supportive environment in which to pursue this project, as did the Harvard Law School.

Our tenure at the Department of Justice during the Reagan Administration provided many of the ideas and some of the experience that went into this book. Many who served with us in that department were kind enough to read portions of the manuscript to discuss and debate the issues we raise, and to provide assistance during countless hours of conversations. We thank Charles Cooper, William Bradford Reynolds, John Bolton, Mike Carvin, Eric Jaso, and Ron Tomalis. Thanks also to Don Sullivan and Mark Mingo, two advocates in the *DeShaney* case.

The book could not have been completed without the assistance of Dickinson College, the Lynde & Harry Bradley Foundation, and the John M. Olin Foundation.

Our thanks are also extended to the good people at Free Press: Peter Dougherty who first encouraged and counseled us, and Bruce Nichols, who patiently guided us through to publication.

Eric Fennel researched the tragic story of Joshua and pulled materials together. His assistance was essential. And of course, there throughout the process, keeping us in line and on target was Vickie Kuhn. Her patience and persistence, good humor and kind heart made this book possible.

Finally, we dedicate this book to our wives, Kathy and Brenda. They have always been there, in quiet times and in turmoil. They are the source of our joy and comfort; our gratitude is too great to measure.

CASE INDEX

INDEX

DATE